The Film Greats

By the same author

THE MATTER OF MANDRAKE
THE HOUNDS OF SPARTA
TALES OF THE REDUNDANCE KIND
END PRODUCT
A SERIES OF DEFEATS
TO NICK A GOOD BODY
THE HOLLYWOOD GREATS
THE MOVIE GREATS
HAVE A NICE DAY
STICKY WICKET

Barry Norman

The Film Greats

HODDER AND STOUGHTON
BRITISH BROADCASTING CORPORATION

British Library Cataloguing in Publication Data

Norman, Barry
    The film greats.
    1. Moving-picture actors and actresses—
Biography
    I. Title
    791.43′028′0922   PN1998.A2
    ISBN 0 340 35270 1
    ISBN 0 563 20383 8 (BBC)

For Emma with all my love

Preface

What is a star? Or, to put it another way, what is star quality? A long time ago when I first set out to make the TV documentaries on which this book and its two predecessors, *The Hollywood Greats* and *The Movie Greats*, were based I thought I might, by a close study of people who were certainly stars, learn the secret. And when I had learnt it I was going to write down the recipe and patent it and sell it under licence to ICI or Du Ponts and make a fortune on the royalties.

Fat chance. Today, twenty-five documentaries later, the only thing of which I am sure is that people either have star quality or they haven't and if they haven't nobody can give it to them. In the words of Sam Goldwyn: "Producers don't make stars. God makes stars and the public recognises His handiwork." What is curious, though, is the disparate people to whom God grants this rare and lucrative gift of star quality.

If, for example, you compare the subjects of this book you will find that just about the only personal quality they had in common was charm; sometimes, indeed in many cases, it was a charm that could be turned on or off depending upon whether its employment would serve any useful purpose. It's not a trustworthy quality, charm; people who have it know it and use it and in any case it is not in itself the secret of star quality. I doubt if anybody could become a star without charm but at the same time it's possible to have charm and not be a star.

For quite a long time, until in fact I started writing this book, I was convinced that another vital ingredient of star quality was sex appeal but now I am not so sure. I don't think, for example, that Bing Crosby had sex appeal; he had much else working for him but not that.

As for talent, I discounted this very soon as having anything at all to do with the matter under discussion. Everyone dealt with in the following pages had a certain amount of talent but the quantity and quality of it varied widely from one person to another. At the top of the list I, personally, would put Henry Fonda but the rest, if you judge them simply on the range of their acting ability, can be shuffled into any kind of order of merit depending on taste.

Of course, what else they had in common was staying power. Once established they remained established unto death but staying power is not an ingredient of star quality—it's a by-product. Stars stick around while better actors who are not stars disappear.

So what then caused me to pick on what is, after all, a pretty eclectic list? Well, simply that each of them was a star and each of them interested me. I liked their work and I wanted to find out more about them or, more specifically, I wanted to find out more about the kind of people they were. Contrary to what the publicity men would have us believe, stars do not walk on water, nor, on dry land, is daylight visible between their feet and the ground. On reflection I don't now believe, as I once believed, that they are necessarily better looking than the rest of us either. What happens, I think, is that having become stars they set a standard for what, ideally, other people should look like. This is not always so, of course; some stars are amazingly beautiful or handsome by any standards but a good many of them are not, or at least were not considered so in the early stages of their careers. Both David Niven and Bing Crosby, for example, were rejected at one time or another because they were not thought to be good-looking enough.

Thus behind every starry façade there lurks a fairly ordinary human being—as much prey to doubts, worries, fears and neuroses as the rest of us—who, thanks to this indefinable thing called star quality, has been boosted to extraordinary prominence and subjected to a degree of admiration and adulation that must be almost impossible even to imagine unless you have actually experienced it.

And the thing that interests me is how they cope with this and how, if at all, it changes them. What sort of people were they to begin with—and were they better or worse at the end? And what effect did their stardom have on those close to them?

At which stage I should perhaps point out one more factor that all the people under review have in common—each of them is dead. There is, however, nothing sinister in this fact. I mention it only because it is brought up every time I make the programmes which go under the generic title of *The Hollywood Greats* and there is invariably the odd cynic who chunters on darkly about it not being possible to libel the dead. Well, this is true. But on the other hand I have no wish to libel the dead (or the living, come to that). Indeed, there would be precious little point in it. The only reason for making the documentaries, or writing the books which are an extension and development of the documentaries, is to come as close as possible to the truth about the people concerned. And it is easier to do that and to assess them when both their lives and their work are done. I do not claim, and never have claimed, that I have discovered the whole truth about any of these people: it's impossible to do that for there are many kinds of truth. Depending on the experiences of the person to whom you are speaking the same man (or woman) can either be the nicest human being who ever trod the face of the earth or the most unspeakable bastard. So all I can claim is that there is nothing in this book which I do not believe to be true.

One more point: what follows is, as you will discover, divided into seven chapters. Five of these deal with actors, one with a director and another with Hollywood itself. The director is Cecil B. de Mille who, whatever you may think of his work, is undoubtedly one of the great names of the film industry and who may or may not have been the actual founder of Hollywood as the heart and headquarters of the movies but who was frequently regarded as such, not least by himself.

As for the chapter on Hollywood, well, this consists of impressions, interviews, quotes and general observations—the results of many visits there over the last decade. Hollywood evokes in me a most ambivalent response: I love to visit the place and I love to leave it again. I don't think I could live there, even if it would have me. But if, as somebody said (and I like to think it was Dorothy Parker), Los Angeles is "seventy-two suburbs in search of a city", Hollywood is still the most fascinating, the most bizarre, the most dangerous and the most glamorous of all those suburbs.

Acknowledgments

My grateful thanks to all those who took part in the television programmes which formed the basis of this book—and my special gratitude to Judy Lindsay, Sue Mallinson, Charles Miller, Chris Mohr and Margaret Sharp.

Contents

Preface 7

1 David Niven 17

2 Steve McQueen 53

3 Henry Fonda 87

4 John Wayne 121

5 Cecil B. de Mille 155

6 Bing Crosby 189

7 Scenes from Hollywood Life 229

Index 255

Associated Press Ltd., p 55 (bottom)

Camera Press Ltd., pp 54 (bottom), 56 (top and bottom), 90 (bottom), 122 (bottom), 123 (bottom)

Columbia Pictures, p 89 (bottom)

The Estate of Cecil B. de Mille, pp 156, 157 (top), 158 (top and bottom), 159 (top)

The Kobal Collection, pp 17, 20 (top), 21 (top), 53, 57, 87, 88 (top), 91 (top and bottom), 121, 123 (top), 124 (top and bottom), 125 (top and bottom), 155, 157 (bottom), 159 (bottom), 191 (bottom)

The Napthine-Walsh Collections, pp 55 (top), 122 (top)

National Film Archive, p 18 (bottom)

Paramount Pictures & the Estate of Bing Crosby, 189, 190 (all), 191 (top), 192 (top), 193

The Photo Source, pp 18 (top), 21 (bottom)

Popperfoto, p 192 (bottom)

Private Collection, p 19

Radio Times Hulton Picture Library, p 88 (bottom)

Rex Features, pp 20 (bottom), 89 (top)

Warner Bros Inc., p 90 (top)

The Film Greats

David Niven

The "perfect English gentleman",
to say nothing of officer.

With Primmie, his first wife, at
Jamie, their younger son's,
christening.

With Merle Oberon. Was she
perhaps the "Great Big Star",
with whom he had his wild fling?

Niven and Sons—David Jr and Jamie.

Niven and Hjordis, his second wife. Meeting her was the best thing that happened to him on the set of *Bonnie Prince Charlie*.

Niven's second family—with Hjordis and their adopted daughters, Kristina and Fiona.

In *Separate Tables* with
Deborah Kerr. He was not
sure he could play the
role—but it won him an
Oscar anyway.

David Niven on his
seventieth birthday in 1980.

Just before David Niven was released from the clinic in Minneapolis where he had been undergoing tests, he phoned his younger son Jamie in New York.

"The good news," Niven said, "is that I haven't had a stroke. The bad news is that I've got motor neurone disease."

"Oh, my God," said Jamie. "What does that mean?"

"It means," said his father, "that I'm going to die and I'm going to die very soon."

He then boarded a plane for New York and found himself sitting next to Tom Brokaw, quite possibly the best of American TV journalists, who was at that time the main presenter of the breakfast show *Today* and who is now anchorman on the NBC News. Now Niven had been told in precise detail what effect motor neurone disease, which is incurable, would have upon him. He would lose the use of his voice, of his hands, of his legs; he would have the utmost difficulty in swallowing, even in breathing. Already his voice tended occasionally to become a little slurred, to such an extent indeed that when a few weeks earlier he had appeared on the *Michael Parkinson Show* on BBC television some people had thought he was drunk.

And yet, as Tom Brokaw recounted later to Jamie, "your father was fabulous. He just made me laugh all the way back to New York." Well, not quite all the way perhaps because . . . "halfway across the country he turned to me and said, 'The most terrible thing has happened to me today . . .' " and then he told Brokaw what the doctors had told him. It was a most uncharacteristic act on Niven's part because he was never a man to share his troubles even with his friends, let alone strangers. But in the circumstances the desire to unburden himself to somebody must have been overwhelming, although to reveal what in journalistic terms would have been an amazing scoop to someone in Brokaw's position might have been, to put it mildly, unwise. It says a great deal for Tom Brokaw's innate decency that he chose to regard the information he had been given as confidential and told nobody about it except Jamie, a decision which, as Jamie pointed out "gave Daddy an extra year in which the press and other people weren't hounding him".

On reflection, though, that anecdote also says a great deal about David Niven and the enormous affection in which he was held. Everybody liked him; nobody would have wished to hurt him or cause him distress. He was, in my experience, unique among actors in that it was impossible to find anyone who had a bad word to say about him. To one involved in a spot of investigative reporting—

which is not to be confused with muck-raking or an act of icono-clasm, but which has nothing to do with eulogising either—it could have been most galling to find every interviewee's face light up with remembered pleasure at the mention of Niven's name and to hear them chuckling happily even before a single question had been asked.

I say, it could have been but in fact it wasn't because I knew David Niven, too—not very well, alas, and not nearly as closely as I would have liked. But I knew him well enough to have noticed a most remarkable quality in him: he had the effect, while you were in his company and for some time after you had left it, of making you feel that life was a much more enjoyable and cheerful business than you had previously supposed. Sir Ralph Richardson had some-thing of that quality, too, but not I think quite to the same extent as Niven.

"What were his faults?" I would ask of each of the interviewees, desirous of producing a rounded picture in which due prominence was given to the warts as well as the beauty spots. "Come on, put a bit of effort into it—he must have had faults, for God's sake. Nobody's perfect." And then articulate men like John Mortimer, barrister and playwright, and Peter Ustinov, actor, director, novel-ist, playwright and heaven knows what else, would flounder about, at a loss to find anything to say at all. Well, they would say, no, no, he wasn't perfect, certainly not—for they had no wish to malign the man—no doubt he did have all the faults and frailties that are common to the rest of us; it was just that they personally couldn't think of any, that was all.

Niven's elder son, David Jr., actually went away for five minutes to search his memory in an honest attempt to find something derogatory to say about his late father, while I tapped my foot impatiently and urged him to get on with it. But when he returned all he could say was that Niven could be verbally harsh and cutting when he had drunk too much gin and what kind of criticism is that, I ask you? I mean, everyone is unpleasant after drinking too much gin. What's more, when David Jr. and other interested parties pointed out this grievous fault, Niven stopped drinking gin and never touched the stuff again. He drank plenty of other things, it must be said in his defence, but he swore off gin.

The question is: how did this paragon—if that is not too harsh a description of an extremely lovable man—come about? Well, his great friend and perceptive journalist Roderick Mann believed that Niven had actually invented himself. "Everyone would say that he was the quintessential Englishman and he wasn't, really, because I never met another Englishman like him. I mean, he was the kind of Englishman that everyone thinks exists but doesn't. Perhaps there was an English type like that before the First World War but not now." The fact is that Niven did all the right things and showed all the right attributes to establish himself, whether intentionally or otherwise, in the public mind as the archetypal English gentleman. At the outbreak of World War Two he abandoned his Hollywood career, just as he stood on the brink of stardom, to return to Europe and fight; he was invariably charming, witty and erudite. He was, as Roderick Mann said, "like an extension of the most popular prefect at a public school. People used to say, 'Oh, he *can't* be like that; it's a mask.' But it wasn't a bloody mask—he really *was* like that. I've been out with him when we both got sloshed and that charm never slipped. In fact he got even more charming as he got drunker sometimes."

But if the Niven that everyone knew and whom, as far as I can tell, everyone loved was indeed self-invented one can only conclude that the invention was just about flawless. To have projected, as he did, a certain kind of persona for seventy-three years without ever being caught out in an uncharacteristic act of meanness or pettiness rather leads one to the belief that the mask, if there was one, was simply an identical replica of the face that lay underneath.

At this stage I should point out that what follows owes only a little to Niven's own two works of autobiography, *The Moon's a Balloon* and *Bring on the Empty Horses*. There are two reasons for this: in the first place I do not wish to be accused of plagiarism and in the second place his reminiscences (whether wholly true or not and I will return to that later) are so widely familiar that any repetition would be redundant. My object, in the TV documentary that spawned this chapter, was not simply to promote further Niven's own self-mocking, self-denigratory image of himself but to discover, as far as possible, what kind of image he presented to other people.

He was born on March 1st, 1910, in Belgravia, London, the perfect setting for one of his upper-class demeanour, the youngest of four children of William and Henrietta Niven. For the record he was christened James David Graham and was semi-orphaned in 1915 when his father was killed at Suvla Bay, Gallipoli. A year later, the widow Niven—who, incidentally, was French—married one Sir Thomas Comyn-Platt. Jamie Niven said: "I know he hated his stepfather," but apart from that Niven was never greatly inclined to reveal too much about his youthful likes and dislikes, although

the actress Ann Todd, who knew him well as a young man, said:
"He adored his mother. She was a lovely, lovely person."

It would appear (and here I must acknowledge a debt to Niven's
own memoirs) that the antipathy he felt for his stepfather was
mutual and the young Niven was sent off to a succession of boarding
schools, good or bad depending on the family finances at the time.
Eventually he went, as well-brought-up young gentlemen of his
generation automatically did, to a public school—to Stowe—where
he was extremely happy. This is worth mentioning because happiness appears to have been a comparatively rare commodity in his
youth and such of it as there was seems to have been provided
largely by his mother and his public school—unless one counts
Nessie. Nessie, according to Niven, was the seventeen-year-old
Soho tart whom he met when he was fourteen and who, he says,
generously and without charge introduced him to the delights of
sex. It must be said, however, that there are those among Niven's
close friends who believe that Nessie was either another invention
or, at best, a romanticised memory of a casual encounter.

But whatever part Nessie played in his life and whether or not
she coached him to become an accomplished boudoir athlete, Niven
developed into a more conventional kind of sportsman and gained
his colours at Stowe as both a cricketer and a Rugby player as well
as performing nobly in the boxing and fencing teams.

Friends who knew him about that time from the Isle of Wight,
where the Comyn-Platts had a holiday home, remember Henrietta
as both "a tall, fine-looking, very pretty person", and "a very
formidable woman, very big. She had the most glorious great big
eyes and I, for one, was terrified of her." She also, considering that
we are talking now about the 1920s, must have been a rather tolerant,
free-thinking woman because one of Niven's boyhood friends recalled: "David and his brother Max used to bring their girlfriends
down for the weekend and they used to go out dancing at night and
come back in the early hours of the morning and create absolute
hell, waking up the entire household. So his mother, in her wisdom,
built on a guest wing to the cottage, which had all the mod cons
and various bedrooms for the guests and it was known, of course,
as 'the Sin Wing'."

So, by the time Niven aged about seventeen went on to the Royal
Military College at Sandhurst, there to prepare for a career in the
regular army, it seems safe to assume that whether it was thanks to
Nessie or whether he was self-taught, he was already sexually
proficient. At Sandhurst he was a model cadet, played in the Rugby

XV and appeared in a couple of college concerts, in which he wrote his own sketches, and even played the lead in a production of the play *It Pays to Advertise*. Such histrionic outings, however, were only diversions; at that time the idea of making a career as an actor would have seemed laughable. But nonetheless he was interested in the stage and certainly in young actresses and it was while he was at Sandhurst that he met Ann Todd.

She was in a play in Portsmouth—one of the first plays she ever appeared in—and Niven went to watch her every night. Miss Todd believed, as nice young women did in those days, that a gentleman and a lady should be formally introduced; Niven tried to find a shortcut past this system. So he got hold of a programme of the play and drew upon it two hearts, one at the top, one at the bottom. And from the bottom heart (Miss Todd's) he drew an arrow bearing love to the top heart (his). Miss Todd didn't like this approach and vowed to have nothing to do with him. But at the end of the week the play's author, Ian Hay, arrived in her dressing room and "behind him came a beaming Niven". Somehow he had managed to ingratiate himself with Hay and the introduction was effected; nor did Ann Todd ever regret it, for they became lifelong friends. And though her heart never did send up an arrow of love to his it would not have displeased Niven's mother if something of the sort could have been arranged.

Still, the Niven Ann Todd remembers from that first meeting was "very cocky. *Very* cocky. Very full of himself but now, thinking it over, I suspect very insecure inside, really." Nevertheless they became "very sort of brother and sister".

Ann Todd's role in the play was that of a schoolgirl in tunic and plaits and Niven had a photograph taken of her in this costume which he kept for years in his wallet, though not for such sentimental reasons as one might assume. "It was there," she said, "only for one reason, which was that when, now and again, he got into trouble with the ladies, he'd produce this photograph and say, 'Oh, by the way, I forgot to tell you—I'm engaged and here's my fiancée.' And he'd bring out this awful picture, sort of sepia-coloured, and show it to them."

But what was he like in those days, apart from being cocky, full of himself and insecure? "Well," she said, "he was just a lovely person. People adored him even when he was very young."

Up to this point Niven's career seemed assured: he was going to be a soldier and it's quite possible that if he had been accepted into the regiment of his choice, the Argyll and Sutherland Highlanders, he might have ended up as some respected but more or less obscure old general, pretty well unheard-of by the world at large. But he was not accepted by the Argyll and Sutherland Highlanders (which he had chosen partly because, despite his image as the quintessential Englishman, he was Scottish by descent) but was posted instead to the Highland Light Infantry in Malta.

His great army friend, Michael Trubshawe, said: "David *could* have been a good soldier; he had all the makings of a good soldier but the tragedy of the thing is that he didn't go to the regiment of his choice but to the HLI. Now in those days there were two battalions—one was called Home Service and the other was further afield. Our battalion in Malta really came under Home Service and there was absolutely nothing to do. Very quickly, I think, David became depressed by this situation. There were really only the four P's—parade (i.e. square-bashing), polo, piss-ups and poking. Now none of these four, enjoyable as they might be, is really guaranteed to help a keen soldier along the line. Whereas, if he'd gone to the 2nd Battalion, the 74th, who were in India, he might well have seen active service on the frontier and been able to apply the skills and training and dedication that he had learnt at Sandhurst. But it all faded. For instance, if one went into his room in barracks in Malta you wouldn't find him reading the manual of military law or the King's Regulations; you'd find him reading *The Tatler*. I've no doubt at all that he could have been a very good soldier because he had the love of the Jocks, the troops, and that's what all soldiering is about. It's not very difficult to be popular but to be respected is an entirely different matter and the makings of a good officer and David always commanded respect."

Trubshawe, formerly of Cambridge University and a smart cavalry regiment, was as bored in Malta as Niven was and the pair of them combined happily in some most unmilitary activities.

Once they went to a fancy dress ball at the Opera House in Valletta, clad as goats. They wore goatskins over their heads and backs and had attached beneath them football bladders with gloves tied on—"to make the thing thoroughly realistic"—and as they crawled about on all fours their batmen followed behind, scattering black olives in their wake. "Well, what we hadn't realised," Trubshawe said, "was that the goat is virtually a sacred animal in Malta and there was absolute uproar, pandemonium and panic. So down the main street of Valletta disappeared two officers of the Highland Light Infantry dressed as goats, with everything dingling and dangling and waving in the wind . . . They nearly called out the friended by the society hostess, Elsa Maxwell, who thinking he might make some sort of film actor—a poor girl's Ronald Colman perhaps—presented him to the director Ernst Lubitsch, who was not exactly overwhelmed by what he saw and told him to forget it. Maxwell's next idea was to find her protégé a rich wife but potential rich wives were even less impressed than Lubitsch had been and so Niven reverted to Plan A, the idea of becoming a movie actor, which had begun to appeal to him quite strongly.

Indeed, the seed originally planted back in England by Priscilla Weigall had clearly taken root quite early because Ann Todd recalled that . . . "One day he said to me, 'I want to ask your advice. I don't think I want to stay on in the army; I've decided to be an actor.' I said, 'Oh, but you can't do that, Niven. You can't act, I mean don't be ridiculous—you can't *possibly* act. After all, if you had to go and begin acting you'd have to say something serious and I don't think you could even say "I love you" seriously. The audience would just pass away with laughing. No, no, you stay in the army . . .' "

So much for professional advice. Niven, no doubt having forgotten this, decided to listen instead to the words of Elsa Maxwell and, armed with an address book full of useful names, made his way by a roundabout route—via Cuba and Panama, in fact—to Hollywood, where he arrived in late summer of 1934.

The contact book proved helpful enough socially but did little for his professional aspirations, partly because he had no resident alien's visa and was therefore unable to work. He also, as an incidental embarrassment, had no money either.

Ever resourceful, however, he checked in at the Roosevelt Hotel on Hollywood Boulevard and introduced himself to the part-owner and general manager, one Al Weingand. "David said he had a problem," Weingand recalled. "He had no money. Well, he was a very engaging, attractive guy and we had plenty of spare rooms so I told him that I would stake him to a room for one month and I'll never forget the monthly rate then was sixty-five dollars. During that month he didn't have much to do and we would go out to lunch or he would have dinner with me and my wife." Weingand did not though believe Niven was a sponger—"The poor guy was just broke."

It says much for Niven's personality that he could enjoin a complete stranger to put him up for a month and even take him out for meals. But it is also greatly to his credit that eventually, Weingand said, "he paid me back in full. Every cent."

But before the debt could be repaid he had to overcome the

problem of acquiring a work permit. His social peregrinations had brought him into contact with a number of prominent film directors and producers, some of whom showed interest in him but none of whom was able to employ him until he acquired some kind of official status. On Al Weingand's recommendation therefore he went to Mexico and—these things being more easily managed there apparently—set about getting his resident alien's visa, which duly arrived early in 1935.

Equipped with this he presented himself at the offices of Central Casting which, in those days, were to be found on Hollywood Boulevard. Central Casting was, and is, the agency which provides the studios with extras, people who stand in the background saying "Rhubarb, rhubarb" to each other while the stars get on with the action. Niven, being only twenty-five and full of optimism was undeterred by the sign outside which said: "Don't try to become an actor. For every one we employ we turn away a thousand." So he was taken on and registered as "Anglo-Saxon type No. 2008". Having thus pigeon-holed him to its own total satisfaction, the agency—or so he later claimed—promptly cast him as a Mexican. As a step up on the way to stardom it wasn't much but at least it was a start.

And in that he was luckier than most. There were literally thousands of registered extras in Hollywood and few of them averaged as much as three days work a week. So Niven, who reckoned he appeared anonymously in well over a score of Westerns, was already shooting better than par for the course. But still it was a long way from stardom or even from a humble speaking role in a movie.

Nevertheless, he continued to put himself about and was even given a screen test at MGM and perhaps it was because of this that a rumour came to be spread abroad that Irving Thalberg, MGM's immensely powerful head of production, was thinking of casting him in *Mutiny on the Bounty* (the Clark Gable–Charles Laughton version). This story was recounted to Sam Goldwyn, who was then running his own studio, and he—possibly wishing to spike MGM's guns; the G. in MGM, after all, stood for Goldwyn, one of the studio's founders—promptly signed the virtually untried Niven to a seven-year contract.

Nowadays that seems a most implausible sequence of events but Hollywood in the mid-1930s was truly a land of opportunity. Production was high and so was the demand for new faces and so, with a bit of luck, a well-groomed, good-looking young man might

reasonably hope for a chance in the movies. Never mind whether
he had acting ability or not; if he had the right appearance acting
ability wasn't necessarily considered essential—at least not to start
with. It was something which, popular belief had it, could be
acquired later. That this supposition was incorrect was proved by
the number of good-looking young men (and women) who appeared
briefly in films and were then rightly returned to the oblivion whence
they had come.

Having signed Niven, however, Goldwyn could find no immediate use for him and not wishing to have him lolling about as an
unemployed burden on the payroll, he lent him to Paramount. Thus
it was with that studio that David Niven began a career which was
to last for the best part of five decades: his first speaking role in a
film was in a now generally forgotten drama called *Without Regret*
in 1935. Niven's great moment came in a scene with the star, Elissa
Landi, on a railway station. "Goodbye, my dear," he said. It's
possible that audiences walked away choked with emotion at the
poignant delivery of this line, though history fails to record any
such response. But at least he must have done his tiny bit reasonably
well because Goldwyn himself then employed him in *Barbary
Coast*, wherein he was notable mostly for being thrown out of the
window of a San Francisco brothel during a riot. (He did, actually,
have a line of dialogue, too, but that was drowned in the background
noise.) Still, he must have looked the part as he hurtled through
the window because Columbia then borrowed him for another tiny
role in *A Feather in her Hat*, and he finished 1935 back with
Goldwyn again as a failed crook and all-round wastrel in *Splendour*.

Well, at least he was on his way. He had appeared in four films
and earned 5,200 dollars and, what's more, better times were on the
way. In 1936 he played his first starring role as Bertie Wooster in
Thank You, Jeeves. Admittedly this was a B-picture made by 20th
Century-Fox but it offered, at last, a real part and one that gave
him an opportunity to show the inborn talent for light comedy that
was to bring him such a lucrative career for the next forty-odd
years. The Niven that most of us now remember was probably too
sophisticated and worldly-wise to be acceptable as Bertie Wooster
but the Niven of 1936 may well have seemed tailor-made for the
role. In any event it was an important landmark for him because,
as a result, he was now regarded as an actor who could be entrusted
with several lines of dialogue at a time. Thus 1936 brought him a
total of five films, among them *The Charge of the Light Brigade*, a
curious epic directed by Michael Curtiz in which the Light Brigade

seemed to spend most of its time on the North-West Frontier of India and in which Niven played Errol Flynn's friend, a role he was destined to fill off-screen as well as on.

But life was not all work for Niven—indeed, he always ensured that it never was—and his social, to say nothing of his sexual activities, were also decidedly hectic. It was around this time that he became involved—according to his memoirs—with "a Great Big Star" who swept him off his feet, took him to New York, kept him away from his studio and his obligations thereto, got him into serious trouble with Sam Goldwyn and then, having all the clout of a Great Big Star, persuaded Goldwyn to forgive him.

Now there are cynical people who maintain that this lady never really existed and that Niven had invented the whole episode because it made a very good story. But others, more trusting perhaps in the author's veracity, have speculated ever since the book was published as to her identity. Niven himself, a gentleman to the end, refused ever to name her and it seemed that the secret may have gone with him to the grave. But my own investigations have perhaps cast a little light on her identity.

Since his early days in Hollywood Niven had remained a close friend of Al Weingand who was, in turn, a close friend of Ronald Colman. And with Colman Weingand had acquired San Ysidro, a ranch near Santa Barbara in southern California, which they had turned into a hotel-cum-weekend resort. It was, and still is, an extremely comfortable and respectable place but in the 1930s it was also used by the Hollywood movie colony as a kind of discreet fornicatorium, a quiet little spot in which they could conduct illicit, or anyway extra-marital, love affairs. And Niven, being among those who took advantage of this facility, was wont to go there with a lady who might, conceivably, have been the Great Big Star of his memoirs . . .

Weingand said: "There was quite a lot of frolicking at the ranch and David sometimes came up with an attractive girl . . ." Yes— and no doubt he turned up with many an attractive girl but there was, surely, one attractive girl in particular . . .

"Well," said Weingand, "there was and they had quite a romance going on at the time. Merle Oberon was a very popular and new actress then and she and David would come up and spend a few days or a weekend at the ranch. I thought that would end up in a marriage. It was a serious affair, not just a shack-up deal—and we hotel men get to know the difference."

So then did he believe that Miss Oberon, the wife at the time of

Sir Alexander Korda, was the "Great Big Star" of the memoirs? "I think so. I personally know of no other."

It's true that to describe Merle Oberon as a "Great Big Star" in 1936 would have been to stretch the point a little. But she was certainly a star—a much bigger star than Niven—and she became an even greater star later on.

Well, whether or not Miss Oberon was the Great Big Star of Niven's reminiscences she definitely shared his bed at San Ysidro —not, in truth, that this made her in any way unique, for by all accounts enough women must have shared his bed in those carefree bachelor days of the 1930s to have worn a groove in his mattress. By 1938, at which time he had appeared with some degree of noticeable effect in more than twenty films, he had set up home with the glorious but ill-fated Errol Flynn, who by then was separated from his wife, Lily Damita. The house they occupied was rented from Rosalind Russell who, knowing her tenants well, immediately dubbed it "Cirrhosis-by-the-Sea". In fact, it was in Beverly Hills and not really by the sea at all, unless you are prepared to concede the fact that the Pacific Ocean is only a fast twenty-minute drive away along Sunset Boulevard.

By Niven's own admission the house rapidly became "a hotbed of fun and bad behaviour". Booze and women flowed in equal abundance and if most of the women flowed towards Flynn, who was an acknowledged star, there were still enough leftovers and Flynn-discards to keep the more modest Niven ticking over quite happily. Miraculously, he even had enough strength left after the boozing and the bedding to make five films in 1939, among them *Wuthering Heights* with, significantly or not, Merle Oberon and *Raffles*, another of his comparatively few top-starring pictures in which he portrayed the cricket-playing, upper-class burglar.

But before that year was out the drinking and the womanising had to be shelved, at least temporarily—as indeed did the film-making— because war had broken out in Europe and Niven had volunteered to take part in it.

At this point, in order to get some idea of the weight of the man, it's worth considering his position. He was twenty-nine years old, had appeared in twenty-two films and while by no means a star was surely quivering on the brink of stardom. He was leading a comfortable, even—by most people's standards—a luxurious life; there was no compulsion on him whatsoever to volunteer for active service; most of his British contemporaries in Hollywood signally failed to do so and his employer, Sam Goldwyn, strongly urged him against any such course of action. And yet, without hesitation, he immediately made plans to abandon his career and return to England to fight. Now why did he do that?

In his excellent book *Niven's Hollywood*, Tom Hutchinson provides as plausible an explanation as any: "There was a debt of honour to his own father killed during the first war and there was the irony of all those mock heroic roles in movies with stories from British history. His Englishness had been a passport to work and social success in Hollywood: now that debt, too, was called in."

What it boiled down to then was that old-fashioned thing, patriotism. As Michael Trubshawe said: "David knew rightly that (a) as an Englishman and (b) as a regular officer there was only one thing he could do. And it was not an easy thing to do because he'd got farther than the bottom rung of the ladder by then: he was halfway up and the money was coming in and the parts were coming in. No, good God, he came back to rejoin the army and do what he conceived to be his job."

On his return to London, however, he was not exactly welcomed with open arms and hearts; indeed his reception was such that in his place even the Prodigal Son might have been tempted to say, "oh, sod it", and leave home again. The press greeted him with jeers on the lines of "Relax! The Dawn Patrol is Here." At first he even encountered great difficulty in finding an outfit that would accept him. He rather fancied the RAF but they turned him down and finally he had to pull a few strings before he could even be taken on as a second-lieutenant by the Rifle Brigade.

What Niven actually did during the war has never been made quite clear, mainly because he was always extremely reticent about it. Certainly he appeared in two propaganda films, *The First of the Few* in 1942 and *The Way Ahead* in 1944, but he had quite definitely not returned to his homeland to do that kind of work. "Far, far from it," said Michael Trubshawe. "Good God, no. He turned down so many requests through his commanding officer to make films that in the end the adjutant-general, who was a very big shot indeed in the War Office, sent for him and said, 'Now, Niven, I want you to make a film, you know. Will you do it?' And David said, 'Well, sir, if I'd wanted to make films I'd have stayed in Hollywood.' And the adjutant-general said, 'I thought you'd say that, Niven. Well, if you won't volunteer I'm afraid I shall have to give you a direct order. Is that understood?' And David said, 'Sir, that is understood,' and he went and did what they asked him to do."

Reluctantly. Because Niven was essentially a fighting soldier. Apart from his time with the Rifle Brigade he was also attached briefly, though mysteriously, to military intelligence, before volunteering for the Commandoes, an outfit not generally known for its willingness to take on recruits strictly on the strength of their photogenic profiles and twinkling blue eyes. And with the Commandoes he appears to have been involved both with the Dieppe raid of 1942 and the Normandy landings of 1944. Whatever he was doing in the army he was obviously doing it well because he ended the war as a colonel and was awarded the American Legion of Merit for his work in communications between the British and US invasion forces.

Afterwards he rarely spoke about the war, although he did admit to his son David that he was "scared to death for much of the time and just glad to get out alive and in one piece". And even Private Peter Ustinov who, in 1944, served in the curious dual capacity of Niven's batman and co-author with Eric Ambler of the script of *The Way Ahead* knew little of what else Niven had done between 1939 and 1945. He told Ustinov some tales of the army but "you could never quite believe them because they were such good stories."

But apart from ending the war as a colonel, Niven also ended it as a married man and a father. First at the Café de Paris then later at (a) a lunchtime concert at the National Gallery or (b) in a slit trench during an air raid at RAF Heston, depending on which of Niven's own conflicting accounts you choose to believe, he had met a WAAF officer named Primula (known as Primmie) Rollo, the daughter of Lady Kathleen and Bill Rollo. The slit-trench meeting makes the better story because, according to Niven, he jumped into it and landed on Primmie's dog which promptly and not surprisingly bit his backside. Ten days later he and the dog's owner were married with Trubshawe as their best man. The year was 1940. In December 1942 David Jr. was born and his godfather Noel Coward presented him with a silver cocktail shaker on which was inscribed: "Because, my Godson dear, I rather/Think you'll turn out like your father." It was not perhaps the kind of gift for which the average baby can find an immediate use but no doubt it came in handy later.

However, by August 1945 Niven was demobbed and the following morning at 5 a.m. was on the set at Denham studios to make what is still one of his most enchanting films, *A Matter of Life and Death*. It was another loan-out by Sam Goldwyn who had forgiven him for breaking his contract for such a frivolous reason as a war and had generously given him a new, five-year contract at a handsome figure.

Niven, aged thirty-five and worried about his future having made only two films in six years, was properly grateful for this continued faith. When the movie was completed (and it was chosen as the first Royal Command Film, as well as proving a success on both sides of the Atlantic) Niven, now a father for the second time—for Jamie had been born in November 1945—set sail for America to fulfil his obligations to Goldwyn. Just as he had arrived to a cool reception in England in 1939, so he departed with an equally unfriendly send-off from the Inland Revenue, who neatly deprived him of virtually all his savings before he departed.

There now followed what, in retrospect, must have been very nearly the worst period in his life; perhaps the last few years when he was struggling against a most debilitating illness were harder but the year or so after his return to Hollywood had a vivid nightmare quality of its own. In the first place he had been warned by David Selznick that he would find changes—new directors and producers, new, ambitious young actors, new competition. In the second place the immediate films he was offered—and which he accepted gratefully—were *The Perfect Marriage* with Loretta Young and *Magnificent Doll* with Ginger Rogers, and what they had in common was that both were the purest tosh. Hardly a hero's welcome and depressing enough on their own but far worse was to come.

In May 1946, Niven and Primmie went to a party given by Tyrone Power. There was a barbecue and then Power and his guests, noted and presumably sophisticated movie stars, decided to play sardines. In the course of the game Primmie opened the door to what she thought was a cupboard, stepped through and fell down a flight of stairs into a cellar. She was taken, unconscious, to hospital where the next day, after an emergency brain operation, she died. She was twenty-five years old.

It could be argued that Niven never truly recovered from her death, a death which as Peter Ustinov said was "so absurd and so dreadful. The idea of dying when you're trying to find a place to play hide and seek is really so asinine that it makes one angry with fate. She was obviously very suited to him."

Michael Trubshawe, who perhaps knew her better than any of Niven's other friends, said of her: "She was an absolute darling. She was kind, she was fun and she was a wonderful mum. They were tremendously happy and her death absolutely shook the old boy to the core, all the stuffing was knocked out of him."

Niven's sons were obviously far too young at the time of their mother's death to have any real memory of her but David Jr. said:

"Every time he spoke about her it was with tremendous love and affection." Jamie said: "He always spoke of her as a fabulous woman but he didn't really talk much about her, maybe because it was something that really bothered him a great deal. We all got the message that he loved her and we all got the message that it hurt him terribly when she died. But he didn't talk about her all the time. In fairness, you know, he was married for thirty-five years after that to another woman and I'm not sure that always talking about your first wife would have been terribly well received at home."

Niven's immediate response to the loss of Primmie was to turn to his friends. He rang Ann Todd, who was in New York, and asked her to fly out to stay with him and this she did. "It was extraordinary to see him. He became very bitter against life and fate and he was in a very, very bad state."

Ann Todd stayed with him for two or three weeks and after that it was Douglas Fairbanks and his wife who offered comfort and hospitality. Fairbanks was godfather to James Niven and of Primmie he said: "She was charming, absolutely charming. Very pretty, typical English rose, very sweet—absolutely adorable." When Niven felt that he couldn't contemplate staying any longer in the house where he and Primmie had lived he left his sons with their nanny and took refuge with the Fairbankses. "He stayed for weeks and weeks and my wife actually answered all the letters of condolence that came to him because he couldn't face it. He was terribly distressed and remained so for a very, very long time."

Obviously in time the sharpest and most immediate distress passed but, in Roderick Mann's opinion, something of it remained even until the end of Niven's life. "He would talk to *me* about her, anyway. I think he fantasised about how it would have been if she'd lived."

But when, at last, Niven recovered from those first deep pains of grief there was work to return to—though he could have found little consolation in that. *The Other Love*, with Barbara Stanwyck, and *The Bishop's Wife*, with Cary Grant and Loretta Young, were both stinkers but even they seemed more than acceptable compared with *Bonny Prince Charlie*, which he made in 1948 on loan to Alexander Korda. Niven had no wish to be connected with this enterprise. In the first place a return to Britain presented him with tax problems and in the second place, being no fool, he could recognise a potential disaster when it loomed up before him and a disaster was what *Bonny Prince Charlie* turned out to be, taking up almost a year of his life and causing one of the less caustic critics to observe that the star looked about as comfortable as "a goldfish in a haggis". But despite his misgivings he had no choice in the matter since, by the terms of his contract, he was more or less obliged to go where Goldwyn sent him.

Still, the film could not be accounted a total loss because one day on the set he met Hjordis Tersmeden, a Swedish model and aspiring actress. Niven described this encounter as a "coup de foudre" or, to put it more simply, love at first sight, which is indeed what it must have been for ten days later—shades of his first marriage—on January 13th, 1948, they were married at Chelsea Register Office, Michael Trubshawe again serving as best man.

"It must be admitted," said Trubshawe, "that Hjordis was very, very beautiful—an absolute knockout—and David succumbed." Nevertheless the speed of the marriage rather took the best man aback. "I think he was what you might call 'caught on the rebound' —you know what I mean?"

Douglas Fairbanks, on the other hand, said that he had been hoping that Niven would remarry. "He was a fish out of water; he was lonesome."

So with a new and beautiful wife to assuage his loneliness Niven returned to Hollywood—to "the Pink House", the home he had bought for Primmie but which she had never lived to occupy, and to more indifferent films. Worst of all, the ribald reception given to *Bonny Prince Charlie* notwithstanding, he was lent again to Korda to make *The Elusive Pimpernel*, which many perceptive critics believed to be even more dreadful than the previous Korda epic. *The Times* was so concerned about it as to say that "film audiences are in danger of forgetting what a really accomplished actor Mr. Niven is." Nor were things any better when he returned to Hollywood to find himself on loan again, this time to an American independent company, to make a frightful turkey called *A Kiss for Corliss* with Shirley Temple. The truest criticism of it came from Niven himself who described it as "a disastrous teenage potboiler".

By this time, however, he could take no more. Certainly he had been working regularly since his return from the war but to what end? His reputation seemed to grow increasingly tattered with each successive film and so he decided to rid himself of Samuel Goldwyn, a task which must have appeared unflatteringly easy. He went to see Goldwyn to say he wished to end the contract and Goldwyn said, "Okay". Now to some extent Niven had been egged on to do this by vague promises of employment from various hotshot producers but once he had done the deed he discovered, as many another actor had discovered in a similar position, that the hotshot producers suddenly remembered that, actually, they didn't really have any work for an unemployed freelance.

He was therefore firmly in the middle of the worst phase of his career, a time when some people even spoke darkly of him as "box-office poison", though it was not Niven, who always gave of his best no matter how dire the part, that was poisonous: it was the films which he had perforce to accept—films like *The Toast of New Orleans* and *Happy Go Lovely*, in both of which he was called upon to drift around looking elegant and quizzical, which isn't much of a contribution at any time. He was even so desperate to re-establish himself that he made a mildly disastrous venture on to Broadway, co-starring with Gloria Swanson in a flop called *Nina*. After that there were more films—*Soldiers Three* (from the story by Kipling —a long, long way from the story by Kipling), *The Lady Says No!* and *Appointment with Venus*—but all of them mediocre at best.

One explanation for the fact that he plunged desperately, if not happily, into a succession of movies which might quite easily have wrecked the career of a less resilient actor, was provided by his son, David Jr: "The first reason that would come to mind is the fact that maybe he needed the scratch. It helped pay the rent and keep food in all our mouths and clothes on our little tiny bodies. So I think, quite honestly, that a lot of it was work done just to make ends meet." Furthermore Niven had a pretty rich lifestyle to maintain. "I mean, he did everything first class; he didn't stint on anything. He always had lovely homes and plenty of people looking after those homes and plenty of people who were being entertained around those homes."

Jamie Niven said: "He always had that wonderful expression that he used about the films he made: first of all, who's in it? Second of all, where is it? Third of all, when is it? And last of all, how much?" But that came later, when he was back at or around the top again. In the late 1940s and the early 1950s, the first two questions were luxuries he couldn't afford—when and how much? were the only important factors.

Nevertheless, things began to improve considerably with *The Moon is Blue*, a most risqué comedy for the time (the mention of a girl's virginity caused the raised eyebrows of shock in the censor's viewing room), directed by Otto Preminger. Niven's performance as a suave seducer reminded cinema audiences (and no doubt readers of *The Times*) that he was indeed an accomplished actor. And the film's wide success enabled him to alternate between Hollywood and Europe (where, for instance, he made *The Love Lottery* and *Carrington VC*) not as a peripatetic mummer frantic for work but as a star of some international renown. And in 1956 that renown became even greater when he appeared as Phineas Fogg in Mike Todd's truly mammoth production of *Around the World in Eighty Days*, certainly the most expensive film (when you take comparative costs into consideration) in which he had ever appeared and one of the remarkably few in which he was cast as the undoubted star.

It's one of the odder facts of Niven's career that although he was widely regarded as a star he was not, in fact, a star at all, if you accept the definition that a star is one whose name invariably appears at the head of the billing. If you look at a list of Niven's films you will find, far more often than not, that his name appears third or fourth. Even after *Around the World . . .*, which won the Oscar for the year's best film, he was next to be seen supporting Ava Gardner and Stewart Granger in *The Little Hut* and though he headed the cast in *The Silken Affair* he was soon back in a supporting role in *Oh Men! Oh Women!*, whose stars were Dan Dailey and Ginger Rogers.

I suppose the two actors with whom Niven is most often compared and with whom he is frequently bracketed are Ronald Colman (as whose successor Sam Goldwyn originally saw him) and Cary Grant, an even greater master of light comedy than Niven himself. But Colman and Grant were stars by any definition while Niven, though certainly a star as far as the public was concerned, was actually regarded by the studios as a kind of prince of supporting players.

Still, by the mid-1950s Niven was, if not exactly at the top then well within hailing distance of it, a position he retained with the occasional upward and downward lurch for the rest of his career. By then, too, he had inserted his foot pretty firmly in television's doorway by forming, along with Dick Powell and Charles Boyer, Four Star Playhouse, which for a good many years was prolific in making films for TV.

In 1958 Niven achieved what was for him, and is for any Hollywood actor, the pinnacle of his career when he played the seedy Major Pollock in the screen version of Terence Rattigan's play, *Separate Tables*. Again it's worth noting that although he played one of the four equally important roles in the film, the main stars were Rita Hayworth and Burt Lancaster—or at least those were the names most widely used to sell the picture to cinema audiences.

The story, briefly, tells of two couples, Hayworth and Lancaster, and Niven and Deborah Kerr (with whom he had earlier appeared in *Bonjour Tristesse*). The chief link between the two pairings is that all of them are staying in the same private hotel in Bournemouth. Niven's was a very serious role, something he had not really essayed for some time and Deborah Kerr said: "I think he was a tiny bit scared. I remember him coming to me and saying, 'You know, chum, I don't know whether I can do this. I mean, this is serious stuff, isn't it?' But, of course, he did it superbly. Superbly."

Delbert Mann, who directed the film, recalled that originally all four parts were to be played by Laurence Olivier and Vivien Leigh, with Olivier also directing. But that fell through and Lancaster and Hayworth took over two of the roles, with Niven and Kerr taking the others. "I would think," said Mann, "that David's was the most untypical role he ever attempted. He was extremely nervous about it: it was a big challenge for him but whatever insecurities he might have had about the role he covered with the joviality and jollity that were so much a part of his character. I do know that he worried about the part a great deal and would come to me and ask questions and we'd have to go off in a corner and have intimate discussions about the role and the background to it." But against that as an actor to work with he was . . . "Absolutely adorable, wonderful. He was a total, total professional. He came prepared; he had something to offer in rehearsal and on the set and he was a giving, loving, caring actor. He gave to the other actors, he was open to the director's suggestions. It was for me a kind of ideal working relationship, the likes of which I have had very few times in my career."

Delbert Mann believed that the winning of an Oscar would, nevertheless, have come as something of a shock to Niven. "I have no idea whether he expected to win it. I would seriously doubt it, knowing David and his habit of putting himself down. But for my taste it was certainly well deserved."

Deserved or not—and Niven's opposition in 1958 was Tony Curtis in *The Defiant Ones*, Paul Newman in *Cat on a Hot Tin Roof*, Sidney Poitier in *The Defiant Ones* and Spencer Tracy in *The Old Man and the Sea*—he carried off the Academy Award for best actor.

Speaking of Niven the man, Delbert Mann said: "I felt very relaxed with David. I felt I got to know him quite well. But I'm not really sure I knew what was going on in his mind."

That kind of comment was made by many others who also felt relaxed with Niven and believed they knew him well. There was always a part of him that was intensely private, that was masked even from the people closest to him. John Mortimer said that was one of the things he liked most about Niven and was what "made him such a good actor to play in *Separate Tables*, to play the sort of part in which you're always cheerful on the surface but underneath you're not. David certainly had terrific sadness in his life but he didn't burden others with it."

David Niven Jr. explained that part of his father's character by saying: "I think it was to do with the generation he belonged to. He felt that his problems were his own and why should he bore other people with them. Everybody has problems and his life was certainly not without them but he felt that he was best equipped to figure out how to solve them and he didn't see why he should cry on other people's shoulders."

But if Delbert Mann was unsure how well he really knew Niven the man he had no doubts at all about Niven the actor. "I would rate him absolutely the highest. I worked with a lot of very, very good actors and I would place David absolutely in the top category."

Delbert Mann's encomium is probably the highest Niven ever received. His own tendency was to disparage his acting ability with such rhetorical questions as "Can you imagine being wonderfully overpaid for dressing up and playing games?" He even told his sons to answer any criticisms of his ability that might be proffered by their schoolmates by retorting: "Well, he's a very, very bad actor but he absolutely loves doing it." In truth, he was a long way removed from being a bad actor. First of all, said Deborah Kerr, he took his acting "a great deal more seriously than he appeared to do". And beyond that . . . "He was very much better than he gave himself credit for and, of course, he was a superb comedian."

A comedian, yes—specifically a light comedian, which makes his Oscar for the essentially "straight" performance in *Separate Tables* something of a curiosity. To Douglas Fairbanks he was "an *excellent* light comedian"; to Bryan Forbes, who directed him in his penultimate film, he was "in many respects a very underestimated actor"; to John Mortimer (who wrote the script for *The Guns of Darkness* in 1962) he was "wonderful. He learned the technique and the throwaway part of film acting perfectly"; and Peter Ustinov, a little less fulsomely, remarked: "I think he regarded the whole thing as a job but I think, too, he began to regard himself as an artist. He was very conscious of his limitations, he knew what he could do and what he couldn't do and within that he certainly was an artist. He

43

knew when he would like to do a scene again because he wasn't satisfied and so on."

On that subject, the dispassionate (albeit affectionate) views of Jamie Niven are rather interesting: "I don't think he's going to go down as the world's greatest actor. I don't think he can be compared with Olivier and Burton and Richardson and people of that kind. I think he was a very competent professional and he enjoyed his work. But he didn't let it get blown out of proportion; he treated it very much as a nine to five kind of job and he didn't bring the work home with him. He thought he was a competent light comedian, which would probably be the general assessment, and he thought he was lucky because he did something that he enjoyed and that he was relatively good at. There were moments, I think, when he thought he was very good. He thought he was good when he made *Around the World in Eighty Days* and *Separate Tables* but he was very self-effacing; he wasn't an arrogant man. So therefore he probably felt that he wasn't as good as some of the great actors and I think that's right, I think that's a fair statement. I don't think he was—but he was very competent and he was a tremendous professional."

Strangely there is much to be said for all these somewhat disparate points of view. When the part was right for him, Niven *could* be wonderful; he *was* an excellent comedian and *was* a consummate professional. But, as an actor certainly, he did not have the stuff of greatness in him: what he sold, far more than technical virtuosity, was the personality of David Niven, an immensely attractive personality, and for most people that was enough.

But some time after he picked up the Oscar for *Separate Tables* and with success now dancing attendance on his career, Niven encountered a temporary setback in his private life. In July 1959 he and Hjordis decided to live apart. The fault, he acknowledged, was his: his new-found status as an Academy Award winner had drawn him temporarily into the familiar trap of putting his career above all else and when, later on, he said that at one stage he had become rather bigheaded it was probably this period that he was referring to.

The separation, however, lasted for only three months and a little while after the reconciliation—in fact in the spring of 1960—the couple decided to move to Europe. One reason for this was that Niven was a little disenchanted with Hollywood, feeling that he had seen the best of it in the pre-war years. This, of course, may well have had much to do with the fact that he was now fifty and beginning to feel, as many people do, that the world was a better place when he was young. But the main reason for the move was financial. David Jr. said: "He was in the ninety per cent tax bracket and he really didn't have very much money. He'd done a lot of pictures but he had very little in the bank. As a matter of fact, as he explained it to us, the reason he decided to leave was that he didn't even have enough money to repaint the Pink House. So with the money he was going to have to raise to have the Pink House repainted he was able to buy a house in Switzerland where he was able to keep ninety per cent of his earnings instead of giving ninety per cent to the government."

Actually, it was Deborah Kerr who helped persuade him to choose Switzerland rather than some other European tax haven. She and her husband, Peter Viertel, lived at Klosters and one day on a visit to Hollywood they found Niven in a low mood bemoaning the fact that everything there seemed to be going down the drain, including his bank balance. "What does one do?" he asked. "Where does one go? You can't save a nickel here." And it was at this point that the Viertels planted the idea of Switzerland in his mind. Indeed, he rather took to Switzerland—he enjoyed the social life and he enjoyed ski-ing, at which he was not particularly adept, although he formed his own ski-ing club, its emblem a ham on skis, of which he was the sole member.

And speaking of members . . . John Mortimer's favourite Niven anecdote is of the time he was ski-ing downhill and discovered when it was too late to stop that he had forgotten to zip up his pants. "His vital organs became frozen," said Mortimer, "and he looked down and saw what he described as a very small, Eton-blue acorn. He was in terrible agony and arrived in the square at St. Moritz doubled up in pain." With great presence of mind, however, Niven bundled himself into a taxi and asked to be taken to the nearest bar. Others in a similar predicament might have gone to a hospital but not Niven. Shuffling into the bar he demanded of the barman: "What do you do when your balls freeze?" The barman suggested a double brandy. Again others in like circumstances might have drunk the stuff but not Niven. He took the double brandy into the men's room and lowered his frozen parts into it and he was just beginning to thaw out when various other people came in to use the facilities and discovered the great actor apparently urinating into a brandy glass.

But the episode of the frozen balls came later. Long before then he had made one of his better films of this period, *The Guns of Navarone*, in 1961 and he and Hjordis had adopted two daughters,

45

Kristina and Fiona. According to Michael Trubshawe: "They wanted a family of their own but Hjordis was unable to have children." The result was that, since she didn't work herself, she had little to occupy her time, especially when Niven was busy on a film. "And then, it's the old story, David would come home tired and wanting to put his feet up—the old carpet-slipper treatment—and Hjordis would want to go out. In the end I think they decided for the sake of both of them, and especially for Hjordis, to adopt a couple of children to keep her happy and busy during the daytime. That's how it came about and it was highly successful."

Niven, by all accounts, was as loving and attentive a father to his two new daughters as he had been to his sons. But the two boys, though welcoming the girls into the family, were not unaffected by the change.

James Niven said: "I got on very well with Hjordis at the beginning but after the adoption our relationship changed a lot—not from my standpoint but from hers. I think from that moment on the relationship deteriorated enormously: she just wouldn't talk to you, she simply cut you dead all the time and that was a tricky thing to live with. I coped with it as best I could and we would try to make a joke of it. There were days that were good and days that were bad but there's no question—her relationship with me changed dramatically the day she adopted a child."

Perhaps that's understandable—a woman coping with two young children of her own (if not biologically her own then at least hers by choice) is likely to have less time and attention to spare for two teenage stepsons. Niven himself was unaware of the changed circumstances vis-à-vis Jamie and Hjordis, partly because nobody told him about it and partly because the situation was more or less resolved quite quickly when Jamie went away to boarding school and later to university. "So I really didn't have to see very much of her after that." As for the girls . . . "Dad was terrific with them, a fabulous father."

Meanwhile, Niven's career rolled on—a couple of Italian films were followed by the likes of *55 Days in Peking*, *The Pink Panther* and *Bedtime Story*, in which he appeared with Marlon Brando. None of them was particularly memorable, although Niven's own performances were as gilt-edged as ever. And so the next dramatic change in his career came in 1971 with the publication of the first volume of his memoirs, *The Moon's a Balloon*. It was Roderick Mann who started him on this enterprise after years of listening delightedly to his anecdotes. Niven was even more than a raconteur of near genius . . . "He was a great mental gymnast in that he would take some quite ordinary anecdote and spice it up and the stories were so good that I used to say 'You've *got* to write a book.' Well, he didn't for two or three years but finally he sat down and in longhand he began to write." When the book was finished and the working title, "Three Sides of a Square" had been changed to *The Moon's a Balloon*, Mann took it to his own agent and then to Hamish Hamilton the publishers, who were delighted with it. But then a rather considerable problem arose: it was suddenly remembered that some fifteen years earlier Niven had written a novel called *Round the Ragged Rocks* and was obliged to offer any new work first to the publishers of that book. Unfortunately, by the time this was discovered he had already signed a contract with Hamish Hamilton. What to do? Well, according to Roderick Mann, Niven wrote a letter to the publishers of the novel, a small American firm, purporting to come from his agent and saying, in effect: the actor David Niven has sent us a heavy tome of theatrical reminiscences (in itself enough, as Roderick Mann, said "to strike terror in the flinty hearts of any publishers"). And the letter went on: we understand you have a two-book deal with Mr. Niven but we hesitate to send this tome to you without your express wishes, since it's very heavy indeed and we estimate it weighs about five pounds.

"And this went on and on," said Mann, "and in the end the Americans said, 'No way—we don't want to know.' So David was off the hook."

The Moon's a Balloon was immediately and immensely successful, much to Niven's own surprise, as indeed was its successor *Bring on the Empty Horses* and from then on he regarded himself as a writer as much as an actor. Both his sons say he found the act of writing "terribly, terribly difficult". He could neither type nor dictate so everything had to be written in longhand, a considerable task when, as David Jr. said, "the words didn't come easily and being the sort of perfectionist he was he rewrote and rewrote and edited and re-edited many times before he handed the manuscript to the publisher."

Nevertheless, it was his writing that gave him the greater satisfaction, possibly because he regarded it as work, unlike acting which he always declared was simply fun. David Jr. said: "The satisfaction he got from his acting came when he received his Academy Award: there at least he was acknowledged by his peers. The success he got from writing possibly gave him more pleasure because it was something that he did all by himself. Also it gave him a whole new lease of life and he was thrilled, absolutely thrilled, that people wanted to buy his books."

It's worth noting, too, that the success of his books owed more to the quality of the writing than to the name of the author, useful though that was in publicising and selling them. John Mortimer and Peter Ustinov, both excellent writers themselves, pay tribute to his talent and Ustinov believes that "he'll be remembered for his books almost more than his films because films always date, whether you like it or not. He had a very meticulous eye for the comic and the absurd."

These gifts were not quite so apparent in his novel, *Go Slowly, Come Back Quickly* but they were outstanding in the two volumes of reminiscences. Yes, but how true were the amazing stories he told therein? Roderick Mann believed, as I suspect most people do, that they were "slightly made better. I'd had adventures with David and then years later I would hear him telling the story and I'd think: Well, I know that, I was there, that wasn't the way it happened. But it was much better the way he told it. He was just incapable of being boring or allowing himself to be bored."

And so with his books being constantly reprinted, with film offers continuing to come along at the rate of at least one a year and with the producers of television chat shows eagerly seeking his services as a raconteur, Niven enjoyed perhaps the most fecund decade of his career. But it's one of the less agreeable characteristics of fate that there is always a price to be paid for success—or, as the Americans put it in a slightly different context, "there's no such thing as a free lunch." The bill for the apparently free lunch that Niven had been enjoying for most of the 1970s was presented in 1979 and it was a very stiff bill indeed.

He was in France playing his last important film role in *Better Late than Never*, directed by Brian Forbes, when the illness which, eventually, was to kill him first became apparent. Bryan Forbes said: "I became aware of it when we were doing a scene on the beach and he suddenly said, 'Forbesy, I can't run. My legs won't work . . .'" And then his voice began to fail. "He couldn't articulate certain words . . . he found it very difficult to get his mouth round certain words, which is the most terrible thing for an actor."

About the same time he appeared on the *Michael Parkinson Show* when some people thought he was drunk and others, more charitably and knowing Niven was too professional ever to appear drunk in public, suggested to Jamie that something was wrong. Jamie phoned his father and said: "I saw a tape of the show and, I've got to be frank with you, aren't you concerned?" It was then that Niven admitted that he was indeed concerned and put forward the theory that he had suffered a stroke. Soon after that he underwent the tests that showed him to be a victim not of a stroke but of motor neurone disease.

Niven had never much liked the idea even of growing old. He accepted, of course, that it was inevitable but, according to Roderick Mann, he used to say: "I have a vision of myself as a young man of twenty-five and then I see this old poop prancing about on the screen and I can't bear it." The idea of being not simply old but infirm was almost intolerable to him. "I've always thought," he wrote in a letter to his publisher, "that was reserved for old farts but I sense now that young farts of seventy-two are coming into the firing line!"

That was in 1982 when he was close to the end; in the intervening years since 1979 he had fought with great courage against the debilitating effects of his illness. What affected him most of all was the inability to communicate. At one point he said to John Mortimer: "I think it's having talked too much all my life that's given me this voice."

Jamie Niven said: "He coped with it amazingly well and with a certain amount of humour. You've got to remember that this is a disease that is psychologically frightening because your mind is fine but your body is melting away and you know it and there's nothing you can do about it. And so you have to deal with the fact that you're dying slowly and that your ability to communicate with your fellow man is eroding."

Niven continued to write to his friends, first in his own hand until—in his own phrase—he was "fucked up gripwise, as they say on Madison Avenue", and then by dictating to a secretary.

In 1982 he even appeared, for the last time, in a film—*The Trail of the Pink Panther*, quite the worst of that lengthy series. When he was making this his voice was so far gone that his part was dubbed later by the American impressionist Rich Little. Had he been fit he would have strolled through the role; as it was it must have been unbearably arduous for him. So why did he do it? God knows, he didn't need the money. Perhaps he believed that if he was still able to work he could not be, no matter what the doctors said, as ill as he seemed. Or perhaps as Jamie Niven put it: "He'd committed to make the movie before he realised how ill he was. I don't think it was an ego thing—that he wanted to make his last movie. I think it was just typical that he'd made a commitment and the financing had been organised and he felt that he shouldn't let the producer down."

When the filming was completed Niven retired to his second home in the south of France and, in effect, waited for death. Roderick Mann went to visit him two months before he died. "That was awful. I almost couldn't bear to go. Roger Moore had been to see him and said, 'You've got to go because he's asking to see you. Just bite the bullet and go,' so I went and it was horrendous because he couldn't speak. I literally couldn't understand what he was saying and he had shrivelled in his clothes. And we went and sat in the garden and I just looked at him and he looked at me and he smiled —he was twinkling away, you know, still, because the brain had stayed active. But it was very grim and very sad. And then when I left he stood in the drive and waved, right until the car was out of sight. He knew I wouldn't see him again and I knew it, too."

David Niven died on July 29th, 1983, in his home in Switzerland at the age of seventy-three. He had chosen to go to Switzerland, according to his son Jamie, "because he felt he could breathe better up in the mountains". Right to the end he refused to go on any kind of life-support system and when that end came, Jamie said, "I was happy for him because it was over and I was saddened because I had lost him. I felt that he was at peace and that was good because he had suffered so much."

Hjordis, his wife of thirty-five years, was not with him when he died. She was herself under considerable strain at the time and since his death she has lived almost as a recluse at their home in the south of France. To David Jr. she said that she would never again visit the house in Switzerland because it was there that Niven had died.

The funeral, held in Switzerland, was, as Jamie put it, "a mad-house. It was a tiny little village and 350 photographers and most of the local people came. But it was a beautiful service and very touching. But it was a very hard thing to do—to bury your father in front of 350 photographers who don't let you alone. You felt like you were sharing it with the whole world. It was not a very private moment for any of us. I'd never realised how popular he was, I'd never realised that he was loved by everyone as much as he was."

Two stories which may help to explain why Niven enjoyed such universal popularity. The first was told by John Mortimer, who one day had invited him to lunch at the Mortimer house in the Home Counties. "We were having lunch at one o'clock and my son arrived at half-past twelve and said, 'I think I've seen David Niven about four miles away, walking down a country lane.' And what had happened was that he had arrived too early and was too shy to knock at the door and so he'd gone for a long walk to fill in the time, holding, as I remember it, a large pot of caviar that he had brought as a gift for us."

The second, and even more revealing, anecdote was told by Jamie Niven. "After he died we received some wonderful flowers from the porters at Terminal No. 1 at Heathrow Airport, with a card that said: 'To the finest gentleman who ever walked through these halls.' Some time after that I went to the terminal and thanked the head man there and asked him if there was anything particular that he remembered about my father. And he said, 'Absolutely. Your father had one man in particular who always used to take care of him here. One day there was a mad crowd of people in the place, just horrible, and your father jumped into his car and disappeared and didn't tip the man who looked after him. Well, the fellow thought that was a bit odd for Mr. Niven but he understood how it had happened and didn't worry about it. But forty-five minutes later your father walked back in to find the guy. He'd got halfway to London when he realised he hadn't tipped him and had come back to do so." Jamie added that this was "typical of the way he felt about people. He was humble. He wasn't a proud, arrogant, difficult man."

It was probably this kind of quality that made David Niven a star in the public mind and kept him a star even though he almost certainly appeared in more bad films than any other actor of similar stature. In nearly half a century he featured in eighty-nine pictures, in roles ranging from a cough and a spit to leading man, and very few of them made any noticeable contribution to the art of the cinema. He was indeed less an actor than a great screen personality; most of the time he simply played himself but that, granted his small but finely honed talent as a light comedian, was enough to save a multitude of mediocre films from total disaster.

John Mortimer felt that he had no illusions at all about himself as an actor. "I believe he thought it was all a huge joke—that he'd strayed into it from Central Casting because he hadn't anything better to do." Maybe. But there was undoubtedly more to him than that: he was the consummate professional, always on time, always word perfect. A man who truly believes that acting is a joke doesn't take that much trouble. Niven was proud of his craft but knew his limitations, although the ease and lightness of his touch on screen may have concealed a greater degree of talent than even he was aware of. At this stage, however, it hardly matters: what he left on screen was the indelible image of a hugely engaging character and

I suspect that generations of movie-goers will continue to watch his films, bad though many of them are, simply because the very presence of Niven makes them feel better.

I believe that the truth about David Niven is simply this: no matter what he achieved as an actor or as a writer, his greatest success was as a man and that's probably the greatest success of all. Certainly it's the most difficult to achieve. To be spoken of, as he is, with universal affection is an extremely rare accomplishment. People who knew him remember him chiefly as a friend; they remember him laughing and causing laughter; they remember his loyalty and kindness, his modesty and his sensitivity to the needs of others. I could quote each of them at great length but perhaps the essence of what all of them said is best summed up in the words of John Mortimer: "He was a model of how people who are famous and who enjoy the terrific privilege of stardom or public acclaim should behave." As an epitaph it serves him well.

Steve McQueen

McQueen in *The Cincinnati Kid*—then in his
prime at thirty-five and probably the highest
paid actor of his time.

The young McQueen at an age when, on balance, he preferred motorbikes to girls.

With his first wife, Neile, who could cope with the bikes but not, in the end, with his girlfriends.

At the première of *Papillon* with
his second wife, Ali MacGraw,
the wrong choice if he liked his
women "barefoot, pregnant
and in the kitchen".

McQueen with his third wife,
Barbara Jo, a few months
before he died of cancer.

The family man, maybe not singing but certainly smiling in the rain with his daughter, Terri.

And at home, in Beverly Hills, with Chad.

As Tom Horn in his last film before illness struck. McQueen's somewhat shrivelled appearance was due to a crash diet.

Steve McQueen died, aged fifty, in the early hours of November 7th, 1980, still owing his friend Bud Ekins five rare motorcycle magazines that he had borrowed and neglected to return and still, according to James Coburn, clutching "the first dollar he ever earned".

McQueen was notoriously tight-fisted and even, on occasion, grasping. Whenever he made a film the company, naturally, provided his wardrobe, in his case more often than not blue jeans. Depending on the amount of violent action in which the script called upon him to be involved, five or six pairs of jeans would normally be thought to suffice for one picture. McQueen would demand twenty pairs.

"He was a natural born hustler," said John Sturges, his director on such films as *The Magnificent Seven* and *The Great Escape*. "I mean, he always made us get him *two* electric shavers. You'd think the guy would have his own electric shaver but, no, Steve would insist that we get him two new ones. Well, how many electric shavers do you need?"

Norman Jewison, who directed McQueen on *The Cincinnati Kid* and *The Thomas Crown Affair*, said: "He was crafty, you know. He was very frugal, never had any money on him. Just before leaving the set he would say, 'Gee, have you got a coupla dollars? I gotta stop and get some gas.' And I'd give him five or ten dollars and then I realised after being hit two or three times and watching him hit a few other people that it was a game. He took a delight in playing it."

Nevertheless, game or not, the money was never repaid. And yet . . .

Towards the end of his life he was living on a small ranch near Santa Paula in southern California and learning to fly at the local airfield. At that time he owned a couple of planes, an impressive array of motorcycles and a small fleet of assorted cars, some of which he had raced occasionally in the past. McQueen had always been obsessed with machines, especially those that travelled fast or were becoming rare. Among the cars was a 1951 Hudson Hornet, which had cost him a great deal of money but for which he could find no room on the ranch. He therefore garaged it at the airfield in the care of Sammy Mason, the man who had taught him to fly and also introduced him to religion, two interests which, though not necessarily complementary, were equally important to him at the time.

One day at the airfield he said: "Sammy, I don't need that Hornet any more. I want you to buy it from me."

Somewhat appalled at the prospect, which was likely to prove extremely expensive, Mason said: "Steve, I can't afford to buy that car."

"What's the matter?" asked McQueen. "You can't afford a dollar?"

Mason found that he could indeed afford a dollar and the deal was struck. It was, as Mason said to me, an amazingly kind act on McQueen's part and difficult to equate with his apparently greedy demands for more electric shavers and jeans than any one man could possibly want. On the other hand that greed becomes a good deal easier to comprehend when you consider that McQueen did not keep the spare shavers and jeans for himself but almost certainly gave them away, unobtrusively and without publicity, to the inhabitants of the Junior Boys' Republic at Chino, a kind of reform school, a house of correction for disturbed, difficult and mildly delinquent boys, some fifty miles south of Hollywood.

In any assessment of McQueen's character the importance of the Junior Boys' Republic cannot be underestimated for it was there, beginning when he was nearly fifteen, that he had spent the fourteen most formative months of his early life.

The story of McQueen's childhood has a drably familiar ring to it. At the age of nineteen his mother, Julian—so named because her parents, Victor and Julia Crawford, had wanted a son and saw no reason to change the Christian name they had already chosen when a daughter arrived inconveniently in his stead—had married one William McQueen, against the wishes of both her father and her mother. It was a marriage of necessity rather than romance for Julian was already pregnant at the time and a few months later in a hospital in Indianapolis she was duly delivered of a son, Terrance Steven. The date was March 24th, 1930.

William, the father, was a feckless young man, a former pilot in the US navy who was now employed—when he was employed—as a stunt pilot with a flying circus. His interests extended to speed, flying and games of chance and he approached fatherhood with such a sense of responsibility that he named his son after one of his gambling companions.

The small, young family stayed together for six months after which, no doubt satisfied that he had done all that could be expected in the way of rearing his child, William McQueen took off and was never seen again. (Many years later, inspired by curiosity, Steve tried to find his father but arrived at William's last known address some three months after he had died.)

As a parent Julian was no great improvement on her husband for when Steve was not quite three years old she dumped him on her uncle, Claude Thomson, who had a farm in Indiana, and left him there until he was twelve, while she went off to seek her fortune in Los Angeles.

Young McQueen enjoyed life on the farm and, left to himself, would probably have settled down happily enough to some kind of career in agriculture. But in 1942 around Christmas time and now remarried to a man named Berri, Julian turned up to retrieve her son, greatly to the boy's displeasure for he hardly knew his mother and instinctively disliked his stepfather. Nevertheless, he had no choice but to go and live with them in a down-market, multi-racial area of Los Angeles.

There, lacking care and affection—his mother had become an alcoholic—Steve went to the bad; or anyway the fairly bad. He would cut school, at which he showed little aptitude, and tended to run wild with a bunch of juvenile delinquents. He was picked up by the police a couple of times, for such offences as stealing hubcaps, and once he appeared before the juvenile court, charged with theft. He was given a conditional discharge. At fourteen, pushing fifteen, he was not exactly an embryonic John Dillinger; his crimes, after all, consisted largely of the aforementioned theft of hubcaps and getting drunk and in later life he explained his behaviour by saying that he was looking for a little love. There was not, however, very much of that about in his home. Indeed, there was so little of it that eventually his stepfather declared him "unmanageable" and had him committed to the Junior Boys' Republic at Chino.

He arrived there on the morning of February 6th, 1945 under the name of Steven Berri, though to the authorities at Chino he was more familiarly known as No. 3188.

Today the Boys' Republic is more like a summer camp than a detention home. The inmates are given a sound, formal education and in their spare time tend the farm on which the place is situated. Discipline is strict but appears to be leavened with compassion and a high degree of understanding. Perhaps it was so in McQueen's time, though initially he didn't take the trouble to find out. He was small, tough, truculent and a loner and he wasn't about to put up with life in a boarding school for wayward boys.

Twice he ran away, once returning of his own accord, once being returned under protest by the police. For these misdemeanours he was punished by being given the more unpleasant tasks—digging ditches and cleaning latrines. He also found himself singularly unpopular with his fellow inmates, who deeply resented the fact

60

that McQueen's daring attempts at escape only led to their privileges being restricted.

Later he was not much given to discussing his time at Chino but . . . "He did tell me," said his son Chad, "that they were very strict there. If you'd done anything wrong they would use a long paddle with holes drilled in it and they would lean you over a barrel and schwack you right on the butt. And I think it was good for him. I mean, he really straightened up there, as far as he told me. When you go to a Boys' Republic that's your last chance to make something of yourself before you go down the toilet—and he took that chance."

Yet it was not the punishment that caused young McQueen, at this crucial point in his life, to take a long, careful look at himself and decide to change what he saw. It was rather the perception and interest of one of the school instructors, Lloyd Panter, who detected potential in this surly youth and pointed out to him that if he didn't pull himself together and adjust to discipline he was likely to be unhappy and in trouble for the rest of his life. And No. 3188 was smart enough to heed this advice.

So for the remainder of his fourteen-month stretch, which ended in 1946, when he was sixteen, he knuckled down to life at the Boys' Republic and became a model inmate. What Lloyd Panter had shown him was kindness, a commodity which—like love—had been in short supply since he left his uncle's farm, and it took young McQueen some time to adapt to it. "My first reaction," he said, somewhat poignantly, later on, "was that the guy was crazy. I couldn't accept that anyone would be interested in my future or my welfare."

By the time McQueen left Chino his stepfather was dead and his mother, planning to remarry again, had moved to New York. Her son joined her there, doing odd jobs in Greenwich Village, developing an interest in motorcycles with various biking friends, and eventually in a mood of restlessness, taking a job as a seaman aboard a Greek tanker. This was not a well-advised move because conditions on board were decidedly primitive and when the ship docked in the Dominican Republic McQueen went ashore, never to return. He worked his way back to the United States doing rough labouring jobs and by the time he reached South Carolina he decided that what he really wanted to do was join the Marines.

He was under age at the time but, with his mother's approval, he enlisted in September 1947, becoming a tank driver and mechanic. He liked the work but his career in the Marines was somewhat erratic, for he was continually being promoted from the lowest rank of private to private first-class and then being demoted again, having committed some unmilitary bêtise.

"For instance," said John Sturges, "there was one occasion when he was up in the north, just above the Arctic Circle, and it was really cold and he wanted to heat up a can of beans. So he started up a jeep and stuck the beans in the exhaust pipe. Well, they were warming up nicely when suddenly a general arrived and there was a snap inspection of the troops. The general was just walking down the line when the can exploded and wiped him out—beans and tomato sauce all over his uniform. So Steve went back to buck private again. He was always doing crazy things like that."

The ups and downs of promotion apart, McQueen was happy enough during his spell with the Marines, which ended in April 1950. But there was one aspect of it, which, though he was certainly not aware of it at the time, may well have had far-reaching and indeed tragic consequences later. For a while he worked in the engine rooms of ships in the San Diego dockyard. The conditions there were hot and stuffy—and there was asbestos dust in the atmosphere. The disease that killed him thirty years later was a comparatively rare form of cancer which is generally believed to be "asbestos-related".

His service in the Marines over, McQueen was left once again facing the prospect of earning his living. He was unqualified for anything very much except tinkering about with machinery and he did a little of that, as well as a short spell as a lifeguard in Miami. Mostly, though, he hung around New York doing odd jobs—selling encyclopaedias, tending bar and the like. Sometimes he would augment his income with a little light shoplifting or rolling the occasional drunk.

The director Mark Rydell, who knew him at that time, said: "He was like a delinquent."

On the other hand he had no desire to be a delinquent, for the lessons he had learned at Chino had stayed with him, and the GI Bill of Rights, which provided grants for ex-servicemen who wanted to study or generally improve themselves, gave him the chance to learn a trade that might provide a steadier income than petty crime.

A girlfriend who was greatly smitten by his blond, blue-eyed good looks, had suggested that he might become an actor and he found the idea interesting but felt there were other options open to him.

"He asked me one day," said Mark Rydell, "whether he should go to the Neighbourhood Playhouse drama school or whether he should be a tile layer. He didn't know what to do because with the money he had from the GI Bill he could have gone to either school, acting or tile-laying. And he finally decided on the Neighbourhood school because there were more girls there and that's what produced Steve McQueen, the actor."

He was, Rydell said, deeply interested in girls and "he was very attractive to women. He had a wonderful animal quality, a primitive quality, and he was very sensitive and quite talented and strong and powerful."

Thus equipped he duly enrolled at the Playhouse drama school where he stayed for a year before moving on to the Uta Hagen-Herbert Berghof Dramatic School in Manhattan, where he studied for two more years. He earned money on the side as a male model and by driving at nights for the post office.

In 1952 he made his professional stage debut in New York State with a touring company's production of *Peg O' My Heart*, starring Margaret O'Brien. McQueen's role was a small one and the play was not a success; neither was his stint in a touring version of *Time Out for Ginger* with Melvyn Douglas in the leading role. McQueen asked for a rise in order to buy a new car and was promptly fired. But one or two other bits and pieces of work came his way, on television and in stock company productions, and around 1955 he joined Lee Strasberg's Actors' Studio, being one of five people chosen from several thousand applicants.

What effect, if any, the Actors' Studio had upon him is difficult to say, because McQueen was not often there. Slightly bigger, slightly better roles were being offered to him on television; he made his Broadway debut in a short-lived play called *The Gap*, with Gary Merrill and Sam Jaffe and in the summer of 1956 he finally began to attract critical attention when he took over successfully from Ben Gazzara as the lead on Broadway in *A Hatful of Rain*.

That same year he met Neile Adams, a highly promising twenty-one-year-old actress and dancer who was then appearing in the chorus of *The Pyjama Game*. It was Mark Rydell who brought them together.

"I had the good fortune to be dating Neile," he said, "and I introduced her to Steve McQueen one day in a restaurant and that was the end. I lost her immediately."

Neile's impact on McQueen and his on her were equally dramatic. The following night he accosted her on her way into the theatre and she invited him to her dressing room—"that impressed him because I had an enormous dressing room and he had a little, teeny one down the street"—and after that they started going out together. Neile explains the instant mutual attraction as "weird". She said: "I guess we both had the same sort of childhood background and the minute I saw him I knew him. You know? And I guess he felt the same way about me."

Clearly he did because they met in July of 1956, when he was twenty-six, and married in November. Before then, however, McQueen had made his film debut as a nineteen-dollar-a-day extra with one line to mumble in *Somebody Up There Likes Me*, the boxing picture which bestowed stardom on Paul Newman. And Neile had gone to Hollywood to play a featured role in *This Could be the Night*, directed by Robert Wise.

"Steve phoned me up one day," she said, "and he said, 'I think I'll come out there and make an honest woman of you,' and I was so naïve I didn't realise that meant getting married. As a matter of fact, when he got off the plane he already had the wedding ring. I really wasn't ready to get married but he was so persuasive and persistent and in the back of my head I thought, 'Well, if it doesn't work out we can always get a divorce.' So I said to Robert Wise, 'Can I get off work early tomorrow, because I want to get married?' Everybody thought I was crazy because I was a sort of half-star on Broadway and I was under contract to MGM and I had a BIG future, so why did I want to get married?"

Nevertheless—perhaps consoled by the thought that a swift divorce was always possible—she and McQueen set off in search of wedlock. It wasn't easy. They were turned away from the first church they tried because no banns had been posted and while they were looking for another one they were stopped for speeding by a police car. McQueen explained that he was in a hurry to get married; the fuzz, cynical as ever, refused to believe him; and he and Neile ended up at the police station trying to persuade the precinct captain of the reason for their haste. He, fortunately, turned out to be more sympathetic and more romantic than his underlings and began phoning all the local churches to find one that would be prepared to perform the ceremony. Eventually they found a Lutheran minister who was willing to leave his own dinner party to marry the couple. He had to open the church specially to do it but, said Neile, "the two policemen who had arrested us escorted us there and we were married with the policemen as witnesses. Now the minute we got married, I was fine. I was suddenly resigned to the fact that I was married. And then Steve turned round and looked at me like he thought he had gone out of his mind. He wouldn't come near me for God knows how long, not until we'd got to Mexico for the honeymoon anyway."

But what kind of a man was this, whom she had married? It was a question she asked herself at the time, because she hardly knew him. Looking back, nearly thirty years later, she said: "He was a wild man. He would do *anything*. You just couldn't dare him because he would do it. He was fearless . . . well, not fearless but the kind of person who had to capture fear by facing it. Whereas you or I might say, 'Well, I'm not going to do that because I'm scared,' he would do it." But at the same time he was "a male chauvinist pig of the first order".

In those days Neile was the potential star; McQueen was merely her consort and he resented it. "He was the type of man who could not stand to have his wife making more money than he. And, of course, when tax time came around and I could show that I was making 50,000 dollars to his 4,000 dollars . . . that was very difficult. And what I would do to sort of cool it down was this: I would always come home after a hard day's work, if I was on a film, and make dinner for him. Or, if I was doing a show, I'd make his dinner before I went to the theatre."

Fortunately, however, there was also a credit side to the balance sheet . . . "He was very romantic, very attentive, very volatile. We had an intense, passionate relationship. We fought hard and we played hard and we loved hard—there was never anything in between."

McQueen continued in the role of, as it were, Mr Neile Adams for more than a year but in 1958 his career began to look more healthy. To begin with, he played his first starring role in the cinema in a film called *Never Love a Stranger*, which was written by Harold Robbins and was awful. Nevertheless, McQueen's *was* a starring role and he swiftly followed it with two others—in *The Great St Louis Bank Robbery* and *The Blob*, a ludicrous sci-fi movie about a glutinous mass that attempts to swallow the world. Remarkably, McQueen's performance in this nonsense was praised as "natural" and "dignified", two qualities difficult to achieve in the circumstances.

Despite all this cinema activity, however, it was television that provided his real breakthrough. In September 1958 he was asked to appear in a pilot programme for a potential new series about a bounty hunter. McQueen was perhaps a touch on the small side (being only five feet seven inches) for the physical role that the producers had in mind and they didn't consider that he was "all that great-looking". But he did have an air of truculence and brooding menace that attracted them and they were pleased enough with his work in the pilot to offer him the starring role in the series. It was called *Wanted—Dead or Alive* and it ran on the CBS network for three years and by the time it was "rested"—as they say, euphemistically, in the TV trade—McQueen was a household name.

Meanwhile, he had twice become a father; his daughter, Terri, was born in February 1959, and his son, Chadwick—or Chad—in December 1960. He was an erratic father, Neile said: "Sometimes he would give them a lot of love and sometimes he would withdraw it—almost on a whim. But that was part of his eccentric personality because essentially the kids always knew that they were loved."

McQueen's eccentric personality also made it imperative for Neile to employ a nanny, whether she wanted to or not because . . . "Steve would wake up in the middle of the night—midnight or one, two o'clock in the morning—and he would have the urge to go motorbike riding. And I'd have to sit on the back of that bike and we'd go off into the mountains or wherever. So I constantly had to have somebody in the house to look after the kids because in everything he wanted gratification right *now*. If he felt like going out riding at that time he went—and I had to go with him."

Motorbikes and later, as he grew rich enough to afford them, motorcars were always an obsession with McQueen. The people whom he admired and with whom he felt most comfortable were bikers like Bud Ekins and grand prix drivers such as Stirling Moss. Ekins, a champion motorcyclist and stunt rider, said: "Steve was a top amateur. He never rode long enough to be put into the expert class but he was certainly a top amateur." McQueen would probably have claimed no more than that for himself, although less know-ledgeable friends such as John Sturges, James Coburn and Don Gordon, who appeared with him in *Bullitt*, insist with perhaps more enthusiasm than accuracy that he would have been a world champion —either on a bike or in a car—if he had so desired.

The closest he came to any such distinction was when, along with Bud Ekins and others, he was part of the official American team in the international six-day motorcycle trials in Germany in 1964. At noon on the third day the American team was actually winning; but then disaster struck. Ekins ran into a bridge and that finished his participation. And at about the same time McQueen damaged his exhaust pipe when he struck a rock in some woods. With great presence of mind he snatched an axe from a passing woodchopper, hacked off the broken exhaust and continued the race. But, alas, it wasn't his day because, while trying desperately to make up lost time, he contrived to crash into somebody else and that was the end of the competition as far as he was concerned. It was a great disappointment to him because he had trained hard for the event.

Bud Ekins said: "He gave up work for almost a year beforehand just so he could practise for the trials. He practised changing tyres, riding the bike and all the other things you have to do to become a good team member."

Such dedicated preparation was much in character, for there was never anything of the dilettante about McQueen; whatever the enterprise he insisted on carrying it through as well as he could, which was why he had already begun to acquire a reputation as a difficult actor to work with during the three years and 117 episodes of *Wanted—Dead or Alive*. He had frequent rows with the directors and producers about the interpretation of the character he played. Once he threatened to walk out in mid-series and only agreed to carry on when everyone else agreed to capitulate and let him have his own way. McQueen's explanation of this apparently temperamental behaviour was simple: "I'm not out to win any popularity stakes: I'm out to get a job done."

The television series had made McQueen a household name in America but he was wise enough to realise that TV fame is ephemeral and lasts only as long as the show you are in. The cinema offered something more substantial and so during the time he was playing a bounty hunter he also made three films. The first of these, *Never So Few*, a World War Two adventure story set in the Burmese jungle, co-starred him with Frank Sinatra and began a long association, both professional and personal, with the director John Sturges. "Steve was always a very nice young man," said Sturges. "I liked him. He was eager, enthusiastic, intuitively a very good actor and exuberant about his work. He was certainly not an intellectual; Steve didn't read much; he didn't know very much about what was happening in the world but he enjoyed life and we became very good friends. He was sincere and likeable and neither pompous nor terribly concerned about his own importance."

The combination of McQueen's agreeable personality and his performance in *Never So Few*, which stole the notices away from Sinatra, prompted Sturges to put him under contract for his next film, *The Magnificent Seven*, the hugely successful adaptation of Akira Kurosawa's *Seven Samurai*. It was this film that truly established McQueen, aged thirty, as a star but, as is so often the way, it almost came about by accident. His role as the tough, laconic gunslinger riding just behind Yul Brynner as the seven desperados rode off to conquer Eli Wallach's Mexican bandits was originally fairly small. Brynner was the nominal star of the picture and the rest of his gang were there by way of support. But as the filming progressed it became desirable, as Sturges saw it, to look at the action from two points of view—Brynner's and that of somebody else. And so for two reasons, one that the McQueen character was the only one of the seven, apart from Brynner, who survived and two, because of Sturges' conviction that McQueen was destined to be a star, it was his part that grew.

Sturges had said that he was "intuitively a very good actor" but there was rather more to it than that. He had not always been intuitively very good at all and indeed he owed a great deal of his success to Neile. "In the early days," she said, "he didn't quite know whom to imitate—either Marlon Brando or James Dean. He was caught in between. So I said to him, 'Look, it's just not right; it's not you. We've got to put *you* on the screen. You have a wonderful personality and a wonderful smile. Somewhere along the way you've got to show that smile.' And then we had to figure out what he should wear because he wanted to look different. So we hit on the idea of a sweatshirt—this was in *Never So Few*—but with the sleeves cut off and we spent I don't know how many hours cutting up sweatshirts to get the sleeves just the right length so that his biceps showed but without looking too obscene or Hollywoody. So I guess in a way I was the orchestrator of his career, not because I was all that bright but because I knew instinctively what was right for him."

Once these details had been settled McQueen, certainly in John Sturges' experience, needed very little direction; "I didn't tell Steve much about anything, though he did need what he called 'the fix'. He kept coming to me saying, 'God, John, give me the fix.' And what this turned out to be was his viewpoint on the character he was playing. Once he'd sorted that out, once he'd got the fix he was all right."

McQueen earned 50,000 dollars for making *The Magnificent Seven* and he was still earning 90,000 dollars from the TV series. By then he was not simply a star but already on the brink of superstardom—"the natural successor," as one critic put it, "to James Dean"—and his next two films, *The Honeymoon Machine* in 1961 and *Hell is for Heroes* the following year, consolidated his position. *The Honeymoon Machine* was a comedy about a naval officer using the ship's computer to make a fortune on the roulette table in Venice. It was not particularly good but McQueen's presence saved it at the box office, even though it indicated quite clearly that comedy was not his forte. McQueen realised that, too, and never appeared in a comedy again. *Hell is for Heroes* was a more straight-forward action story about the Second World War and he followed that with the only picture he ever made in England, *The War Lover*, co-starring with Shirley Anne Field.

His time in London was less notable for the film, in which he played a rather dour character, than for his adventures at the Savoy Hotel from which he was politely ejected after one eventful evening. It began with McQueen deciding that he could take an E-Type Jaguar through a U-turn in the hotel's forecourt, a feat normally accomplished only by London taxis which have a remarkably tight turning circle. And indeed he achieved what he set out to do—but only by racing the Jaguar into the forecourt, stamping on the brakes and skidding into the turn. In doing so he rather overlooked the fact that it had been raining hard all day and that he could only manage the U-turn by hitting a large puddle outside the main entrance at about fifty miles an hour with the result that he drenched a considerable number of departing guests in mud and water. The Savoy Hotel was not pleased (nor, come to that, were the departing guests) but they were prepared to overlook this eccentric behaviour and all would no doubt have been forgiven, if not forgotten, had not McQueen, later that night, come close to setting the whole place on fire.

The Savoy can provide some of the best food in London but that evening McQueen had a hankering for a hamburger, a homemade hamburger. He had therefore gone out and bought himself the necessary ingredients along with some kind of primitive cooking stove, all of which he had been obliged to smuggle into his room on account of the fact that the hotel doesn't actually encourage its guests to cook on the premises.

First he had a shower and then, stark naked, put the hamburger on the stove to cook while he lay on the bed and meditated. Unfortunately meditation led to sleep and by the time he woke up the hamburger was on fire and so were the curtains and the bed. Which is why McQueen was next seen in public running, totally nude, down the hotel corridor yelling, "Fire! Fire!" The staff dealt with the fire and McQueen retired to what was left of his bed to sleep. The following morning he awoke to find a coffee tray beside him and a valet busily packing his suitcases. "Hey, man," he said, "what are you doing with my stuff?" The valet paused in his task.

"Oh, good morning, Mr. McQueen," he said, courteously. "Didn't they inform you, sir? You're leaving us today."

John Sturges said: "This kind of thing was always happening to Steve and he'd tell you about it real seriously, as if he couldn't see the funny side of it. But then, when you suddenly burst out laughing and said, 'Hey, man, do you realise what you're telling me here?' he'd stop and slowly he'd grin and say, 'Hey, I guess that's right.' But he never seemed to see how humorous it was until you pointed it out."

By the time *The War Lover* was released in 1962 McQueen had eight films behind him and was an established leading man. But somehow he was still hovering on the brink of superstardom. Of all his pictures only *The Magnificent Seven* had been truly memorable and he needed something else, something big. Again it was John Sturges who provided it. The film was *The Great Escape* in which McQueen was to play a rebellious American prisoner of war in Germany, a loner who constantly tried to escape and was recaptured and spent much of his time in solitary confinement.

In the three years that had elapsed since *The Magnificent Seven* Sturges found a significant change in him. "All of a sudden Steve didn't like anything; nothing was any good. Now this began to affect the other actors, to demoralise them and destroy their belief in the picture. So we had a discussion and I suggested that Steve stopped thinking, let *me* do the thinking. Well, there was a little rumpus but finally he called me and said he was going to act, by God, and he did and then everything was fine."

What had happened, according to James Coburn who, ever since *The Magnificent Seven*, had developed a deep affection and admiration for McQueen, was that "Steve had become *the* star. He was a tyrant—a kind of soft tyrant. He had a special kind of sense; he knew what was right for *him* and he saw to it that everything moved that way. He'd say about a scene or a line, 'I can't do that, I just can't do that,' and they'd rewrite it for him."

Or, as often as not, if it was a line of dialogue that he objected to, he would simply have it deleted. Norman Jewison, who directed him in *The Cincinnati Kid* and *The Thomas Crown Affair*, said: "He was one of the very few actors I've ever worked with who was quite willing to give away lines. Words, he felt, weren't important, or weren't as important as his ability to react honestly and put across the characterisation."

In a sense, of course, this was the "intuitive" side of McQueen at work. Films, after all, are a visual medium. Therefore if an actor can convey what he thinks or what he feels by a gesture or an expression, then words are superfluous. But McQueen was inclined to take this theory to extremes. "He got to a point where he didn't want to say *anything*," said John Sturges. "He was always boiling his lines down, saying 'Do I *have* to say this? Do I *have* to say that?' and I said to him, 'Steve, you simply can't come on here and make faces. You have to say *something*. People do communicate; the audience has to know what you're thinking and who you are,' and then he'd do it. But there always had to be that pitch made, the business of 'Can I get rid of this line? Can I get rid of that one?'" On the other hand McQueen's conviction about the lack of necessity for dialogue in films was more theoretical than practical because . . . "It was kind of phoney. If you said to him, 'You don't have any lines at all in this, Steve,' he'd be *very* upset."

But that, too, was all part of the complicated nature of the man. Don Gordon, who appeared with him (at McQueen's insistence) in *Bullitt* and who says of him "I remember him with love and I don't think I'll ever stop missing him until I die", describes him as "the most complex person I ever met in my life. He truly was like an onion. I wish I could think of a better analogy but that's what he was, an onion—layer upon layer upon layer. Incredibly complex. There was nothing simple about him at all. You had to know when to leave him alone and you had to know when he needed some love, when he needed some caring, some stroking. And most people didn't know that; they didn't know when to leave him alone. But he got a certain look in his eye and when he did, that was the time to just back off and let him be for a while."

During the making of *The Great Escape* McQueen had numerous adventures and misadventures with various motor vehicles, most notably on the night of his arrival in Bavaria from California. At the house which had been rented for him outside Munich were all the costumes he would need for the film, because John Sturges liked his actors to wear the clothes before they started shooting so that they would be used to them and would look natural in them. McQueen, his body unadapted to the change in time, woke up at about 3 a.m. that first day and, feeling the need to work off energy, decided to go for a ride on his motorbike. Dutifully he thought that he might as well grow accustomed to one of his costumes during the ride so he dressed himself carefully as a soldier in the Wehrmacht and then set off. Some time later he discovered, not unsurprisingly, that he was hopelessly lost so he started accosting passers-by and asking them the way to the film studio. As he spoke no German whatsoever he had very little success, though he did succeed in striking a certain amount of terror into the hearts of the local populace, since the sight of a Nazi soldier complete with gun and Swastikas was not particularly common in Bavaria in 1963. Somehow, despite his lack of German money to go along with his lack of comprehension of the German language, he managed—probably through inducing naked fear—to con petrol out of somebody and finally reached the studios only because one man eventually recognised him and set him on the right road.

But again this was merely the kind of thing that happened to McQueen. "On *The Great Escape*," said John Sturges, "he had a very powerful Mercedes and we spent half our time keeping him out of jail. Every time he showed up at work there'd be this collection of policemen who'd come in waiting to arrest him. And we'd have a consultation with Steve saying, like, 'Steve, you just can't drive through flocks of chickens; you just can't cut off into the woods and then come back to the road . . .' He mowed down some trees, he wrecked the car twice; he drove faster than made sense. I remember one night he drove all the way to the Italian border and back. I can still see him showing up at the location, the car steaming and this wild-eyed character driving in at 100 miles an hour." Once when he had wrecked the Mercedes he stepped out of the crumpled remains and said, "Tell them to send me a red one next time."

There was one sequence in *The Great Escape* in which McQueen, wearing the stolen uniform of a Wehrmacht soldier, tries to get away on a motorbike while other Wehrmacht motorcyclists pursue him. Unfortunately at the time this sequence was shot the best stunt riders were away taking part in a championship race in South Africa and the local riders who were recruited in their stead were incapable of keeping up with McQueen. Nor did they even look as if they were riding nearly as fast as he was.

So McQueen dressed himself up as another German soldier, with goggles to hide the upper part of his face and a handkerchief to hide the lower half, and doubled for his own pursuers, with the result that there are moments in the film when McQueen flashes by on a motorbike as himself, hotly followed by McQueen disguised as somebody else.

All of this behaviour was part of his need for speed and danger. It was not a death-wish: he was accused of harbouring that many times and always denied it with anger and conviction. It stemmed from something else. John Sturges said: "Anybody attempting to put forward a creative effort is under a strain. There's a sense of frustration. Well, some people get rid of that by doing exercises, some by playing tennis, some by getting drunk. Steve drove a car."

The Great Escape finally established McQueen among the top movie stars of his time and over the next few years he and Neile and the children moved to ever more lavish homes in the Hollywood area. But stardom—big, big stardom—was beginning to change him. Although he was emotionally as close as ever to Neile, women —other women—were starting to play a more prominent part in his life. When he was making *Love With a Proper Stranger*, for example, he had an affair with his co-star, Natalie Wood, who was then between marriages to Robert Wagner. And eventually it was to be extra-marital affairs such as this that destroyed his own marriage.

In the meantime, however, his career continued to progress. Not all the films he made were of any great merit but he had the happy knack of following the indifferent with the exceptional, so that pictures like *The Cincinnati Kid*, which did for poker what *The Hustler* had done for pool, and *The Sand Pebbles*, an adventure story about an American gunboat involved with Chinese warlords along the Yangtze River in 1926 (for which McQueen gained his only Academy Award nomination), kept him firmly at the top of the heap.

It was while making *The Cincinnati Kid* that Norman Jewison first met him. "I never knew what he was saying half the time," Jewison said, "because he was so hip. He'd say, 'You're twisting my melon, man. I don't know what you mean, man. You twist my melon.' And I didn't know what he was talking about. Later, of course, I realised he was talking about his head, his mind. And then he would go on about 'the juice'. He'd say, 'I'm only interested in who's got the juice, man. Who's got the juice?' And then I'd discover that juice meant power. He was interested in power." Jewison came to the conclusion that McQueen was shrewd, street-smart and crafty but that "he wanted a father. Because of that distressful childhood he seemed to want a father image, someone to tell him what to do. He desperately wanted that kind of relationship and that kind of discipline and I think for that reason he was happier with older directors."

Jewison, however, was only four years senior to McQueen and thus unable to fill the role. "I was more like an older brother and once he accepted that we got along very well. But with other actors he felt threatened; he had all the insecurities of any major film star. In *Cincinnati Kid* he had a scene early on with Edward G. Robinson who, after all, was a star from the old school. And the way the film was set up it was the challenge of youth against age. So before we did that scene I said, 'Eddie, your character would have a drink but, Steve, you don't drink alcohol. You're playing a game of poker, you have to keep your head clear.' And cleverly Steve said, 'No, I don't want to drink, I'll just suck this lemon.' That was *very* clever. He took half a lemon and put it in his mouth and sucked it and that made *me* pucker up just to look at him. I realised what he was trying to do—he was trying desperately to come up with a bit of business that would keep the audience's mind on him rather than on Edward G. Robinson and it worked. Steve was a consummate film star."

But he was also an unpredictable one. When the moon was full, so it was said, he would suddenly take off on his motorbike or in his car and disappear into the desert for two or three days at a time, possibly ending up drinking jugs of wine on some Indian reservation. "What he considered his friends," said Norman Jewison, "were stuntmen, motorcyclists, professional racing drivers, mechanics. He was very warm with minority people—ex-convicts and all those people he felt had been treated badly or didn't have a chance or didn't have an education." The kind of people, in fact, that he himself might have become had he not learned the lessons of Chino so well.

Don Gordon, one of the few actors whom McQueen truly befriended, was not exactly underprivileged, and he certainly was not a minority person because he was among that horde of talented performers in Hollywood who are continually on the fringe of being discovered. One day in 1968 he was summoned to an interview with the British director Peter Yates, who was about to make a film called *Bullitt* and who told the astonished Gordon that he was exactly right to play the leading man's partner. Gordon left the office hardly able to believe his incredible luck but . . . who was this leading man whom he was to partner? He discovered quite swiftly that it was his old friend Steve McQueen.

"So I go to Steve," Gordon said, "and I say, 'I want to thank you,' and he says, 'What for?' So I say, 'For getting me the part in *Bullitt*,' and he gets furious. He says, 'What are you talking about, man? I didn't do that.' And right up to the last time I saw him he was still denying that he got me that part. But I know he did. He did a lot of things like that for a lot of people and a lot of charities; a lot of things that nobody knows about."

This was the other side of McQueen, the side that negated the reputation (thoroughly deserved, let it be said) for meanness and tight-fistedness. And with it went a deeply protective attitude towards his friends. There was an occasion, round about the time of the filming of *Bullitt*, when he and Gordon were sitting in a restaurant and a message arrived to the effect that a very famous Italian producer, who was at a table across the room, would like to see Mr. Gordon. Gordon, being an actor, was very excited, feeling that his big opportunity had come. He was even more excited when the famous producer handed him a film script, decidedly less so when the producer said: "I'll give you 25,000 dollars if you'll hand this to Steve McQueen." Gordon said: "He had the money right there in his pocket. All I had to do was pick up the script and take it over to Steve." To his credit, he didn't. He went back to his own table where McQueen, now excited on his friend's behalf, said: "Hey, man, what was all that about?" So Gordon told him. And . . . "It was like lightning came out of Steve's eyes. And I had to calm him down, hold him down, because he was about to go over and beat up on that guy. Anyway, that producer never did get to him. A very famous producer, he was, but he never could get to Steve after that."

Bullitt was another huge success for McQueen; indeed many people remember him best for it. But, oddly enough, it was a part he was reluctant to play. Neile said she had to "get down on my knees" to make him accept the role. His argument was that he did not want to play a cop because it cut across the anti-establishment image that he had built up in nearly all his other films and it was only when she persuaded him that he could play it as an anti-establishment cop that he agreed to take the part on.

Neile was never quite sure how anti-establishment he really was. She believed that his early childhood on the farm had left him with a basic foundation of mid-Western American values but . . . "He did have a kind of quirk. He would idolise, or put on a pedestal, people like the Hell's Angels. Well, I mean that's so nuts—the Hell's Angels are crazy. But he admired them because they *were* anti-establishment. He was a man of such contradictions I can't even begin to tell you."

James Coburn, on the other hand, saw him as a true rebel. "He was a rebel all his life. That never changed at all. I mean, my God, he would test every form of authority to the nth degree. He was the only guy I ever knew of who talked his agency into taking five per cent, instead of the normal ten per cent." But to some extent that rebelliousness stemmed from a kind of contempt for the people who were prepared to pay him so much money to do a job for which he had very little respect. McQueen was never wholly convinced that acting—putting on make-up and the rest of the make-believe that went with it—was proper work for a man. Perhaps that, too, helps to explain his desire for speed and danger, a more macho image.

Neile said: "Sometimes he would react to his own success with disdain. Or he would push the people who were paying him all this money to the limit, to see how far he could take them. For instance, it got to a point where he would not have a script delivered to his house. He would have it sent to the local gas station as a drop-off point. He would then pick it up from there but before he would read the damned script, money had to be deposited in the bank. And, of course, the people who went along with this he treated with great disrespect."

It was, in short, a try-on but it didn't always work. Certainly it didn't work with John Sturges. Apart from an abortive attempt to get together on *Le Mans*, a film about the twenty-four-hour race, Sturges and McQueen never worked together again after *The Great Escape*. "There was no real reason why not," Sturges said. "In fact, I had a couple of projects that he was interested in doing. One of them he liked very much but then he called me up and said he'd been offered two million dollars to do that disaster movie, *The Towering Inferno* with Paul Newman, and he said, 'Gee, I can't resist two million dollars.' So I said, 'Go ahead.' Besides, later on when it got to a point when Steve wouldn't even read a script without a firm offer of 5,000,000 dollars, I said, 'To hell with that.' I mean, you could decide whether Steve was worth five million or not, and he probably was, but the idea of submitting a script and if he liked it you gave him a cheque for five million and no discussion was not my way of dealing with stars. My way was that you discussed it together and if you both agreed to go ahead, then the lawyers and the other hatchet men got together and came up with a price."

Other directors, however, had perforce to accept the alternative way, McQueen's way, and by the end of the 1960s he was not only a superstar with nineteen films behind him but he was also reckoned to be the highest paid film actor in the world. But nature, life, fate —call it what you will—has an ironic way of counterbalancing such enviable success as he was enjoying by introducing the odd patch of black ice on the apparently clear road ahead. In McQueen's case, as so often with movie stars who climb high and fast, it was in his private life that he slipped up. By the time he went to France around 1971 to film *Le Mans* he and Neile were on the point of divorce.

She said: "It's hard to pinpoint any one thing that caused it. But when the sexual revolution came around—the youth culture, the drug culture—he was getting on for forty and worrying about it and it was then that the problem started to surface, slowly. So it was a combination of things, but what I found hard to take was his jumping from bed to bed. When it was done quietly I could cope with it, although we had a lot of fights, of course. But when suddenly he was looking at me like I was somebody who was keeping him from doing all these wonderful things with the young, then it became difficult. I don't mean he was after twelve or thirteen-year-olds, I'm talking about nineteen, twenty-year-olds—the kids, the hippies, who were singing about everything being free. And he felt that he was not a part of it and I was preventing him from having this wonderful time."

In the last few years of the marriage there had been a lot of women and Neile said: "It's not difficult to see why. Like he said to me, 'You can only say no so often, because there they are at every street corner.' "

Once, when she was trying to understand his behaviour, trying to keep the marriage together, she spoke to McQueen's psychiatrist who said: "People like Steve, the very rich and very famous, are difficult to help because they come here looking for help and you think you're beginning to make a breakthrough. But the minute they walk out of that door there's somebody who is willing to give them everything for nothing." Neile said: "That's right, you know. He comes home and finds he has to work for love, the love of his family, as everyone does. And he says, 'Well, why do I have to work for it when I can just go out on the street and get it for free?' So it was especially hard for somebody from his background. He was attractive, he was a sex symbol, he had money and he had power. It was difficult for him to say no to any woman."

The drugs, too, were another sympton of the male menopause through which he was so painfully struggling. McQueen never became an addict but "he had to try everything that came his way —marijuana, cocaine, heroin—he did all that. And I think it did change his personality eventually. At one point in his life he would just sit there and watch television and smoke grass and drink beer and grow fat."

Other men, even other movie stars, have faced the desperation of reaching forty without recourse to nubile young lovers and the use of drugs but perhaps they do not carry with them the scars and traumas of the kind of childhood McQueen had had. He was always, Neile said, an insecure man—"an incredibly insecure man"—and along with that went an urge towards self-destruction. "If he was happy or content he would do something to make it all go awry." Obviously he was aware of what he was doing because he went to a psychiatrist for five years to straighten himself out but, Neile said, "though he found out why he was doing certain things, he still kept on doing them".

At the root of it all was an almost frantic desire for happiness. "He felt he had to be in a constant state of happiness and, of course, we all know that's crazy but it was his thing. I guess, because he'd been so unhappy as a kid, he felt compelled to be happy all the time." And if he wasn't, he felt cheated.

Neile's final attempt to keep the marriage going came when she flew to join McQueen at Le Mans. His greeting was not too encouraging. "What are you doing here?" he asked. "I'm flying some women in." Neile said: "Well, I'm a woman and I'm here." In truth, once he had recovered from the surprise, he was genuinely glad to see her and they went off to Morocco together to try to straighten matters out. But by then too much damage had been done and in March 1972, after fifteen years of marriage, they were divorced. Twice in later years, when McQueen was between his other marriages, he asked Neile to come back to him but, she said: "He was too late. Also we had become such good friends in a way that went beyond the man and woman thing. We were happy to be in each other's lives but without having to live together."

The film of *Le Mans*, something McQueen, the speed enthusiast, had dreamed of making for years turned out to be a considerable disappointment. John Sturges, the original director, withdrew because nobody could decide what the storyline should be. McQueen, indeed, didn't seem to want a storyline at all, nurturing a vague and unstructured vision of the film as a kind of dramatised documentary. Sturges decided that this was hardly enough and he was not wrong. The finished picture which was later taken over by another director, Lee H. Katzin, had virtually no plot and hardly any documentary content either, consisting largely of shots of McQueen driving a racing car.

Nevertheless, the superstar bounced back swiftly, first with *Junior Bonner* in which he played a rodeo rider and then with *The Getaway*, a crime thriller directed by Sam Peckinpah. McQueen's co-star was Ali MacGraw, a sophisticated, well-educated New Yorker and McQueen's opposite in every possible way. That being so it was probably inevitable that they should fall passionately in love. In any event, inevitable or not, that is precisely what happened and in July 1973 they were married.

For McQueen it was another slightly bizarre wedding. He and Ali, who had been living together for some time, simply decided one morning that this would be a nice day to get married. Together with McQueen's children, Terri and Chad, and Ali's son, Joshua, by her previous marriage to the producer, Robert Evans, they were in Cheyenne, Wyoming, at the time to see a rodeo. What they wanted, they decided, was a quick, simple, civil wedding; so they hauled the local judge off the golf course and persuaded him to perform the ceremony.

McQueen was forty-three and Ali MacGraw was thirty-five and Neile said: "Actually, I think their relationship should have been an affair rather than a marriage." She is perhaps entitled to say such things without being accused of sour grapes because she and Ali are, and have been from the start, very good friends. In any case, with the benefit of hindsight, it seems clear that she was right.

As it had been with Neile, McQueen's relationship with Ali was intensely passionate but apart from the passion and the genuine love that accompanied it they had very little in common. Besides, McQueen had now reached a stage when he wanted to get away from the fuss and the hype of Hollywood and the movies. So they took a house at Malibu, near the ocean, and lived a quiet, reclusive life while they tried to get to know each other and, for a while at least, to be the kind of person the other wanted. But this was inevitably doomed to failure because their interests were so disparate. McQueen was happy tinkering with his toys—his cars and his motorbikes—while Ali began to think wistfully of rather more cultural pursuits: concerts, visits to the theatre, to museums, to art galleries, none of which interested McQueen in the least. As Neile said: "He was incredibly bright but he was no intellectual. The things he loved to read were motorcycle magazines but he wasn't too crazy about reading generally."

Furthermore, McQueen was deliberately taking time out to think and decide what he wanted to do with the rest of his life. He was a millionaire several times over, so money was no particular problem. And he was still one of the biggest stars around, with the demand for his services increasing in direct proportion to his reluctance to make movies any more. But this no longer gave him much satisfaction: more and more he came to believe that acting was women's work and sometimes he felt guilty that he could demand so much money from an occupation for which he often felt something close to contempt.

But there again was the paradox in the man. The only thing he really enjoyed about stardom was the money that went with it. John Sturges said: "I don't think Steve ever particularly wanted to be a movie star but he liked money; he enjoyed having money and he piled a lot of it up. Of course, he wasn't exactly the most generous person in the world. You know, there's an old story that the real definition of eternity is waiting for Jimmy Stewart or Cary Grant to reach for the bill in a restaurant. Well, you might add Steve to that list. But he said a couple of times that he had lived for so long on nothing that money was just something you didn't spend."

Against that he could be extremely generous with his friends and family and very generous with his time as far as the inmates of the Junior Boys' Republic at Chino were concerned. Frequently he would arrive there unannounced and, ignoring the staff completely, would spend hours talking to the boys, encouraging them to make something of themselves.

And, of course, in the matter of cars and bikes he was a positive spendthrift. Over the years he amassed a huge collection of vehicles of one kind or another. But his favourite car, just for day to day driving, was the Ferrari. He always had a Ferrari somewhere around the place and on one famous occasion he bought two in the same afternoon, though this was a matter of necessity rather than choice. He had just taken delivery of a brand new, shiny red model with twelve miles on the clock and he was driving it home, carefully as if it were made of eggshells, when suddenly as he halted at a stoplight he glanced in his rearview mirror and saw a kid in a hotrod staring out of his own window at a passing girl and bearing down on him at about forty miles an hour. McQueen, realising there was nothing he could do, merely crossed his arms over his face and waited for the crunch—which duly arrived. Both cars were a dreadful mess. McQueen got out slowly, walked over to the weeping and shaken youth in the hotrod and said: "Don't worry about it, man. It's cool." Then he phoned for a breakdown lorry to take his crumpled new toy away, went back to the Ferrari dealer and said: "Give me another one—*now*."

A complex man, then, as Don Gordon said, and undoubtedly a hard one to live with. But Ali tried and in doing so won the affection not only of Neile, her predecessor, but also of Terri and Chad. Terri described her as "a terrific lady" and Chad said: "Well, after a while they fought like cat and dog there. But she was fine."

Yet, once again with hindsight (the clearest form of twenty-twenty vision in the world) it now seems obvious that the marriage was doomed to fail. McQueen's friends think so anyway. James Coburn said: "It was a marriage that came from a famous romance and you felt it would last a while and that would be it. Steve was very protective of Ali and worried that anybody might be messing around with her, because being a womaniser himself he was very jealous of the women he married. But I wasn't surprised when it broke up; it never seemed to be a marriage that was made in heaven and, besides, Steve always seemed to believe that wives should be at home, barefoot and pregnant in the kitchen."

This was not the kind of role that the intelligent and independent Ali MacGraw would easily settle for, although the pregnancy part would have appealed to her. Unfortunately, however, it never came about and possibly that is another reason why the marriage began to fail. Ultimately, though, it was McQueen's womanising which, once more, led to a divorce.

John Sturges believes that McQueen's sexual activity outside marriage stemmed from something much more than promiscuity or satyriasis. "Steve was an impulsive type," he said. "He was sort of frantically searching around, compensating to some degree, satisfying his ego, I guess. I would say his relationships with women, his marital infidelities, were in the same category as his driving his Mercedes to the Italian border and back. They were a way of getting rid of the pressures and the frustrations, not just sexual but professional, that went with being creative, being a star. You know, he fancied himself as being very smooth with girls but I thought he was a slob with them and told him so. I wouldn't consider him a smooth operator; he was a compulsive, spur-of-the-moment kind of fellow."

Well, whatever the explanation, too many spurs at too many moments led to separation and eventually, early in 1978, to divorce. During the time that he was with Ali MacGraw, McQueen's career —certainly through no fault of hers—had tended to waver. *Papillon*, the story of a French convict who escaped from Devil's Island, was followed by a co-starring role—not a great deal more than an enlarged cameo appearance—in *The Towering Inferno*. And then there was a true curiosity, *Dixie Dynamite*, a biking film in which McQueen appears, uncredited, as a motorcyclist. He had heard that it was being made, had heard that the producers needed extras who were good on bikes and so, on a whim, had turned up to register as just such an extra with Bud Ekins. He was paid 225 dollars for one day's work (which, at a conservative estimate, is probably about one-thirtieth of what he would have got if his name had been above the credits) and he caused consternation on the set when he signed his name to the extra's contract and thus revealed his identity.

And he also starred, even more oddly, in a screen version of Ibsen's *An Enemy of the People*. It is said, perhaps apocryphally, that this came about because he was under contract to make a film for First Artists, was not particularly eager to fulfil the obligation and picked up a book that Ali happened to be reading and said: "This will do." In any event it was not a success and wasn't even released, theatrically, in America, though it had a limited distribution in Britain. In fact, McQueen was rather good in it—almost unrecognisable, admittedly, behind round spectacles and an enormous beard but also appealing and believable. His performance, indeed, lends weight to the belief—or anyway suspicion—held by many people who knew him well that he could have been a far better actor than even he realised.

Financially, however, *An Enemy of the People* was a disaster and McQueen immediately returned to mainstream cinema with *Tom Horn*, based on the life story of a former cavalry scout who, somehow, was framed for murder and allowed himself to be hanged. For this role he had got himself back into some kind of physical shape, shedding the excess weight he had gained during the reclusive years when he had sat and pondered his future. But in the film he looks curiously shrunken, scurrying around like a bushy little chipmunk. He acts well but the old, physical presence has gone.

Before and during the making of that picture, two important events occurred in his life. He bought a ranch called, ironically as it turned out, "The Last Chance Ranch" and he met Barbara Jo Minty, a successful twenty-four-year-old New York model, who had a passion for horses. Because she was not, and had no desire to be, an actress she was very different from his previous wives and mistresses but at the same time, with her long, dark hair, she looked remarkably like both Neile and Ali; indeed, from some angles she could easily be mistaken for Ali MacGraw's younger sister. Just as importantly she, like McQueen by then, was not greatly impressed by superstardom. So by early 1979 they had entered into a relationship which, in January the following year, became permanent when they were married at the Ventura Missionary Church.

By that time McQueen had found two more interests to add variety to his life—flying and religion and both came to him from the same source. Maybe the interest in flying stemmed indirectly from the fact that this was the period when he was trying, unsuccessfully, to trace his father who had been a flyer himself. Or perhaps it was simply due to the fact that his ranch was very close to the local airfield. In any event, McQueen took up flying—and religion—with the same fervour that he had earlier brought to motor racing in all its various forms.

His instructor in both was Sammy Mason, a master pilot who was really involved with more advanced students, those who wished to learn aerobatics and the like. But McQueen was persuasive and eminently charming and finally talked Mason into teaching him to fly. Mason is a devoutly religious man and, although no proselytiser, makes no secret of the fact and this, too, began to attract McQueen's attention. One day he said, "Sammy, I'd like to go to church with you next Sunday," and he did—and continued to attend for several weeks afterwards until he announced: "I want you to know I've received Christ. I've made my own decision and now I'm a Christian." This, it is worth mentioning, happened before the onset of his fatal illness; in other words he did not turn to God in a last, frightened attempt to save his own life—he turned to Him out of conviction, out of belief.

After that declaration Sammy Mason noticed a change in him: "It was very noticeable. There was a very evident peace in his life. He was more at ease and calm. Before then he had been an uptight kind of person but I noticed he was becoming more confident in himself, knowing now that he had God and God wasn't going to let him down."

Unfortunately, this new-found contentment was not to last long. Around September 1979, McQueen started work on what was to be his last film, *The Hunter*, the story of a modern-day bounty hunter. It all began confidently enough. True, McQueen had been troubled with a persistent cough but it had been diagnosed as a form of "walking pneumonia" and he was inclined to ignore it. He was, in fact, so confident of the future that he adopted a teenage girl. Her name was Karen Wilson, she was thirteen and she appeared in one scene of the film, a scene in a tenement. McQueen became interested in her, learned that she was living in poverty and that her mother was dying of cancer and immediately set about arranging the adoption.

But by the time the filming was over, he was seriously ill. He had begun to cough up blood and in hospital in Los Angeles tests revealed the presence of mesothelioma, a form of lung cancer caused by exposure to unsafe asbestos. Whether it was his time in the naval dockyards while he was in the Marines that had planted the seeds of this disease is impossible to ascertain. For, as Neile said, there were many occasions when McQueen exposed himself recklessly to asbestos. "Sometimes when he was motor racing," she said, "he wouldn't have a proper face mask and he'd just dip a towel into some kind of asbestos liquid and put that over his mouth. And then, too, he would wear asbestos suits in those racing cars. So maybe that had something to do with it."

It was after the diagnosis of cancer that he married Barbara Jo and then set about finding a cure. At the Cedars-Sinai hospital in Los Angeles he was told that nothing could be done for him but he refused to accept that. He heard about an unconventional cancer treatment being carried out in Mexico by an American named Dr. William Kelley. Kelley had gone to Mexico because he had been banned from practising in Texas without a proper medical licence. His treatments, which included special diets, positive thinking and, in some cases, the injection of live sheep cells, were regarded with suspicion by American doctors. But McQueen felt that he had nothing to lose by trying them. His first course of treatment in Mexico was in March 1980, and two weeks later he returned to his ranch at Santa Paula looking amazingly fit.

But the remission did not last long. Soon he was back at the Cedars-Sinai hospital where, once again, specialists who had been flown in from many parts of the world declared that there was nothing they could do for him.

All this time he had refused to confess, despite rumours throughout the international press, that he was suffering from cancer. But in October he finally admitted it—having first broken the news privately to Terri and Chad. In a press statement he said: "The reason I denied I had cancer was to save my family and friends from personal hurt and to retain my sense of dignity. I say to all my fans and friends, keep your fingers crossed and keep the good thoughts coming. All my love and God bless you."

The following month he returned to Mexico, desperately ill, for a final operation to remove a five pound tumour from his abdomen. The operation took place on November 6th and the tumour was indeed removed. But by this time Steve McQueen was too weak to recover and thirteen hours later, at 3.50 a.m. in the morning of November 7th, 1980, he died.

His body was cremated at Ventura and a few days later Sammy Mason and his son Peter flew out over the Pacific Ocean, according to McQueen's wishes, and scattered his ashes from the plane.

In his will he left nearly nine million dollars, mostly divided between Barbara Jo and his two children and with special provision for Karen Wilson. There was also a bequest of 100,000 dollars to the Junior Boys' Republic at Chino, which has used the money to build a Steve McQueen Gymnasium. And he left instructions to Barbara Jo that she was to give Ali MacGraw any help she needed in a lawsuit she was fighting over a film.

During the peak years of McQueen's stardom I was involved in writing about movie stars for newspapers or talking about them on television but he and I never met. At the time it didn't bother me very much but now I regret it. I think I would have liked him; he may very well not have liked me but I think I would have liked him. I think, in fact, that given only the slightest knowledge of his background it would have been very difficult for anyone not to like him.

Certainly he seems to have left behind an impressive residue of affection. The wives I have spoken to, Neile and Ali, admit to loving him still and both are warm in their commendation for Barbara Jo, who has never spoken publicly of him, for the love and support she gave him in those last difficult months.

Others, who were less close to him, speak of him now with an interesting mixture of affection and reserve. Mark Rydell, for instance, who directed McQueen in *The Reivers*, says: "I miss him as a friend and as a star, because he was a wonderful, magical, magnetic personality. But he was very difficult, very strong-willed. He was monumentally gifted but he was the only actor I've ever directed who had me on the ropes. He was the one who had me up all night calling Norman Jewison for advice! But I have to tell you that if I had that chance to work with him again and again and again I would do it, because he had magic—real magic." And then, after a pause for reflection, he added: "I admired him but he wasn't my kind of guy. You know? He wasn't the kind of guy I would have spent a lot of time with. He was a miracle talent and a terrible pain in the behind and I often got angry with him and had battles with him. But I admired him very much and I wish he were around now."

A miracle talent? Well, perhaps that's pricing it a little high. He was always, after all, Steve McQueen and most of the time he played Steve McQueen. I'm not saying that was bad—but it was limited. He was a reactor more than an actor and thus dependent on the quality of those playing opposite him. It was therefore to his credit that in the days when he could call the shots he was not afraid to surround himself with high-class performers—Edward G. Robinson, Paul Newman, Dustin Hoffman, Faye Dunaway, Eli Wallach and the like.

As Neile said: "He was a fabulous movie star. And he did regard

85

himself as a good actor—limited, but good." But that, too, is an over-simplification. Ali MacGraw said of him: "He was an extraordinary man, complicated and heartbreaking. He hadn't nearly done all his stuff and I'm not sure he had really grown up either. He was the overwhelming force in my life; that five years with him is a period that I will never forget and maybe never get over. He was incredibly sensitive, vulnerable and intelligent. But he was always intimidated everywhere he went, even though you knew that all the people in the room only wanted to meet *him*."

It was that vulnerability, thinly disguised by a veneer of toughness, that gave him his international appeal, an appeal that transcended language; that and a kind of remoteness, an attitude that said, "Stay there. Don't come any closer."

Norman Jewison, I believe, summed it up. "I don't think I ever really knew him," he said. "I think Neile knew him—maybe the women knew him. The women in his life probably knew him better than the men."

And yet for a while there, as he strutted about on the screen in his super or even megastardom, we all felt we knew him, not because he was any great actor but because of the person he was. Every cinema-going generation seems to demand a rebel, an anti-establishment figure, to identify with and idolise and McQueen's background and screen persona produced him made-to-measure for such a role. He was not so abrasive as Bogart, nor so mannered as James Dean but he followed logically in their line of succession. He had a quality of wary stillness that made you watch him at all times. He was laconic, he was sceptical, he was cool. And in his private life, as well as in his best films, he appeared to take no nonsense from anybody, least of all from those who had the juice, the power. And along with that he had good looks, a sudden brilliant smile and sex appeal that stemmed from a curious mixture of innocence and street-wise toughness. Given his time over again, I suspect he might have chosen to be a champion motorcyclist or racing driver but if so he would always have been fighting against the odds because from the word go and despite the unlikely background from which he came nature quite clearly intended him to be a movie star.

Henry Fonda

Fonda as the romantic leading man,
before he became the conscience of
America.

Margaret Sullavan, the first wife, whose less than benign influence may have helped spoil his next three marriages.

With Frances, his second wife and the mother of Jane and Peter.

With Susan (wife No. 3),
who was told that tears are
disgusting. . .

. . . And Afdera (wife
No. 4), who couldn't think
of a single good reason to
divorce him.

With Shirlee, his fifth and final wife. With her, he said, he had at last "hit a home run".

Fonda, Jane and Peter in what, at one time in their relationship, would have been an extremely rare moment of fond togetherness.

Two of Fonda's best and most memorable roles, forty years apart. As Tom Joad in *The Grapes of Wrath*. . .

. . . and in his final film *On Golden Pond* for which, at last, he won the Oscar he had deserved so often.

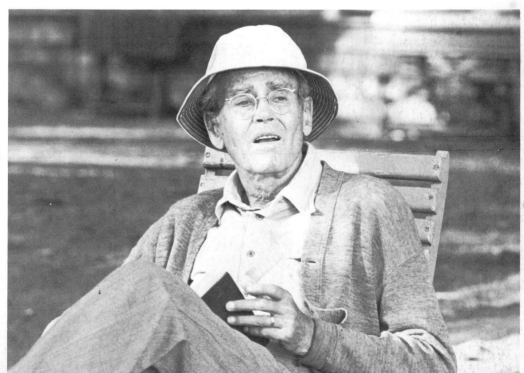

One day, when he was on his honeymoon, Henry Fonda took his new bride to the beach: the sort of thing husbands often do in such circumstances, as Fonda would have known better than most because he was already on his third honeymoon, one for each wife so far. Susan, the latest Mrs. Fonda, only twenty-two years old and naturally anxious to please her man, took his watch and laid it carefully on a piece of driftwood so that sand wouldn't get into the works.

"It was quite a rare watch for that time," she said. "It showed the hour, the day, the month, what time the moon came up and went down and it did everything but dance." Having performed this thoughtful uxorial duty Susan joined her husband in the sea, emerging some time later to find that the tide had come in and the driftwood had vanished and so had the watch.

"I was devastated," she said. "I ran up the beach and said, 'I've lost your watch,' and I burst into tears and I just felt terrible."

And Fonda eyed her coldly and said: "Don't cry. Crying is disgusting."

At which point . . . "I turned round and cried some more. He didn't like displays of emotion. Boy, did he ever marry the wrong party."

Well, he was good at marrying the wrong party; he had a positive gift for it. By the time he had finished his experiments in matrimony he had been on five honeymoons and it was only with his fifth and final bride that he found a lasting contentment and happiness. That the other marriages failed was, in at least three cases out of four and as he would readily have pointed out himself, largely his own fault. For it was a curious paradox of his nature that while he was a man of immense charm, a most honourable and decent man capable of arousing abiding affection in others, he found it virtually impossible to display any kind of deep emotion, especially love. That he could feel love there is no doubt; but a love, however passionate, that is never allowed to reveal itself is something of a handicap to a successful marriage.

Fonda was aware of this shortcoming but unable to understand it himself. Or, at least, he said he was unable to understand it but since he hardly ever seems to have shared his innermost thoughts with anybody I suppose it's quite possible that he had in fact worked it all out but chose not to disclose his findings. James Stewart, who was probably his closest friend for more than fifty years, claimed that in all that time they never discussed either marriage or politics which, if true, is remarkable.

Oddly enough there was nothing in Fonda's early background to explain his emotional reticence, although there was certainly one incident that helps to account for the staunch and humane liberalism that he practised all his life. He was born (on May 16th, 1905) and brought up in Nebraska, the heartland of America, his birthplace being Grand Island, although he only lived there for six months before his parents, William and Herberta Fonda, moved to Omaha, where Fonda Senior became a printer. There, too, Henry—or Hank, as he was known to his intimates—was joined by two sisters, Harriet and Jayne.

The Fondas, originally of Italian descent, were Christian Scientists, not particularly well-off but not poor either: a solid, sober, hard-working, affectionate and caring family. The affection was probably implicit rather than overtly explicit but the caring, in a general, social sense anyway, was given practical demonstration by William when in September 1919, he took his son, then aged fourteen, to watch a lynching.

This event, which the local law was presumably unable or unwilling to prevent, must have been reasonably well publicised because the Fondas, father and son, made a special journey downtown to watch it. The victim was a young black man who had been accused of raping a white woman. He had not actually been found guilty of this crime but legal niceties mean little to a lynch mob. On this occasion they dragged the terrified youth out of the courthouse and strung him up from a lamp post. William Fonda's motive in taking his young son to watch this appalling act had nothing at all to do with morbid curiosity: he simply wanted the boy to understand, graphically and unforgettably, what hatred and intolerance could lead to. And Hank never did forget.

This dramatic and horrifying episode apart, however, the young Fonda's upbringing appears to have been placid and unexceptional. He was unusually shy, perhaps, but otherwise much like any other youthful middle-class Nebraskan. At the age of eighteen he went to the University of Minnesota in Minneapolis to study journalism but exhausted himself by doing various odd jobs to work his way through college. As a result he did badly in his exams, dropped out of university, returned home—and by accident became an actor.

A friend of his mother's, one Dorothy Brando—the mother at that time of a year-old son called Marlon, later to become something of an actor himself—was running an amateur theatrical group called the Omaha Community Playhouse and she asked Hank if he would join the company.

John Houseman, who was later to direct Fonda on stage in a triumphant portrayal of Clarence Darrow, the legendary American lawyer, said: "The reason he found acting such an enormous satisfaction and joy was that he was a very timid, diffident and slightly insecure young man who suddenly discovered that the minute he went out there, even in a not very big part, he was somebody else. When he went through that door on to the stage he became somebody else; he didn't have any of the problems of his own life to deal with; he dealt with the problems of the character he was playing. I suppose all actors are like this to some extent but I've never known anyone else for whom it was so totally, completely true."

Fonda's own explanation was, typically, more laconic: "I liked the feeling of being up there after I realised that all eyes were not on me all the time. I lost most of my self-consciousness and began to relax."

Initially William Fonda was less than enthusiastic about his son's new interest, arguing that he should be out pursuing a career instead of frittering away his time on amateur theatricals. But after Henry won unanimous applause in the title role of *Merton of the Movies* (playing a grocery clerk who prayed each night that God would make him a film star) even the elder Fonda gave his support and Hank began to seek and find jobs with various small theatrical companies.

But it was not until 1928, when he was twenty-three years old, that the next significant opportunity came his way. He was taken to see the University Players—a bunch of Ivy League graduates and undergraduates from Harvard, Yale, Princeton and the like—in a production of *The Torch Bearer* by George Kelly. He was immediately enchanted by them all and by none more than Joshua Logan, who was playing a comic character called Huxley Hossefrosse.

Logan said: "I stepped onto the stage and said, 'Anybody here, David?', which was my first line and I heard a howl of laughter out in the audience. It sounded like somebody sobbing in a high voice and being strangled at the same time. It was a terrible sound but so funny that the whole audience laughed at it and after that every time I said a word this funny howl came and the audience roared with laughter. At the end I got a tremendous hand and I was a huge success but only because of this terrible thing that was happening and I didn't know who it was. I went backstage and was taking my make-up off in our communal dressing room and the orchestra leader came in and said, 'I'd like you to meet somebody, a friend of mine from Omaha. His name is Henry Fonda,' and this funny,

long-legged, long drink of water came in. He had this cherubic face
—perfect, handsome, beautiful almost—and a funny, long, wiggly
body. I can't explain it: he caved in at the chest and came out at
the pelvis and he wore black stockings and . . . well, in those days
plus fours were the big thing but his were more like minus twos.
He really was an odd-looking man with this beautiful face and he
looked around the room and said, 'Were you Huxley Hossefrosse?',
pointing at me, and I said, 'Yes' and he let out this terrible yell,
this appalling laugh and I knew immediately who he was and I've
loved him ever since."

The affection was mutual and Fonda at once began a four-year
association with the University Players which was to prove significant in all manner of ways. First, it gave him experience and
exposure in a variety of roles; secondly it led to lifelong friendships
with both Logan and James Stewart who, in fact, replaced Fonda
in the company when he left; and thirdly it led indirectly to his first
meeting with a beautiful and gifted young actress named Margaret
Sullavan. In April 1929, and in between University Players' seasons
he appeared in a musical at Harvard. Margaret Sullavan was also in
the cast and she and Fonda promptly fell in love. It was by no
means an easy relationship for Miss Sullavan was a volatile and
high-spirited character who appeared to be attached to a remarkably
short fuse. Nevertheless, the romance flourished and on Christmas
Day 1931 they were married at the Kernan Hotel in Baltimore. She
was twenty and he was twenty-six and Joshua Logan was at the
wedding.

"They got married in the big old dining room where the whole
company ate. It sounds grand but it was the saddest big dining
room you've ever seen in your life. We sort of ate like people in the
army—we went by with our plates and they slopped the food on. I
would say it was the most pitiful little marriage ceremony ever.
Then they went off on their honeymoon but they didn't stay on it
at all. They got quite lonely that night without the rest of us and
they came back the next day."

The marriage itself was almost as brief as the honeymoon. Temperamental differences, squabbles, tantrums and shouting matches
became so frequent that within four months they had parted. Joshua
Logan said he was not surprised that the marriage came so swiftly
to an end: "I was surprised that it took place at all. You ask if they
were at all suited to each other. Well, I don't know that either of
them was suited to anyone. They were very special people. On stage
they were magic together but they had their own ideas and though

they seemed to get along very well together the moment they were married there were difficulties. I never knew exactly what but mostly I'm sure they were intellectual difficulties."

And yet there was more to it than that. In his biography—*Fonda: My Life*, written by Howard Teichmann—Fonda told how he had heard that his wife was having an affair with a producer named Jed Harris. Many nights after that he would stand watching their apartment, knowing the lovers were in there together and waiting for Harris to leave. But all that would happen was that the bedroom lights were turned out . . .

Teichmann quotes Fonda as saying: "I couldn't believe my wife and that son-of-a-bitch were in bed together. But I knew they were. And that just destroyed me. Never in my life have I felt so betrayed, so rejected, so alone."

Afdera Franchetti, the aristocratic Italian socialite who was later to become Fonda's fourth wife, believed that that was the most destructive and in many ways the most telling experience in Fonda's life, leaving him with emotional wounds that would take thirty-odd years and four more wives to heal.

"Somehow, I think, he never got over that," she said. "That marriage had an enormous effect on him—more than any of the others. It conditioned him for life, so that he couldn't show his emotions and was always a little bit afraid of being hurt again. I don't think she played around with other *men* but she was a very young and bewitching woman and she did play around with the one other man and in a very cruel way. And Fonda was also young and sensitive and not very sophisticated and it scarred him for life."

Soon after his separation from Margaret Sullavan Fonda left the University Players and worked for a while, mostly as a backstage odd-job man, with a theatre company in Maine. But in the autumn of 1932 he went to New York and moved into an apartment with Joshua Logan and two other actors, James Stewart and Myron McCormick, where they set up a kind of small-scale commune. According to James Stewart, "The fellow who was working sort of bore the financial burden and then, when we were all working, we'd put money into a general fund to take care of expenses when we all got fired."

Memories of who did most of the working at that time differ rather sharply. Stewart remembered Fonda as being "the busiest of us all. He had parts in summer stock, in small theatres in New Jersey and in small, try-out theatres." By contrast, Joshua Logan remembers him best as the communal cook but thought that, as an actor, "he certainly should have been losing confidence because everybody else worked except Fonda. James Stewart worked every minute of the time and so did Myron McCormick and so did I—as a company manager or a box-office manager, whatever job I could get. But Fonda couldn't get anything."

Obviously, though, he did manage to find the occasional job but nothing that amounted to very much until in March 1934, he did a comedy sketch with Imogene Coca in a show called *New Faces*. The agent Leland Hayward was sufficiently impressed to arrange a 1,000 dollar a week film contract for him with producer Walter Wanger. The only slight snag in this deal was that there weren't actually any films for him to appear in so he stayed on Broadway where, at last, the long-awaited big break came his way. He was given the leading role in Marc Connolly's play, *The Farmer Takes a Wife*. It was an immediate success (as, too, was Fonda) and 20th Century-Fox swiftly acquired the film rights, seeing it as an ideal vehicle for Janet Gaynor. They did not, at the time, have any plans for Fonda. Instead they offered his role to Gary Cooper and then Joel McCrea but as neither of them was available they decided that the man who had created the part on stage might just as well do it on screen, too, and so they borrowed him from Walter Wanger. Thus in March 1935, two months short of his thirtieth birthday, Henry Fonda went to Hollywood, assuring everyone that it was just for a short time and that he would be back on Broadway very soon. But in that he was wrong.

Fonda's performance in *The Farmer Takes a Wife* still looks a little overblown, a touch stagey, but it would have been much further over the top had it not been for the director, Victor Fleming, who, early in the shooting, took his new young star to one side and pointed out that in the movies there was no need to hit the back row of the gallery. A different kind of acting, a more relaxed and realistic kind of acting, was needed for the cinema and Fonda learned the lesson quickly. He was to improve with each succeeding film but even in that first one and despite his tendency to overplay it's possible to see clearly the beginnings of the Fonda style, a kind of acting that is so subtle and natural as not to seem to be acting at all. Hollywood, the critics and the audiences were all duly impressed and Fonda's return to New York and Broadway was indefinitely delayed.

It was, said James Stewart, simply a part of the "tremendous creative talent" of the man that he adapted so swiftly to the demands of the cinema. "His career just took off. It really happened pretty quick and in a year or so he was recognised as a very important leading man in pictures." Certainly he was busy enough: Fonda made three films in 1935, another three in 1936 and four in 1937.

Around this time, too, James Stewart also received the call to Hollywood where he and Fonda shared a house, double-dated with Lucille Ball and Ginger Rogers, built model aeroplanes and for a while entertained a scheme to dig a tunnel from their garden into that of their next-door neighbour, a certain Greta Garbo who, even in those early days, insisted that she wanted to be alone and thus presented a challenge to the red-blooded and probably randy young men in the adjacent house. Stewart maintained that, in his recollection, they did actually start digging the tunnel but had to abandon it when they encountered some such obstacle as a gas main or a sewage pipe.

But this bachelor existence did not last long, at least not for Fonda. One of the films he made in 1936 was *Wings of the Morning*, a romantic tale in which he co-starred with the French singer and actress, Annabella. It was made in England (the first Technicolor picture to be shot here, in fact) and it soon became evident that Fonda's interest in Annabella was more than merely professional. She, naturally, was flattered and, to some extent anyway, pleased, rather to the displeasure of her husband. Rumours, greatly exaggerated but nevertheless confusing began to drift across the Atlantic about the alleged romance that was taking place on and off the set. Joshua Logan was among those who heard the rumours and took note. What he did not hear, however, was that Fonda's amorous interests had changed direction.

He had met and fallen in love with a twenty-seven-year-old American widow, Frances Seymour Brokaw, whose multimillionaire husband, George, had died earlier that year, leaving her with a daughter.

The Seymours (Seymour being Frances' maiden name) were a socially and politically prominent New York family, supposedly descended from Lady Jane Seymour. Frances and Fonda travelled through Europe together on an extended courtship. He proposed marriage in Budapest; she accepted in Paris and they returned to New York together to get married. Joshua Logan was to be the best man, although until the couple actually arrived he was by no means sure who the bride was to be.

"I think Fonda was still slightly in love with Annabella," he said, "and I couldn't quite work out whether it was Annabella he was talking about when he said he was going to be married."

The wedding—the big social event of the season in New York—took place at Christ Church on Park Avenue on September 17th, 1936. The marriage lasted some thirteen years and produced Fonda's two famous children, Jane and Peter, but as with Fonda's first venture into matrimony Joshua Logan could never understand why it happened at all.

"Frances became his wife and the mother of his children. She was a beautiful girl but I never believed they ever had anything to do with each other. Well, it's apparent they did because of the children. But she never talked the same language as he did: she always talked about houses and dresses and jewels and money and sex and various things that he would never mention. She never saw plays or movies and I couldn't quite see why they were so close together. They built a beautiful house and had a wonderful life and wonderful kids but I just never saw them having fun together."

Since the marriage did last a considerable time (certainly by Hollywood standards) it seems reasonable to suppose that the couple, especially in the early days, enjoyed a fair amount of fun together. After the wedding they moved back to California and rented a house off Sunset Boulevard while they planned to build a home of their own. (In those early days their closest neighbours included Fonda's agent, Leland Hayward, who was now married to Fonda's first wife, Margaret Sullavan. This is not altogether an amazing coincidence. The upper levels of Hollywood society consist of a comparatively small number of people. Everyone knows everyone else and sometimes it's possible to imagine that, sooner or later, everyone marries everyone else.)

In those upper levels of society, the Fondas were swiftly accepted, not so much because he was a promising young star but because she, being a millionairess in her own right and very well connected, was recognised as having class, a commodity always in short supply and therefore much prized in the film community.

And so with his social success assured, Fonda swiftly began to increase his reputation as an actor, first showing his versatility by stepping out of character to play a killer in Fritz Lang's *You Only Live Once*, then moving on to co-star with Bette Davis in *That Certain Woman* before returning to the theatre—always the medium in which he felt happiest—to play the title role in *The Virginian* at the Westchester Playhouse. Encouraged by the play's reception he returned to Broadway in *Blow Ye Winds* but the experience was not a happy one because the production closed after only thirty-six performances and Fonda was obliged to return to Hollywood where,

in 1938, he appeared in five films, opposite such notable leading
ladies as Bette Davis again (in *Jezebel*), Joan Bennett and Barbara
Stanwyck.

Although by this time he had made fifteen films and was already
thirty-three years old he was not yet considered big enough to carry
an important picture on his own, perhaps because he worked for a
variety of studios who used him as a foil for their own contract stars.
But in 1939 his status improved immeasurably when John Ford cast
him in the title role of *The Young Mr. Lincoln*. Initially, he was
reluctant to take the part, feeling that Abraham Lincoln, who had
always been his hero, was simply too big a character for him to
portray. Ford, however, talked him into it, largely by pointing out
that as far as the film was concerned Lincoln was not the great
emancipator of America but merely a smart, though unassuming,
young country lawyer. Thus reassured Fonda gave one of the finest
performances of his career.

The picture opened in February 1940, in which month Fonda
became a father for the second time, now having a son—Peter—to
join his daughter, Jane, who had been born on December 21st, 1937
and who, in honour of her supposed ancestor, was known as Lady
Jane for the first few years of her life.

According to Joshua Logan, Fonda's reaction to fatherhood was
one of delight. "I remember he was certainly terribly happy when
the children were born," he said. Logan was not asked to be
godfather to either of the Fonda offspring, though he had served in
that office for the children of Leland Hayward and Margaret Sullavan who, when the Fondas moved into their new home, had also
moved nearby. There was consequently a certain amount of to-ing
and fro-ing between the two families but, Logan said, "the Fonda
children were always a little bit distant towards us compared with
the others. They were beautiful and fine and well cared for but we
never got very chummy with them."

A possible explanation for this apparent aloofness is that Jane
and Peter had inherited their father's shyness, although Afdera
Franchetti suggested that it may also have been due to the fact that
they were already somewhat self-contained children, having little to
do with their own parents. She said: "Henry was very busy and
according to him so was his wife. She was a very domineering,
intelligent career woman. So she looked after the business matters
and he looked after his career and the children were cared for by
nannies."

At this point, however, the Fondas appeared to be an exceptionally happy and settled family and Hank's career was advancing rapidly. After *The Young Mr. Lincoln* he had made *Drums Along the Mohawk*, a John Ford Western that did his reputation no harm, and then in 1940 he starred, once more with Ford directing, in what is probably his best-remembered film, the adaptation of John Steinbeck's *The Grapes of Wrath*. It was Fonda's performance as Tom Joad that established firmly and indelibly his screen image as the epitome of the honest, liberal American, the caring idealist. It also won him his first Academy Award nomination as best actor although, surprisingly, the Oscar went to his friend James Stewart for his performance in *The Philadelphia Story*. It says much for the power of Fonda's portrayal that Stewart himself actually voted for him. And Joshua Logan, remembering the film more than forty years later, said simply: "Fonda was superb in *The Grapes of Wrath*. That last scene was his signature—Fonda at his very best as a young man."

So at last, as an Oscar nominee, Fonda was accepted as a real star, one whose name above the title was guaranteed to draw at least a respectable audience and capitalising on this he made thirteen films between 1940 and 1942, the last of which was *The Ox-Bow Incident*. At this time, he was under long-term contract to 20th Century-Fox and it is a reflection of Fonda's prestige that *The Ox-Bow Incident* was made despite the studio's reluctance and misgivings. No doubt Fox could see little future in a story in which a cowboy (Fonda) was unable to prevent the killing of three men by a lynch mob. Fonda, who never really got along with Fox and actively disliked Darryl Zanuck, the studio head, insisted on it being made anyway, his enthusiasm for what was certainly a grim movie no doubt stemming from the hatred of mob violence that had been kindled in him more than twenty years before when he and his father watched the black man being lynched in Nebraska.

In the event *The Ox-Bow Incident* was his last film for three years. By the time it was released in 1943 he was in the American navy, which service he had joined in August 1942, on the grounds that he had no desire to fight the Second World War on a back lot but wished to be where the action was. He was trained as a signalman, commissioned as an officer, and by 1944 was assigned to the staff of Vice-Admiral Hoover on active service in the Pacific. Towards the end of the war, when his ship, the *Curtis*, shot down a Japanese plane, Fonda and another officer swam out to the aircraft to retrieve its map and flight plans and for this action, and for his work in plotting the course of Japanese submarines, he was awarded a

Presidential Citation and the Bronze Star. Altogether his was a most respectable war record, and in 1945 he was given an honourable discharge and returned to Hollywood and family life.

But the family he rejoined at the age of forty was by no means as settled as it had appeared before he joined the navy. In the first place, Peter, who was only two when his father went to war, hardly recognised him. And in the second place Frances, reacting as many a wife did in wartime, had eased her own loneliness by indulging in the occasional affair. She was now thirty-six and worried about ageing and losing her looks. At the same time, Fonda himself had changed during those years apart; he had become if anything even more introspective than he had been before and was now prone to outbursts of rage that stemmed perhaps from the tensions and frustrations that he felt at home. Although he and Frances stayed together, the marriage was decidedly shaky.

But for him, as always when his private life was beset by problems, there was the consolation of work. He picked up his film career pretty much where he had left it and between 1946 and 1948 he made seven films, none of them of the quality of *The Grapes of Wrath* but at least two of them—*The Fugitive* and *Fort Apache*, both directed by John Ford—of better than average quality.

This spate of activity culminated, to Fonda's great relief, in the end of his contract with 20th Century-Fox, which took him out of the clutches of the detested Darryl Zanuck and left him free to consider a proposition put to him by his old friend, Joshua Logan.

Together with Tom Heggen, Logan had written a play called *Mister Roberts*, based on Heggen's short stories about naval life in the Pacific during the war. Fonda, an old navy man himself, asked if he could hear it. His interest in the project was fairly dispassionate because he was virtually committed to making another film but Logan read it to him all the same and, when he had finished, asked: "What do you think of it, Hank?" Fonda replied: "I'm going to do it, I'm going to play it."

Logan pointed out that there was, by way of a snag, this movie that Fonda had also said he would do, to which Fonda replied: "I've got the toughest agent in the world and if he's any good at all, he'll just talk me out of it. If he doesn't, I'll leave him."

The agent proved to be quite as tough as his client had predicted and in February 1948, Fonda opened on Broadway to ecstatic reviews in what proved to be the biggest stage success of his life and one that was mainly responsible for keeping him away from the cinema for seven years.

The part of Mister Roberts was ideal for him because it demanded all the characteristics of integrity, decency and honesty with which he was already associated in the public mind. But even so it was not staged without difficulty. As Joshua Logan said: "Roberts was the hero that everyone followed." But as he also said . . .

"At first Hank was suspicious of me; he didn't realise that I'd had as much experience in my field, the theatre, as he'd had in his. He thought I was still a member of the University Players or the Princeton Triangle Club or something and he kept saying, 'Are you really sure you mean that, Josh? This *is* Broadway, you know.' "

This kind of remark is practically guaranteed to irritate a Broadway stage director but Joshua bore it stoically until one day, during rehearsals, Fonda asked: "Do you understand Roberts?"

Logan, who could take no more, replied: "Understand him, you arsehole? I *wrote* him! You come to my house tonight and I'll tell you all I know about Mister Roberts and then you can decide whether I understand him." Fonda accepted the invitation, Logan harangued him deep into the night and at the end . . . "Hank got up, didn't say a word except 'Thank you very much', shook my hand and left. But after that he never gave me another moment's worry. He listened to everything I said from then on."

Fonda was often difficult and argumentative in the early stages of rehearsal, especially in the theatre. But his attitude and his suspicions were caused by his constant search for a kind of perfection rather than big star temperament. "He was arrogant," Logan said, "but he was arrogant the way he was when I first met him. He was always arrogant."

The success of *Mister Roberts* and the clear signs that the play was destined for a long run led to considerable domestic upheaval. The Fondas sold their home in California and moved to Greenwich, Connecticut, but there family life deteriorated even further. The rift between Fonda and Frances became even wider and he found increasing difficulty in communicating with his children. Jane has told of "long car rides in which not a word would be spoken. I would be so nervous that my palms would be sweaty from riding in absolute silence with my own father." And the writer, Radie Harris, recalled a night at the circus when she sat next to Henry, Jane and Peter, and again no word was spoken. "He didn't buy them hot dogs, candy or souvenirs. When the performance was over they simply stood up and walked out. I felt so sorry for all three of them."

Worse still, Frances was now showing signs of mental illness. She had begun to live virtually as a recluse in her own home, staying in her room endlessly checking business accounts and not even joining her family for meals. By August of 1948 she had entered a hospital in Massachusetts to undergo treatment and though she was released after eight weeks she returned there again early in the new year and from that time onwards, as the clinical depression from which she suffered worsened, she was almost a permanent resident.

It was against this background that, early in 1949, Fonda met and fell in love with Susan Blanchard, stepdaughter of the lyricist Oscar Hammerstein II. Fonda was then forty-four and she was twenty-one, but the age difference, according to Susan, meant little. "He was a very nice, shy, simple man. In a sense I think he was less sophisticated than I was. He was a product of the American mid-West—very honest, very straight and honourable and, at least at that time, I think rather naïve. An American Gothic."

True to those mid-Western principles Fonda decided that he was not going to indulge in some clandestine affair with Susan Blanchard; instead he went to Frances, who was then enjoying a remission of her mental illness, told her he was in love with someone else and wanted a divorce, a request which she agreed to calmly enough and in October she started the legal proceedings. But the following month she suffered a relapse and returned to hospital. Her health had declined to such an extent that it was feared she might become suicidal, which diagnosis proved only too accurate, for in April 1950, in a sanatorium in New York she killed herself by cutting her throat with a razor blade.

On the face of it Fonda's reaction to his wife's death was astonishing: that same night he simply went on stage as usual in *Mister Roberts* and, as usual, gave an immaculate performance. Joshua Logan said: "Frances' death was a shock to all of us and a terrible blow to Hank. And yet he went on and played and played very well. I'll never understand how he was able to do it."

Fonda's own explanation was that plunging himself back into work was the only way he could have got through the night. And Susan Blanchard said: "I think he didn't know what else to do. He was not a man to break down in public, ever—and not really in private either." Nor, during the time that Frances was ill, had he ever discussed her condition with Susan. "I never knew what his thoughts were. I knew that she was ill but he simply didn't talk about it. He was not a man given to revealing his innermost thoughts." Therefore when he insisted that the show must go on within hours of learning that his wife was dead . . . "It was very much in character. He was a person who always did what was expected of him. He never let anybody down and he was extremely professional. Also I think he was emotionally numb at that time and the only way for him, let us say, to survive was to work."

When Frances' will was read it was discovered that she had cut her husband out of it altogether and had left the bulk of her estate to her three children—a daughter by her first marriage, Jane and Peter.

Barely nine months after the suicide, just before the new year, Fonda and Susan were married in New York. Their honeymoon in the Virgin Islands was marred first of all by the episode of the watch and then, far more seriously, by the news that Peter Fonda had been involved in a shooting accident. He and another boy had borrowed a shotgun and, according to Susan, "Peter had the gun right against his gut and was trying to force a bullet into it when it went off and shot him in the stomach. He was very lucky because the bullet missed all the vital organs."

The incident, which terrified Henry Fonda, did not, however, serve to bring him any closer to either of his children. His relationship with them, Susan said, "was very good towards the end of his life. I think they resolved a lot of the problems they'd had between them." But at the time of her marriage to their father . . . "they'd rebelled, like any children do, and it was more difficult for them because he wasn't the kind of man who could talk easily. I don't think they were in awe of him. I think they desperately wanted to please him but because he wasn't demonstrative there was great frustration for them. There was mutual love between them all, very much so, but I think he felt a lot of things that he couldn't verbalise. He wasn't the sort of father who would come into a room and throw his arms around his children. I don't know . . . I often wonder what his own childhood was like in terms of his relationship with his parents. You know—whether they were very authoritarian. I was always trying to find out but he said he didn't remember a lot. I'm not sure whether that was so. Perhaps he didn't want to remember."

Fortunately, however, the relationship between Susan and the Fonda children became and has remained close. Because she was not very much older than Jane, or even Peter, she was able to serve in the capacity of friend, rather than stepmother. And so, while his new young wife concerned herself with family and domestic matters, Fonda felt free to immerse himself as deeply as ever in his work, which in Susan's opinion was "the most important thing in his life".

When *Mister Roberts* finished its Broadway run, he went on tour with the play; and when the tour ended he returned to New York to star in *Point of No Return*, another hit which ran for 364 performances in 1952 and 1953 and when that, too, was over he found himself in his third consecutive stage success, playing the reluctant defence lawyer in Herman Wouk's *The Caine Mutiny Court Martial*.

By then he had also become, legally if not physically, a father for the third time. He and Susan had adopted a girl, Amy, to whom—possibly because he was older now than when his first family had been born—he showed, for him, remarkable tenderness. "I used to have one day off a week," Susan said, "and then he would take care of Amy and feed her and bath her and dress her. He was very sweet with her. I think he was very good with small children. When they grew older and got minds of their own, when they could talk back —that's when the difficulties started."

Fonda stayed with *The Caine Mutiny Court Martial* until May 1954, at which point he was asked to play his original role in the film version of *Mister Roberts* and because the play had become very special, very personal, to him he accepted immediately. But the filming proved to be far less congenial than the stage production had been, essentially because Joshua Logan had been replaced, as director of the movie, by John Ford. Hitherto, Fonda's professional relationship with Ford had been nothing but beneficial to both of them. By 1954, however, Ford was pretty far gone in alcoholism and his views on how the play was to be filmed were, to say the least, eccentric. He changed the impetus of the story, developed minor characters to the detriment of the others and added an unnecessary amount of broad physical comedy to the action.

As Joshua Logan put it—and it must be remembered that Logan spoke with a certain amount of bitterness because he always regarded *Mister Roberts* as *his* play, the one *he* should have directed on screen: "I could have done a better job with my left hand than Ford did. I must tell you that, because that's the way I feel. He took the play and threw it away and started over again."

And clearly Fonda, too, felt the same way for early in the filming there was, literally, a fight between him and Ford. What actually happened in this fight is open to doubt: I, personally, have heard three different versions of what took place. According to Logan, after one particular day in which the director had introduced all manner of elements which appeared to have nothing to do with the original story, Ford said: "Well, Fonda, how do you think it went?" Fonda replied: "It was shit." At which point, "Ford poked him in the jaw and knocked him across the room. Then they were grabbed by everybody in the place and pulled apart so the fight couldn't go any further. But Fonda never spoke to him again as long as they lived."

Fonda's version, fairly similar, ran as follows: "Pappy (Ford) turned to me and said, 'Okay, what's the matter? I know something's eating you.' And I said, 'Pappy, everyone knows you're the best director in the business but I have to be honest and tell you you're making some big mistakes.' Then I told him what they were and suddenly he rose up out of his chair and threw a big haymaker and hit me right on the jaw. It knocked me over backwards. I was more embarrassed than hurt. I just walked out of the room. Half an hour afterwards Pappy came to apologise. But from then on our relationship was never what it had been."

The most graphic description, however, came from Jack Lemmon, then a comparatively unknown actor who had been cast as Ensign Pulver (for which role, incidentally, he won the Academy Award as best supporting actor). In Lemmon's submission the original script of *Mister Roberts* was to Fonda tantamount to the Bible and people tampered with it at their peril. Ford tampered with it quite recklessly and Fonda began to seethe, to ask of his fellow actors what the hell was going on. The climax came, in the Lemmon version, at about two o'clock one morning. Lights were on, the sound of upraised voices was coming from Ford's room and "naturally little ol' Pulver's got to see what's going on. So I sneak down and look in there, through the crack in the door and they're really going at it. John Ford was about 100 at that time; I don't know but he sure wasn't young. Hank, who was very tall, had got his hand out, holding Ford back. Now Ford is trying to hit him but he can't reach him—he's about six inches short and Hank's holding him off and very calmly but very loudly telling him, 'Don't do it, don't fool around. We did the play for years and we think we know what works and what doesn't work.' And Ford's saying, 'You can't tell me how to make a film.' It was hysterical. And then finally Hank just gave Pappy a push and he went backwards onto the bed and that ended it."

Well, you pays your money and you takes your choice but however the sordid little scuffle resolved itself Ford left the picture to be treated for his alcoholism and Mervyn Leroy took over the direction, throwing out Ford's innovations and reverting to the script as written. Later still Joshua Logan was asked to reshoot a few scenes but the result was, in Logan's words, "a mish-mash. It was nowhere near the film it could have been. It could have been one of the greatest pictures of all time, I think. But Fonda was never as good in the film as he was on the stage. He really was in such a dark mood that he didn't play it well, comparatively."

Nevertheless, the screen adaptation of *Mister Roberts* marked the end of Fonda's Broadway interlude and his return to Hollywood. In 1955 he went to Rome to play Pierre in Dino de Laurentiis' film of *War and Peace* and it was there that his third marriage came to an end.

"I think the main problem," Susan said, "was a difference in personalities. Although we thought alike in many areas we had very different characters. I tried to save the marriage; he did, too, and I don't know that it wouldn't have lasted longer if I'd been more mature and he'd been more able to talk. I tried to get outside help; I went to a therapist to talk about it and I was very concerned because I'd grown very close to the children and loved them very much. It's hard for me to remember now exactly what triggered the end. I really couldn't break it down and analyse it for you. I think we simply weren't emotionally suited to each other. I loved him very much and I know he loved me but it was as if we were sort of passing each other on different levels, not really connecting. He was a very self-sufficient person in terms of his work and the fact that he was a good painter and also did wood carving. He could get lost in these occupations. I needed more human contact than he did and I was lonely. It was like living alone."

So, around August 1955, after five years of marriage, she left her husband in Rome and returned with Jane, Peter and Amy to New York. Many years later Susan said of Fonda: "I think there's a scream inside Hank that's never been screamed, a laugh that's never been laughed." And to me she explained that remark by saying: "He found it almost impossible to really let go. When he was playing a part he could accomplish any kind of emotion; as himself he was very restrained and buried and I think there were a lot of emotions that cover a whole range of feelings—happiness, misery, rage, whatever—that were simply not released."

Did she never find out why? "I was just a young wife," she said, "not an analyst." Occasionally, very occasionally, she had seen Fonda lose his temper and then it was "terrifying. But he was not given to emotional outbursts at all. It's my personal theory that he had a lot of rage in him but he didn't let it out very much."

Thinking back on a marriage that had ended more than a quarter of a century ago she said: "I was afraid of him. It may not have been justified but that's what I felt. I felt that he was judging my behaviour and I always had to sort of watch my step. I always felt that if I was too free and behaved the way I would like to behave and be very open I would not get his approbation and that somehow I would be punished emotionally." If this made Fonda sound Victorian and puritanical well, she said, maybe that's the way he was. "But I think you have to look at it in the context of the kind of upbringing he had, where there were rules and regulations. I think he was very uncomfortable breaking any kind of rules or doing anything that rocked the boat in any way. He was very moved by many things in his life and he certainly had strong emotional responses. But translating these emotions into action in any form was something else again. I mean, many times in his relationship with the children I think he would have longed to be able to talk to them but he couldn't. It wasn't that he was deliberately withdrawn; he simply couldn't cope with heavy emotional Sturm und Drang."

Fonda wept when Susan informed him that she wanted a divorce, but by then it was too late for tears. "I didn't think he would change or I would change. We were both very sad and bewildered. It was really awful."

So she left him. But before the filming of *War and Peace* was finished, before he left Rome, Fonda had already discovered the woman who was to be his fourth wife, Afdera Franchetti, a beautiful Italian aristocrat even younger than Susan. When they met, Afdera was aware that Fonda was married and separated but typically "he didn't talk very much about her; he just said that she had gone." What she liked immediately about him, she said, was his shyness, his reserve, the fact that he didn't behave in any way as a famous film star might have been expected to behave. They courted one another fairly surreptitiously at first because Susan's divorce did not come through until May 1956 and it was ten months later before Fonda and Afdera were married at his home in Manhattan. By then he was fifty-two and she was only twenty-three but the age difference she said (as Susan had said before her) made no difference at all. "Being Italian I had a certain sophistication and he had this young, naïve thing about him, like a student. No, I never felt the difference in age, not even at the end of the marriage."

It was not a marriage that lasted long but it was certainly eventful. On the eve of the wedding Afdera was stricken with terrible doubts, partly because what had been a deliciously clandestine romance was now about to become open, formal and official and she spent the entire night weeping and declaring that she wanted to go home.

The result of all these tears was that her eyes were so swollen at the ceremony and afterwards that she cut them out of all her wedding photographs. For an introverted man Fonda coped with this Latin emotion very well, proving to be a loving and indulgent husband. He never actually said he loved her—Afdera soon realised that such a declaration would be too much to hope for—but he showed it in the way he spoilt her. Once, for example, thinking to please her and make her feel at home, he hired an artist to paint Venetian murals in their home. "At the time," she said, "it irritated me enormously but now I think, my God, I was so lucky." Another time she had "nagged him, casually, since September" about a fur coat she wanted for Christmas. But when Christmas came there was no coat; instead there were dozens of other costly presents and, the pièce de résistance, a Canaletto hanging over the mantelpiece. When no coat was forthcoming, Afdera said, she began to sulk and was ashamed of herself later. But a very young and over-indulged wife, especially one married to a man who is firmly established at the top of his profession, is almost certain to have a distorted sense of values.

And Fonda, of course, was very much at the top of his profession. On his return from Rome he had filmed *The Wrong Man* for Alfred Hitchcock, played an ex-sheriff turned bounty-hunter in *The Tin Star* and then co-produced and starred in the movie version of a successful TV play called *Twelve Angry Men*, a courtroom drama in which once again he played the unbiased, uncorrupted and incorruptible American. The director Fonda had chosen was the then unknown Sidney Lumet, who remembered him as a nervous, fussy producer who disliked the job so much that he decided never to try it again.

But as an actor, Lumet said, "He was perfect. He didn't know how to do anything false; you couldn't even beat him into it. Hank always had the best of American liberalism about him; the whole idea of a man fighting for justice was enormously appealing to him. So his performance was heroic without him ever having to play the hero."

Twelve Angry Men was a critical success but a box-office failure, though it has since developed something of a cult following. For Lumet it won an Oscar nomination for best director and caused him to form a lifelong friendship and admiration for Fonda whom he regarded as equal with Spencer Tracy as the very best of all American screen actors. During the making of the picture Fonda invited him home to dinner and to meet Afdera, which experience remained vivid in Lumet's memory.

Afdera, he said, was "enchanting, very, very fond of him and very, very scatterbrained". The dinner party itself, however, was bizarre. "It was a sit-down dinner for thirty or so. There were four tables of eight. Dessert came and there was a sort of soupe anglaise, I guess, and there was some sauce in there. The centre pieces on the tables were gardenias and Afdera's Italian friends thought of picking out these gardenias and dipping them into the soupe anglaise and throwing them from table to table and pretty soon they were all doing that. And I looked over at Hank and from the expression on his face I knew this wasn't going to work out. His sense of order had been rather violently disrupted."

Afdera dismissed this incident with Latin insouciance. "Once only it happened," she said. "It was one friend of mine, who was in a very bad mood and she did throw an ice cream. That became snowballed in history for ever." A reflective pause and then . . . "The room had just been painted. But it only happened once."

Nevertheless, Sidney Lumet's prediction that "this wasn't going to work out" swiftly became true. By 1961 Fonda and Afdera were divorced. If it was an attraction of opposites that had led to the marriage it was also, ironically, the fact that they were opposites that ended it. Afdera knew that he loved her—"I never had a second's doubt about that"—but felt that the marriage had begun on the wrong footing. They had had no period of struggling together because Fonda was able to offer her everything she could have wanted, so she had no chance to mature, to become a proper wife. She had no need to cook because they had servants; she had no need to watch the pennies when she was shopping because Fonda was already rich. And she had no real rapport with Jane and Peter, who had become less close to their father after his divorce from Susan.

"I think I wasn't unhappy enough before I married him," she said. "Therefore I took for granted all those wonderful things he did for me. If it had been maybe ten years later I might have understood more and tried to work things out better and do what he wanted me to do."

It was Afdera who decided she wanted the divorce. Fonda tried to dissuade her—"because he didn't want another failure. I just wanted to be free. In fact, when I went to Mexico for the divorce I couldn't think of a thing to say against him." In the end the judge and the lawyers settled for the time-honoured compromise in such matters of "incompatibility". As part of the divorce settlement Afdera kept the Canaletto, which she had been given so disappointingly instead of the fur coat. "I was very glad of it," she said.

"Eventually I sold the picture and lived on the money for several years."

Her memories of Fonda, she said, were mostly good ones and her only regret, after the divorce, was that they did not remain close friends. There was no animosity; they merely had few opportunities to see one another. Her feelings for him were of admiration. "His weakness, I think, is that he was perfect, if that is a weakness. Whatever he did, he did well." On the other hand he could be a cruel enemy. For instance, there were several people he instructed her to avoid because of his own antipathy towards them, among them Darryl Zanuck, with whom he had had many a bitter run-in during his years with Fox, and the actor Ward Bond, whose extreme right-wing political views were anathema to the liberal Fonda. "He could be quite ruthless. He scared people a lot, I think. He had this kind of aloof look. I think maybe he intimidated me also. Perhaps he was self-centred but when you're a big star you become self-centred, no? But he was a good man and he had a helluva life."

With four wives down and one to go Fonda thrust aside personal problems, as he invariably did, by plunging ever more deeply into his work. At the age of fifty-six he was in as much demand as ever, not always for leading roles perhaps—in many of the twenty-one films he made in the next ten years he played cameo parts—but even so, possibly because he was such a constant presence on the screen, he was listed among America's twenty top box-office attractions in 1967.

His relationship with his children, however, was still cool. Joshua Logan remembered directing Jane in her first film, *Tall Story* and . . . "Fonda came over to the set and they were photographed together. But I always had the feeling he came as a fan and not out of great fatherly love. I'm sure there was some there; I'm sure that Jane and Peter both felt something towards their father but it wasn't very demonstrative. Hank talked about Jane as though she were another person, quite removed from him. But he considered her the greatest actress in the world."

Meanwhile, Fonda himself was adding to his screen reputation as the quiet man of integrity, appearing variously as the president of the United States, the secretary of state designate, a candidate for the presidency, several high-ranking army and navy officers and an attorney. He had also become deeply immersed in his painting, mostly examples of still life executed with minute, painstaking attention to detail. A lot of actors paint—or anyway purport to paint—but it's generally conceded that Fonda had genuine talent and today his pictures are collectors' items that would fetch highly respectable prices on the open market and not simply for their curiosity value either.

So work and painting and the occasional date with a variety of young women filled his time and, as far as he was concerned, would continue to do so, for after the divorce from Afdera he had vowed never to marry again. His inability thus far to make any marriage work understandably disturbed and puzzled him. Once, looking back on his marital record, he said: "I'm goddamned ashamed of myself." Why then did he marry so often? John Houseman, the stage director, believed it was because "he was a loner and he was very uxorious. He had to have a woman and it had to be a wife. He was not given to promiscuous sleeping around. When he fell for a woman he had to marry her."

Susan Blanchard agreed with that. "I think he was very uncomfortable when breaking the rules. He was not a womaniser, he was not a playboy and I think the reason he married so many times was because he was so conventional. Where he came from one got married and did one's duty and that's the way it was. If he had a relationship with a woman he felt he had to marry her."

Nevertheless, noble though his motives may have been in getting married in the first place, he did seem to show a deplorable lack of commitment to matrimony once the ceremony was over. It's not enough merely to marry a woman; she has a right to expect a certain amount of loving care and attention afterwards and it was in this area that Fonda was a noted failure.

"He was—and he was the first one to say it—a lousy husband," said Jack Lemmon. "And in his opinion, though not necessarily his children's, he was a lousy father, too. For a long time it was something he couldn't cope with. I think that without necessarily being selfish he was a very driven and consumed man about his career and the way he wanted to conduct it. And very often the scales tip over and something has to give—either your profession or your personal life."

Or, as Susan Blanchard put it: "His career always came first."

But all that was to change with the advent into his life of one Shirlee Mae Adams, an airline hostess and occasional fashion model, who was introduced to Fonda one night over dinner in a Hollywood restaurant. Fonda was immediately smitten but this time the courtship was slower. He and Shirlee had known each other a considerable time before they were married in New York on December 3rd, 1965. Fonda was then sixty, Shirlee was thirty-three—another notable age difference which again was of no concern to either husband or wife.

Fonda's own comment on this, his fifth and as it was to turn out, his final marriage as reported by his biographer Howard Teichmann in *Fonda: My Life* was: "After stepping up to bat five times I finally hit a home run." So in the baseball game of love and marriage he had at last made a winning score. He had, on his own admission, mellowed—not before time perhaps at the age of sixty—and besides by the unanimous accord of his friends and even his former wives, Shirlee was the ideal mate for him . . .

Jack Lemmon: "He was devoted to Shirlee and she to him. A lovely, lovely lady. He eventually found a great peace in that relationship."

Sidney Lumet: "She was totally open and direct. She made him feel good and I'm glad they found each other."

John Houseman: "It was an extraordinary marriage that couldn't have been more successful."

Joshua Logan: "She gave him great pleasure and she was very careful of his life. I think she cared more for him than anyone did."

Susan Blanchard: "I think she was a wonderful wife, I really do, and she took such care of him when he was ill—above and beyond the call of duty."

Afdera Franchetti: "In his way he believed in marriage. He was always a one-woman man and it showed when the right woman appeared. I think we were all right in a way but our timing was wrong. With Shirlee the timing and everything was right."

And finally Fonda himself, as quoted by Howard Teichmann: "And we lived happily ever after . . . Every day I wake up and take a look at Shirlee and think, 'This is it. She was worth the wait. I really feel she's the only wife I ever had.'"

So with his personal life now settled, Fonda moved into the 1970s as a hugely respected senior citizen of American show business. There were movies—sixteen of them during that decade—starring roles on television and acclaim on Broadway, notably for his performance as Clarence Darrow in a one-man show that dealt with seven cases conducted and won by that great lawyer, crusader, liberal and humanitarian, a man very much after Fonda's own heart. John Houseman directed it, though not without problems. In the early stages there were occasional tantrums from Fonda as he strove, as usual, for the perfection that in the end, despite all his efforts, escaped him as it escapes everyone else. Even so his performance was magnificent for unlike most movie stars he had the ability to make the transition from film studio to stage with great ease, possibly because the theatre always had the greater appeal for him.

Houseman said: "I think he was completely miserable if, every eighteen months or so, he didn't get back to the theatre. In order to do that he would even appear in summer stock somewhere because he felt the need constantly to renew his contact with live audiences."

Fonda opened in New York as Clarence Darrow in March 1975, and it was during the run of the show that the ill health that was to beset him for the rest of his life first became evident. "When we opened in Chicago," John Houseman said, "he began to lose his voice. Then we opened in New York and he got it back but again he started to lose it." The problem, however, was not caused by his throat or his larynx but by heart trouble. He had an operation for the insertion of a pacemaker and, remarkably soon for a man of seventy, he was back on stage playing not only on Broadway but also in Los Angeles and London.

Houseman said: "That was the beginning of his bad health. After that he went through hell. It was discovered that he had a huge tumour in his pancreas and that was removed, then later he had further complications and his courage in going on working, being in and out of hospital, was absolutely extraordinary."

Fonda's last appearance on Broadway was in 1978, playing a Supreme Court judge in *First Monday in October*. He also went on tour with the play as far as Chicago where he had to drop out because of a hip ailment that was later diagnosed as cancer.

At this point he could, if he had wished, have looked back with justifiable pride on a quite remarkable career. Not one of his contemporaries, or even those in the generation behind him, came close to matching the record of success that he had achieved on both stage and screen. He had made eighty-three films, not all of them good but each of them distinguished by his presence, and he had appeared, usually in the leading role, in seventeen Broadway plays, many of them box-office hits and nearly all of them critical successes. And yet, amazingly, he had not won a single important award. Oscar nominations, yes—he had won those; but the Academy Award itself, never. To other, lesser, actors the Oscars sometimes seemed to have been handed out like gift vouchers on a detergent packet but for forty-five years Fonda had been consistently overlooked. For this neglect his friends offered various explanations. Sidney Lumet, for example, said: "His work was so good for so long that it became expected and also, in the nature of the work, it was never spectacular. He never played the drunk running down

Third Avenue, he never played the lunatic in the asylum, he never played the Hunchback of Notre Dame. The parts were calm, the performances were calm and they needed a little bit of looking at. Another factor is that Hank was never among the biggest money-makers. In the past how a picture did commercially had a great deal to do with the Academy Awards. Very often they went to the four or five biggest financial hits of the year and Hank didn't have many of those."

Jack Lemmon said: "People were never surprised that Hank was nominated or gave a great performance. There was a simplicity in his playing, almost at times as if he wasn't acting at all. There were no great histrionics going on: he wasn't climbing the walls and pouring tears and that. I think the Academy voters just took him for granted and very often some flashier performance would grab them and they'd vote for that."

And so Fonda, the consummate craftsman who often declared that if an audience could detect the seams in his performance he wasn't doing it right, lost out time after time to less able performers who believed that an actor should be seen to be acting.

But as the 1970s came to an end and Fonda himself approached seventy-five, a man in ill health whose mortality was becoming increasingly evident, there was a universal change of heart. The awards and honours that had hitherto eluded him came suddenly in abundance: the American Film Institute saluted his "lifetime contribution to the cinema"; he was given a special Tony for his "outstanding contribution to the theatre"; and he was one of five Americans honoured for their achievements at a special ceremony at the Kennedy Centre in Washington. Furthermore in 1981 the American Academy presented him with a special Oscar in recognition of his "enduring contribution to the art of motion pictures". Well, that's the one they give to almost everybody who manages to live a long time without committing the unpardonable sin of becoming poor or out of work. But the real award, the one every screen actor covets, the Oscar for the finest performance in any one year, had still escaped him. Even that, however, was to come his way.

The circumstances that were to bring him the trophy that crowned his career were in themselves like the ingredients of a film script.

As the 1980s began he was on much easier terms with Jane and Peter, but still not as close as any of them would have wished. But all of this changed with Fonda's last film, *On Golden Pond*.

Mark Rydell, the director of the picture, said: "It was true that, aside from political differences—which, by the way, were resolved long before this film—Henry and Jane had numerous personal difficulties. Henry was a very private man; he was very self-absorbed, a consummate artist deeply interested in his work. I probably would categorise him as less than the greatest father because he was a committed man. And I think that led to resentment and bitterness and feelings of exclusion. I'm not trying to justify or attack him in any way but these things existed and I know that Jane was deeply hungry to resolve these problems with her father."

The way she achieved this was to acquire the screen rights to the Broadway play *On Golden Pond* and offer the film as a starring vehicle for Fonda and Katharine Hepburn. She could hardly have chosen anything more apposite for the story concerned an elderly couple, returning to their holiday home by a lake for what, the audience assumes, will probably be their last summer together. And it is during this period that the father and his daughter, played by Jane Fonda, finally resolve the differences between them that have undermined their relationship for years. As it happened in the film, so it happened in fact.

This, as Mark Rydell saw it, is what took place during the shooting . . .

"Jane was sick to her stomach, literally, every day before she had to play a scene with Henry, because she was so in awe of him and so hungry for his affection, for the father she really needed. He, on the other hand, very careful, very modest with his feelings, was finally indeed overwhelmed by her candour and her need for him. It was just inescapable. They had a quite remarkable psycho-drama that went on every day on the set."

Towards the end of the film there is a particularly touching moment when the daughter pours out the emotion, the love, she feels for her father. And, said Rydell . . . "It was absolutely genuine. I had to cut out great portions of his response. He sobbed, which was not in character for Norman (the role Henry Fonda played). His response was absolutely . . . torrential. He sobbed helplessly when she reached out and touched his arm and said, 'I want to be your friend.' We had to stop shooting; I mean, he was just overcome. And he was very careful with his emotions, very much in control of himself; but this overwhelmed him. And she was a basket case—you know, asking her own father for the affection and consideration that she had longed for for so many years."

Later, when the film was finished, Rydell also had an opportunity to observe Peter Fonda's attitude to his father. "I was invited to the Utah Film Festival to present an award, the John Ford Medallion, to Henry, who by this time had become ill. Jane was working on another picture so they invited Peter to accept the award. It was rather a large occasion, with thousands of people and the press and TV, and it seemed only proper as I got up to talk about Henry that I should say something about Peter and Jane. I said I thought it was wonderful, a testimonial to the strength of the family, that they had been able to overcome the obstacle of having to follow a father who had become a monument, a symbol of America, and had carved out their own lives. And I glanced down, about to introduce Peter, and he was sobbing helplessly. I really had to stall for a few moments until he could pull himself together and when he came up on the stand he took the medallion, his eyes swollen with crying, and he said, 'I'm not going to give this to my father.' I thought, 'My God, what *are* you gonna do?' And he said: 'I'm going to take it home to my ranch in Montana and maybe then he'll come to visit me.' So there was a deep hurt in these children. It's hard really to evaluate but I know that there was injury."

There was one other curiosity about the filming of *On Golden Pond*. Not only was it the first time Fonda and Hepburn had appeared together: it was the first time they had ever met, though each had been in or around Hollywood for the best part of fifty years. When Rydell introduced them, Hepburn said: "Well, it's about time." Later on, as a material token of her esteem, she presented Fonda with a hat that had been worn by Spencer Tracy, with whom she had conducted a very long love affair. Fonda wore it throughout the picture.

The film opened to excellent reviews and even better business. In February 1982 Fonda won the Golden Globe Award for best actor but by then he was too ill to attend the ceremony and Jane collected the trophy on his behalf. A month later he was, at last, named best actor at the Academy Awards celebration and again he was too ill to receive the Oscar himself and Jane stepped up to take it in his stead.

By this time everyone knew that Fonda was dying and I suppose it could have been argued, cynically, that this award—which, whatever you may think of it and of the absurdity of comparing a number of disparate and unrelated performances and declaring that one is better than the rest, is still unchallenged as the most important prize the movie business can bestow—was a farewell present from a grateful industry. But such an attitude would be insulting to Fonda. His performance was indeed superb; true, in the past he had given others equally as good and gone unrewarded but no matter. As Mark Rydell said: "It was not a sentimental award, it wasn't a gift award. He deserved it: he *won* it. And I know that it moved him very much."

Some four months after winning the Oscar, Henry Fonda died in hospital in Los Angeles, with all his family around him. He was seventy-seven years old and he had made eighty-five films in a career that lasted more than four and a half decades. But it was never the bulk of his work that counted; it was the quality. To James Stewart he was, "the finest actor of his generation"; to Sidney Lumet he was "an absolute barometer of truth. His style was totally naturalistic and yet heroes of epic proportions would always come out"; to Mark Rydell he was "the absolute dean of American actors". And Jack Lemmon said of him: "Nobody could make me more proud to be a member of the same profession."

But he was more than just a great screen actor. He was, as Mark Rydell had put it, a monument, a symbol. If John Wayne represented, to the cinema audience, the pioneering courage of America, Fonda represented the nation's conscience. The characters he played were fierce opponents of ignorance, oppression, intolerance and prejudice and they reflected the man himself. It is certainly true that in his private life he was a great deal less successful— except in his last few years—than he was in his career but he was never less than an honourable (and, in my own brief knowledge of him, immensely charming) man and it could well be that all the difficulties he encountered with his first four wives and with his children were due to a crippling and by no means rare inability to express his emotions.

Perhaps, as John Houseman suggested, it was only when he was on stage or on screen that he was able to throw off his inhibitions and, paradoxically, reveal himself. Great artists are rarely simple men and Henry Fonda was a great artist. In its time Hollywood has discovered many stars but only a handful or so of truly fine actors and of those Fonda may well have been the best.

His was indeed the art that concealed art and, in the words of Sidney Lumet, led far too many people for far too long to come away from his plays and his films saying: "Oh well, another great performance from Hank Fonda. What else is new?"

John Wayne

"An American Legend".

Wedding day No. 1, with his wife Josephine and Loretta Young, who lent her house for the occasion.

Wife No. 2, Esperanza (Chata or "Pugnose" to her friends). The marriage was brief—and turbulent.

Pilar, the third and last wife and another Latin American. Wayne was consistent, if not always constant, in his marriages.

Pat Stacy, the secretary who was promoted to girlfriend.

Michael (left) and Patrick, who followed Dad into the family trade as, respectively, producer and actor.

In *Big Jake* with his youngest son, Ethan, portraying quite convincingly his own father's grandson.

In *Stagecoach*, which brought him "overnight" stardom after eleven years. . .

. . . and in *True Grit* which, thirty years later, won him his only Academy Award for best actor.

I met John Wayne only twice; on both occasions we had fierce political disagreements and the second time I believe he had it in mind to hit me.

The first meeting was in Madrid in the early 1960s when he was making an indifferent film called *Circus World* with Claudia Cardinale. Wayne in Spain—indeed Wayne anywhere—was exactly what you would expect: apparently amiable and rough-hewn but mostly huge. He was then fifty-six and beginning to run to fat, or in the rather more tactful words of a *Time* magazine film reviewer, when he walked away from you the back view of his jeans looked like two small boys wrestling in a tent.

The interview (for later publication in the London *Daily Mail*) took place in his trailer and began pleasantly enough. But after a while the conversation turned to politics and I expressed the hope that America would have enough sense not to elect Barry Goldwater to the presidency. In retrospect, of course, this was a daft thing to say to John Wayne but I was naïve at the time and unaware that he had the reputation of being so far to the right that he had never really found a politician worthy of his support since the death of Attila the Hun. Anyway, the apparent amiability vanished very suddenly and he said, drawing himself up to his full six feet four inches, in a markedly cold manner: "Senator Goldwater happens to be a very close personal friend of mine."

At this point, no doubt, I should have backtracked rapidly and returned to the safer ground of the movies but instead I blundered on and ventured a few words of criticism of the late Joseph McCarthy, the notorious Communist witch-hunter of the 1950s.

Wayne heard me out even more coldly than before and then said: "I happen to believe that Senator McCarthy was one of the finest Americans who ever lived", and after that the interview struggled for breath for a minute or two and then gently expired.

Our second encounter was in 1969 on a train travelling from Denver, Colorado, to Salt Lake City. The centenary of the meeting of America's coast-to-coast railways was to be celebrated at Promontory, in Utah, and for a reason which I have never begun to understand the highlight of the festivities was to be the première of Wayne's most recent movie, *True Grit*, for which admittedly he later won his first and only Oscar but which on the other hand had nothing whatsoever to do with railways.

The train wandered slowly through typical Wayne country— rolling plains and snowy mountains all apparently created by God for the sole purpose of making Western movies. News of Wayne's presence on board had spread throughout the countryside and at each wayside halt hordes of people (including, at Laramie, a bunch of Red Indians in a Ford Mustang) turned up to hear him speak warmly of the virtues of being an American.

In between stops the attendant journalists on the train were split into groups of half a dozen or so and ushered into the club car where Wayne held court and granted interviews. By the time I got in there it was mid-morning and the waitress told me, with something like awe in her voice, that the great man had already consumed fifteen miniature bottles of bourbon or, as he called it, "who-hit-John".

I don't think he remembered me from Spain, which was perhaps just as well; not that it mattered, really, because once more the talk turned to politics.

Wayne had just returned from exhorting the troops in Vietnam where his bicycle had been hit by a Vietcong bullet. Wayne wasn't actually within a hundred yards of the machine at the time but nevertheless the consensus among the American media was that he had had a narrow escape and this brush with death was gravely discussed by the local journalists in my group. And when the heroism of the bicycle had been firmly established I asked Wayne what he thought of the situation in Vietnam.

"Well," he said, "I'll tell you: it's easy to stop that war. All you have to do is call up Kosygin on that hot line and say, 'You send one more bullet, one more gun to Vietnam and we bomb Moscow.'"

Unfortunately, I laughed, which was a mistake because I thought he was joking and he wasn't. After that as the talk ranged over politics (in which his views certainly did not seem to have mellowed since the early 1960s) and modern youth, he appeared to take against me rather strongly.

It was a time when students were demonstrating and even rioting across America and Wayne dismissed them all as "just a buncha jerks". His philosophy, forceful if not original, was as follows: "In my day at college you got a D for being a jerk. Now you get an A. That's the difference. Look, if you're a socialist in your first year at college, okay. But if you're still a socialist when you leave you're the dumbest son of a bitch that ever drew breath." He prefaced many of his remarks with "Lemme explain sumpun to ya" and qualified them by saying, "I'm not speaking from up there on the Mount", which I took to be a biblical reference though I suppose he could have meant a horse.

In any event I bore the brunt of most of his references to "goddamn, pinko liberals" and eventually he became so irritated with me that he began to mimic my accent, thereby hoping, I suspect, to amuse and enlist the support of the American journalists present. But Americans are extremely courteous people and they were rather embarrassed by his mockery of me so they all stared out of the window and failed to laugh with him. That annoyed him even more and when I, thinking (wrongly as it turned out) to calm matters, congratulated him on his English accent— which, to tell the truth, was really rather bad—he emitted a growl of what sounded alarmingly like rage and started lumbering out of his chair towards me. Fortunately, an alert band of film company executives interposed themselves between Wayne and me, thrust another bourbon into his hand and put him back in his seat and ushered me very swiftly out of the club car. I expect it was a coincidence but for the rest of the three-day trip I never seemed to find myself within hailing distance of him and we never met again.

I've mentioned all this in some detail largely in order to declare myself: I did not personally like John Wayne. I admired him immensely as a star and somewhat less as an actor but I did not like the man. To arrive at such a conclusion on the basis of two comparatively brief and acrimonious meetings is probably a little over-hasty and no doubt the loss is mine, because my opinion of him does not appear to be shared by the mass of the American populace.

The fact is that nearly five years after his death, John Wayne is just about the biggest and most popular movie star there has ever been. A school in Brooklyn, a cancer clinic at the University of California, Los Angeles, a tennis club and even the airport at Orange County in southern California have all been named after him. There's a nine-foot statue of him at the airport and there is planned to be a twenty-one-foot statue on Wilshire Boulevard, which though not strictly in Hollywood is in the very heart of the general area that is widely considered to represent Hollywood. Furthermore he is one of only eighty-seven Americans to have had a Congressional Medal struck in his honour.

The inscription at the foot of the statue at the John Wayne Airport in Orange County reads: "John Wayne—American legend". And that's what he is, which is really rather odd because, although he made more than 150 films few of them were very good and there have certainly been far better actors than Wayne in the movies. Yet, when you look around, you don't see any twenty-one-foot statues of them overlooking the public thoroughfares. And so it seems reasonable to wonder why all these honours and all this adulation should have been visited upon John Wayne.

The story or, if you prefer, the legend of John Wayne began on May 26th, 1907 in the small town of Winterset, Iowa, where Mary, wife of Clyde L. Morrison, the local drug-store owner was delivered of a son. The father was of Scottish and the mother of Irish descent and with a taste for alliteration and very possibly an odd sense of humour they christened their child Marion Michael. He grew up tall and brawny as any all-American boy named Marion would probably have to be. His father, the pharmacist, was however less robust and when Marion was five the family moved to California where it was believed the drier climate would be beneficial to Clyde Morrison's tuberculosis.

Mr. Morrison was a college graduate but no great shakes as a businessman. He had made very little money as a druggist and he made even less as a farmer which is what he became, as the owner of eighty acres of sagebrush in California. In the words of Michael Wayne, John's eldest son: "They had a great crop but the rabbits ate it all." Still, it was here that the young Marion learned to ride and shoot rattlesnakes, skills which were to be invaluable to him in later life.

The farming experiment rapidly proved a failure and when Marion was nine the Morrisons moved back to town, to Glendale, California, where Clyde resumed his former occupation as a pharmacist, although this time as an employee in someone else's business.

Michael Wayne said: "They were very poor and lived on tuna fish for about six months. Evidently they got a good buy on several cases of tuna fish." (The predictable result of this enforced diet was that ever afterwards John Wayne could barely bring himself to look at a piece of tuna fish.)

The Morrisons' poverty was so evident that a group of firemen took pity on young Marion and every day, as he passed the fire station on his way to school, they gave him a bottle of milk and told him to take it home for his cat, well knowing that he had no cat and was drinking it himself. It was these same firemen who gave him the nickname that was to stick to him for the rest of his life. Though lacking a cat young Marion did have a dog, a big Airedale called Duke and as the pair approached the firemen would say: "Here comes big Duke (meaning the dog) and little Duke (meaning the boy)."

On the two occasions when I met Marion, or Duke, or as I knew
him John Wayne, one of the things that struck me about him was
his apparently anti-intellectual attitude. If you offered him a word
of more than two syllables he would sneer visibly and say: "What
the hell does that mean?"

I can only assume that this was a pose, part of his carefully
nurtured down-to-earth image, because in fact Marion Morrison had
a pretty good education and by all accounts was something of a star
pupil. At Glendale High School he was, as his son Michael said,
"an achiever" and all his life, according to his friends and family,
he was a voracious reader, much addicted to the works of Winston
Churchill. Indeed, the director Andrew McLaglen, who probably
knew him as well as anyone, said: "If you were to ask me 'Was he an
intellectual or not an intellectual' I would say he *was* an intellectual,
because he was an avid reader both in national and world politics
and he could speak on a lot of subjects. People who looked at big
John Wayne and thought he was dumb in any way, shape or form
had another think coming." Perhaps then he was a closet reader,
anxious to keep this unmanly vice secret from the millions of fans
to whom he was the epitome of the more rugged, less cerebral
masculine virtues.

On the other hand it was as an athlete, not as a scholar, that he
won his place at the University of Southern California, to which he
went on a football scholarship in September 1925, by which time
he was armed (thanks to his father) with the three guiding principles
which he tried to follow throughout his life: 1) Always keep your
word; 2) A gentleman never insults anybody unintentionally; and
3) Don't go around looking for trouble. But if you ever get into a
fight, make sure you win it.

He was not, however, armed with much money and was therefore obliged to work his way through college. As a member of
the USC football team, the Trojans, he was one of the benefici-
aries of an offer made by Tom Mix, then the No. 1 Western
movie star and a keen football follower, of summer jobs at Fox
studios. And it was there, while he was working as a general
handyman and labourer, that he met the director John Ford, who
was to become undoubtedly the most decisive influence on his life.
Ford, who was then thirty-one, was making a film called
Mother Machree, on which Duke Morrison was employed as a goose-
wrangler, which is to say that he was in charge of a herd of geese
with the responsibility of pointing them in whichever direction
Ford demanded.

Michael Wayne said: "I guess the geese didn't do exactly what my father or John Ford wanted them to do and Ford got onto my father a little bit about it and my father apologised. But Ford didn't let up on him and finally he said, 'You're a football man, aren't you?' and my father said 'Yes' and Ford said, 'Do you think you could block me?' Now Ford was a very physical guy, about six foot three, but I don't think physically he was a match for my father in those days, or at any time really, but he said, 'Well, get down on your three-point stance,' that's both feet on the ground and one hand out in front of you, and when my father got down, the minute he got down, Ford kicked his hand out from under him and my father went, you know, down on his face and everybody on the set got a big laugh out of it. Well, by this time my father didn't care about Hollywood or anything else; he was mad at Ford and he said, 'May I try that again?' And he got down and before Ford could kick his hand out he drove Ford over some tables and chairs and into a truck that was parked there. And the set was quiet, you know, because . . . 'Oh, my God, he's just done the most horrible thing in the world: hit this great director and really knocked him on his fanny.' But Ford got up, laughed and enjoyed the joke as much as my father did and admired him, I think; admired his spunk and the fact that he wouldn't take any crap from him."

In this violent way there began a lifelong friendship between the two men and it may not be too far-fetched to see in this incident the inception, or even the conception, of the character Wayne was to play so successfully in the movies. Once, when he was talking to me about his career, he said: "In America, I represent manhood", and that's quite true, though it was a rather primitive kind of manhood—rough and tough and boozy. In John Wayne films women were treated with gruff, backwoods courtesy and no man could ever hope to become Wayne's friend unless they had first had a quite brutal fist fight—possibly to ensure that, however close the bonds of the ensuing friendship, the audience could be confident that there was nothing gay about Big John; but possibly, too, because the most important friendship in his own personal life had begun in just such a way.

However, after his summer job, Duke Morrison returned to USC in the autumn of 1926 but within a few months his college career was virtually over. He had suffered a severe shoulder injury in a surfing accident and it soon became clear that he would not be able to play football any more—and that, in turn, meant that he lost his scholarship.

And so he dropped out of college and in the summer of 1927, at John Ford's request, he returned to his labouring job at Fox studios. It was not much of a job but now he had the incentive of Ford's promise that one day he would be given the opportunity to act. In any event he needed work because he had fallen in love with, and intended to marry, one Josephine Saenz, whom he had met the previous November at a Thanksgiving Dance at USC.

She was the younger daughter of Dr. Jose Sainte Saenz, a Spaniard of royal descent, a wealthy businessman and the consul for the Dominican Republic. Unfortunately, neither he nor his wife approved of Wayne and since Josephine refused to commit herself to him without parental approval theirs was a tense and no doubt physically frustrating courtship. Wayne, however, was undeterred and determined that one day he would persuade the whole Saenz family to accept him.

Meanwhile he remained at Fox, essentially in the props department, for the next three years. But in that time he also appeared as an extra in crowd scenes, played an Irish peasant boy in Ford's 1928 film, *Hangman's House*, and gained his first screen credit—as Duke Morrison—the following year in *Words and Music*. More bits and pieces and extra work came his way and then he added another skill to his repertoire when he became a stuntman. The film, *Men Without Women*, directed by Ford, concerned an explosion in the engine room of a submarine and when they came to the scene in which the stars, represented naturally by stuntmen, were supposed to dive overboard the sea was so fierce that the stuntmen refused to do it. Ford thereupon turned to Wayne (who was actually employed as the props man) and said: "Show 'em up!" And his eager young acolyte obediently plunged in.

From then on for his first decade in pictures Wayne looked upon himself as a stuntman rather than an actor and to a large extent he was not wrong to do so, for his apprenticeship was served in Action Man Westerns and Saturday morning serials in which he was called upon to do most of his own stunts and in which anything much more than half a dozen words was regarded as a very long speech indeed and should be cut if possible lest it bore the audience to sleep.

His first break in such films came indirectly through his friend John Ford, who recommended him to Raoul Walsh as the ideal replacement for Gary Cooper (who had declined the role) in *The Big Trail*. The film was a flop—though the Cooper-substitute received good reviews—and its most important outcome was that it caused Marion Morrison (a better name, after all, for a leading lady than a leading man) to become John Wayne. As to how this actually came about there is some confusion.

Michael Wayne's explanation is as follows: "He had an agent and the agent's name, strange though it may seem, was also Morrison. And this guy said, 'Look, you've got to get rid of that Marion Morrison' and my father said, 'What shall I call myself?' and he said, 'John Wayne'." Another and just as plausible theory is that Raoul Walsh borrowed his new star's new surname from a general in the American Revolution who was known as "Mad Anthony" Wayne. That he was perhaps one of the lesser-known generals of the revolution is probably due to his Christian name, since "Mad Anthony" does not, somehow, have the authentic ring of desperate heroism to it. In any case, according to this theory, Walsh was not too keen on Anthony either, considering it to sound too sissy and Italian, and so on to Wayne he tacked the first name John and so it was to remain, though to his friends he continued to be known as "Duke".

Thus equipped with a new name and recognition, of a sort, as an actor the newly born John Wayne plunged confidently into two more flops (*Girls Demand Excitement* and *Three Girls Lost*), then left Fox and moved to Columbia where he developed such a dislike for the head of production, Harry Cohn, that after his brief stay he never worked for the studio again and eventually drifted to Mascot Films (where he appeared in a number of serials), before moving on to Warners (where he made six films) and then signing to make sixteen five-reel Westerns with Monogram Pictures.

By now he was earning 1,500 dollars a film and was at last able to support Josephine, whom he married on June 24th, 1933—some seven years after he first met her—in the grounds of Loretta Young's estate in Bel Air. It had been, certainly by Hollywood standards, an unusual courtship. As Michael Wayne said: "It was kind of a lengthy one. I think my mother's parents were not that anxious to have their daughter marrying an actor. My grandfather was a doctor and head of the diplomatic corps here in Los Angeles and he and my father didn't see eye to eye on anything, especially my mother. As a matter of fact, he sent my mother to Hawaii with my aunt to get her away from my father and my father stowed away on the boat, got caught, got put in jail in San Francisco and eventually got out because the local police chief was the father of a good friend of his. But, yeah, they had a really romantic courtship, you know, fraught with all sorts of obstacles but eventually they got married and went about their business."

133

This business included having four children—Michael, born in 1934, Antonia Maria (known as Toni) in 1936, Patrick in 1937 and Melinda in 1939. Meanwhile, the pater familias was continuing to learn his trade as the star of B-movies and serials as well as becoming, briefly, the world's first singing cowboy under the cringe-making name of "Singin' Sandy". Decently regretting this aberration he dropped both role and soubriquet to join Republic where he starred in yet another series of B-grade Westerns, directed by George Sherman and co-starring Ray Corrigan, who deeply resented his new partner.

Sherman said: "Ray was a great big guy and he was determined that he was going to be the predominant figure in the series. He wore silver belts and silver things on his hat and silver bracelets and he tried to do everything to outshine Duke. But you just couldn't, you know? Duke could walk into a room and the eye would immediately go to him. Wayne was a very graceful man, beautiful on a horse. He was poetry in motion on a horse."

It was while he was still involved in making quickies with George Sherman that, at the age of thirty-one and after sixty-five rubbishy pictures, Wayne at last achieved stardom. The year was 1938, the film was *Stagecoach* and the director was John Ford and he, despite the protests of his producer, Walter Wanger, who was deeply unimpressed by Wayne's track record, insisted on casting him in the leading role of Ringo, the young outlaw.

His co-star was Claire Trevor, who said: "John Ford had great faith in him and had known him for many years, so he wanted to get him in this picture. But I think the higher-ups in the studio were not convinced that John Wayne could do it, so Ford asked me to make a test with him, which I did. That was the first time I met him and he was very tentative and very shy but he had a wonderful quality, I thought." Her admiration for him grew during the shooting but . . . "I didn't know—who could?—that he would be that sensational; not until I saw the picture. When I saw the finished film I was swept off my feet."

Stagecoach was an immediate success but it was more than that: it established John Wayne as a star and lent respectability to the genre of the Western which, hitherto, had been regarded as nothing more than a programme filler. Furthermore it was the first of eleven films (among them such classics as *She Wore a Yellow Ribbon*, *The Searchers* and *The Quiet Man*) that Wayne and Ford put together over a period of twenty-five years. It was a strange relationship, combining elements of father and son, master and pupil, with Ford always the dominant partner.

The style was set during the making of *Stagecoach* when, according to Claire Trevor, Ford "treated him like a child and had no regard for his dignity". In front of the whole cast he would stride up to Wayne, grab him by the head and shake it back and forth while bellowing: "You're acting with your chin. You're not supposed to act with your goddamn chin!" Miss Trevor believes that Ford's harsh behaviour was designed for Wayne's own good. "I really think Ford taught him how to act," she said. "He taught him so many great rules about acting. He taught him the principles and John Wayne took off from there."

Ford may have behaved so rudely because it was obviously in his own interests to get as good a performance as possible out of his leading man. But there is no doubt that a strongly mischievous, even sadistic, streak ran through his attitude towards Wayne. On another occasion during the filming of *Stagecoach* he took his star to see some rushes and in particular a scene in which Andy Devine was driving the stagecoach. "What do you think of that?" Ford asked. Wayne said: "Well, I think it looks kind of phoney; the reins are too loose." Ford promptly took him back to the set, confronted him with Andy Devine and said: "Tell Andy what you told me— that he looks phoney up there driving the stagecoach." The flustered Wayne tried to apologise but the damage was done and from then on there was tension between him and Devine. Many years later Ford admitted to Wayne that that had always been his intention, saying: "I wanted to juice the pair of you up a little bit. I used you."

In both those instances Ford abused and manipulated Wayne for the good of the film but on other occasions he would give him a hard time just for the hell of it. When they were filming *The Three Godfathers* in the intense heat of Death Valley Wayne arrived on set one morning with an appalling hangover, a rare occurrence because although he drank a lot he was usually quite abstemious when he was filming and certainly when he was filming with Ford.

The scene he had to shoot that day was at a dinner table with Ward Bond and Mae Marsh and Wayne was supposed to be ravenously hungry. Harry Carey Jr., who appeared in that and several other films with Wayne, said: "Ford knew Duke had a hangover. Now normally he'd do a scene in one take but this time Ford made him eat that chicken over and over and over again. He'd say, 'Duke, you're not doing it like you're starving! You're starving, remember. Now really go at it.' And Duke would just say, 'Yes, sir' and he'd eat and eat and then he'd go and throw up. And he'd come back green. Ford rode him all that morning. He must have done the scene ten times, eating that chicken and then throwing up."

Wayne's attitude towards Ford seemed to contain a strong touch of awe and even a little fear. In public he always spoke of "Mr. Ford", never of John or Jack. Bill Clothier, the cinematographer who worked with both of them on *The Horse Soldiers* and *The Man Who Shot Liberty Valance*, said: "Wayne called him 'Coach' on the set—'Okay, Coach, anything you say, Coach'—and that was the relationship. But he loved old man Ford and the old man had a way of getting things out of people that no other director had."

Harry Carey said: "Actually he had a very respectful fear of Jack Ford. It would always be 'Yes, sir' or 'No, sir'. After a film they'd go off on Duke's or Ford's yacht together and play cards and get drunk. But on the set it was healthy respect all the way. And in fact Duke was at Jack Ford's beck and call almost all the time. If Jack Ford felt like playing cards with John Wayne and John Wayne was in bed, well, he'd just have to get up and go over to Ford's house and play cards. Like, Sunday afternoon, if Duke decided he wanted to go and see one of his kids and Jack wanted to play bridge or poker, well, the minute Ford called he'd have to go over there."

According to Michael Wayne: "My father had a love for him, a respect for him and also a liking for him. The liking used to be stronger or weaker depending on the situation. One time they didn't talk for two years and my father never really knew why. He just never heard from Ford and my father would call but he never heard back. And then, out of the blue, he got a telephone call and it was as if nothing had ever happened. So it was an unusual kind of relationship but my father always loved and respected him and was always grateful to him for that opportunity in *Stagecoach*. I remember Bruce Cabot said to me one time, 'You know, Michael, I tested for that *Stagecoach* part and I did all the stuff that Ford asked me to do in the test and I jumped up and said, "Well, Pappy, how was I?" And he said, "You were great. You were great, Bruce —but Duke's got the part." ' "

In the three years following *Stagecoach*, Wayne made a dozen films but was not particularly happy with any of them except the one John Ford directed—*The Long Voyage Home*, which was based on four one-act plays by Eugene O'Neill. It was more of a critical than a financial success and it was said to be O'Neill's favourite picture. At this time Wayne was regretting the fact that, unusually for a big star in that era, he was a freelance, with no attachment to any particular studio. He felt the lack of some powerful executive to keep an eye on his career, to boost and publicise him. In the final analysis, of course, this made very little difference but it could help to explain why it took him far longer than most of his peers to reach what is now known as superstardom.

By the end of 1941, however, Wayne had made seventy-seven movies and was much in demand, though his reputation rested largely on *Stagecoach* and to some extent it still does, for it is not easy to think of a better Western. There are, however, other reasons than the quality of that first outstanding success for the special niche Wayne occupies among Western stars. In part he explained it to me thus: "I guess I was the first hero in movies ever to hit a guy with a vase or a chair." Until his advent, it seems, brawls in films had been gentlemanly affairs in which only fists were used. Wayne's claim was that he changed all that and . . . "I guess that's what made my first Westerns different from any that had gone before."

I suppose if Wayne hadn't achieved this dramatic breakthrough somebody else would have done sooner or later. Anyway, he spoke of it with bashful modesty, as if the introduction of real violence into popular entertainment was an achievement in which any man might take a certain amount of pride.

However, back at the close of 1941, America had entered the Second World War—without Wayne—and his marriage was in serious trouble. He was thirty-four and though he tried to enlist in the armed forces he was rejected because of his age and his family commitments and also because of the aftermath of the shoulder injury which had ended his football career. To do him justice he tried very hard to get into the services but even John Ford, who had become a lieutenant-commander in the navy, was unable to help him. So Wayne's war effort was, perforce, restricted to entertaining the troops near the front line and making a number of patriotic movies in which he won countless battles. Ironically, his absence, however reluctant, from the war itself and his consequent presence on so many celluloid battlefields probably did more to create the legend than active service would have done. Along with the Westerns, those war movies helped to build up the picture of Wayne as a hero for all seasons and all spheres of combat.

Meanwhile, on the domestic front Wayne and Josephine were drifting gradually apart. It was a state of affairs that had been becoming apparent for some time but in 1941 Wayne went to Mexico and there became greatly smitten by an actress named Esperanza Baur Diaz Caballos, known professionally as Esperanza Baur and to her friends by the somewhat unflattering nickname of "Chata", which in Spanish means pugnose. For some time Wayne resisted anything approaching a wholly intimate relationship but eventually he brought her to Hollywood as his "protégée". As far as Josephine was concerned that was the clincher; the couple separated and in November 1944 they were divorced, although they remained good friends until Wayne's death.

Considering the difficulties they had had to go through to get married in the first place, the time they had had to wait and the resolution they had shown it is particularly sad that the marriage didn't last. Michael Wayne believes that the chief cause of the failure was the all-consuming nature of his father's career: "Being an actor, especially in the early stages of your career, is very demanding in terms of time. He was trying to establish himself in town; every film that he made was an outdoor adventure story, made on location, so he was gone a lot and I think that perhaps they just went their separate ways. My mother is also a very strong person and created a life for herself. So I guess they gradually grew apart. It was, of course, very disappointing to us, the kids, but we always respected both of them, loved them both, and I never heard my mother say a bad word about my father, while he always had glowing things to say about her. So it was nice to grow up with that kind of feeling and in that kind of situation."

Three weeks after the divorce became final, in January 1946, Wayne married Chata at Long Beach, California. Michael Wayne remembered his new stepmother as . . . "A good-looking, fiery Latin woman and I guess my father was the man to match that fire. She was really very nice to the four children and I guess she was nicer to us than she was to my father, to hear him tell it, anyway."

In any event, Wayne's second shot at matrimony was very different from his first: it was a passionate, even violent, affair in which vast quantities of booze were consumed by both parties. Nor was it helped by the fact that Chata's mother, herself a handy lady with a tequila bottle, lived with them for much of the time and took an active part in all the marital discord.

Chata's problem was that she had no children, had given up her own career and resented her husband's total absorption in the film business. So to get her own back for his apparent neglect, or perhaps simply to attract his attention, she had a series of casual, but strictly non-secret affairs with other men. Wayne, who was obsessed by her —possibly because to him she was often unobtainable—put up with this for quite a long time. But in the end he could stand it no more and in November 1953 they were somewhat messily divorced.

At one point she obtained a court order barring him from the marital home, in response to which he got another court order permitting him to enter the premises to visit their dog, a poodle called Pedro, which in fact he disliked intensely. In the end both parties were awarded a divorce but Chata came out of it all well ahead on points, since Wayne was ordered to pay her 150,000 dollars plus 50,000 dollars a year in alimony.

In fact, however, this did not prove too costly because in the winter of 1954 Chata died of a heart attack in Mexico City.

Those first two marriages—and indeed his third, which followed within hours of his divorce from Chata becoming final—throw some light on Wayne's attitude both to women and to his work.

Claire Trevor, who remained a close friend (though nothing more than that) till the end of his life, believed that he was basically not a womaniser or even a flirtatious man. "He was a romantic. He liked women but he was much more at ease with men. He was a rough, tough he-man. A lot of women found him very attractive—Marlene Dietrich for one—and sort of went on the make for him. But that made him a little shy and frightened, you know? He was a very true man, true to his marriage, to his wife at the time."

Michael Wayne said: "He was attractive to women and he was attracted by women but he was uneasy around them because he liked occasionally to use . . . I guess you'd call them 'vulgarities' . . . and so, though he was always on his best behaviour and was always a gentleman when he was around women, I think it was a little bit of a strain for him."

Along with all this, went a respect both for women and for the state of matrimony. "He was always a one-woman man," said Andrew McLaglen. "If a wife were to leave him he'd fall in love again kind of fast but he usually married the lady."

Wayne himself once told his third wife, Pilar, that he didn't understand women, a confession which hardly makes him unique but which, perhaps, helps to account for his awkwardness and shyness with them, although it doesn't explain his inability to make a marriage work and last.

The reason for that lies mostly in his devotion to his work and his career, which took priority above all else in his life. "He told me that he never wanted more than a week off," said Harry Carey Jr. "I never heard him say, 'Jesus, I'm really tired; I could use some time off.' His vacation was making movies. He *loved* to make movies."

Claire Trevor said: "He was extremely ambitious. Every success-ful actor I've ever known, every movie star had a dedication to his work and Duke had it, too. He wanted success; he wanted to win; he was a perfectionist."

In later years this dedication and striving for perfection made Wayne unpopular with directors of lesser calibre than John Ford, for with them he could be dictatorial. George Sherman believed that working with Ford had spoiled him: "Ford never let him utter one word of criticism about directing, because everybody was terrified of Ford. So when Duke worked with another guy, he figured: this is my opportunity to really get in there and speak out and question things."

In this, however, he was not prompted so much by egotism as by the fact that he probably knew as much about making films as anybody around. Harry Carey said: "John Wayne always knew his lines and he knew yours, too. He'd studied every aspect of the picture business. He knew about editing, he knew about camera work and when he was working with some of those younger directors, he'd say: 'No, no, no, damn it! Jesus, what have you got the camera there for?' You know? But it was because he was so conscientious and wanted to save time. If he had a fault—well, he had quite a few faults—he had a temper and he was very impatient. He couldn't tell anybody how to do something without getting excited."

By the end of the Second World War the dedicated and occasion-ally irascible John Wayne, aged thirty-eight and with a considerable body of work behind him, was already one of the most popular stars in America but his greatest success was still to come.

In the next few years films like *Fort Apache*, *She Wore a Yellow Ribbon* and *Rio Grande* (all directed by John Ford), along with *Red River* (Howard Hawks) and *Sands of Iwo Jima* (Allan Dwan) for which latter production Wayne received his first Academy Award nomination, boosted his career to such an extent that by 1950 he had become America's top box-office star. He was number one again in 1951, 1952, and 1953 and from then until 1968 he was only out of the top ten once.

But by the end of the 1940s he was already something more than simply a movie star: he was becoming a kind of unofficial, self-appointed voice of America. In the latter part of the decade he had banded together with other actors and studio executives to form the Motion Picture Alliance for the Preservation of American Ideals, an organisation that went about peering suspiciously into dark corners of Hollywood for signs of Communist infiltration. In 1949 he became the MPA's president and during his three years in office the association passed resolutions insisting that all Communists should register as such and outlined a number of elements in any film that proved it to carry surreptitious Marxist propaganda.

Wayne himself even complained to the writer Carl Foreman that the scene in *High Noon* in which Gary Cooper ripped off his marshal's badge and threw it on the ground was "like belittling a medal of honour". Against this, though, it should be pointed out that unlike many of his Hollywood contemporaries in the late 1940s and early 1950s, Wayne was not a witch-hunter and certainly never attempted to bar anyone from working on a film because of political beliefs.

True, he was a fervent and lifelong anti-Communist but above all I think he was motivated by the fact that he was a passionate and rather simple patriot. In the words of his son, Michael, he "loved being an American" and indeed in 1968 he addressed the Republican Party convention to tell them so. Frequently he observed that he thanked God for every hour he spent on American soil. "He felt," said Michael Wayne, "that this was the greatest country on the face of the earth. He told me often that in our 200-year history we've given away more to others than the rest of the world combined since the beginning of time."

Whether this expansive claim is true or not (and it would be difficult to prove one way or the other), Wayne did seem genuinely to believe that America was God's own country and gave the impression that he was only sorry that he personally hadn't discovered it, or at least pioneered it. It being rather too late for him to do either of those things he imposed upon himself the task of protecting the American way of life and what America stood for as he saw it. And all those who strayed from his line and from staunchly Republican and capitalist principles were, in his own words, "a bunch of goddamn pinko liberals" who must be regarded as so many pesky redskins attacking the stagecoach and dealt with accordingly.

As he once put it to me: "I'm just an ordinary goddamn American and I talk for all the ordinary goddamn Americans, the butchers and bakers and plumbers. I know these people; I know what they think."

In the early days of his political involvement no doubt he did know and perhaps speak for these people. But later on, towards the end of the 1960s and into the 1970s, he seemed to grow out of touch with them and was still uttering his jingoistic line when jingoism had fallen from favour. And perhaps the knowledge of that helped to account for his political anger and the bitterness of his attitude towards modern American youth during that train journey in 1969 between Denver and Salt Lake City.

Michael Wayne explained his father's involvement in the MPA thus: "It was a time in the film business when the Communist Party was making an effort to take over all of the unions. This was before television and I guess motion pictures were the medium with the largest impact on the public, so this was kind of a logical place for the Communist Party to go in and try to take over. If they had taken over the film business they could perhaps have spread their influence and philosophy across the United States and my father saw this as a great danger. As a matter of fact, I think this was the time when Ronald Reagan was president of the Screen Actors' Guild and he and my father were at the opposite end of the political spectrum. I mean, my father was a very conservative man and Reagan was a liberal Democrat at that time but he asked my father to come in and help him fight this Communist takeover, which he did and he regarded it as a real threat to the United States. I think history has proved him right."

Whether he was right or wrong there is, of course, no reason why an actor should not have political beliefs but Wayne more than any other used the popularity and fame he had achieved to propagate his, even though—as his friend and fellow actor Ben Johnson said —normally "in the picture business you don't take sides hardly. He did and he was big enough to back it up." Because of that, political pronouncements which, had they emanated from almost any other movie star, would have merited only passing interest, had the effect of sounding, in his phrase, as if they came "from up there on the Mount". And so to the rest of the Wayne legend was added the picture of John Wayne, spokesman for America.

But by 1950 politics was not the only new area into which Wayne was expanding. He had also started his own company, Batjac Productions, for which he made a number of moderately successful films such as *Big Jim McClain*, *Island in the Sky* and *Hondo*. His most notable pictures in the first half of that decade though were *The Quiet Man* (another John Ford movie) and *The High and the Mighty*. Immediately after completing the latter production he went to Hawaii to film *The Sea Chase* and it was while he was on location there that he was married for the third time.

His bride on this occasion was Pilar Palette, a Peruvian actress whom he had met while on a visit to South America. They met again at a Hollywood party and began going out together. By the time Wayne went to Hawaii for *The Sea Chase* his marriage to

Chata was all over and so Pilar went with him. On the morning of November 1st, 1954, Wayne received a phone call and then turned to Pilar saying: "That was my lawyer. My divorce has become final: let's get married today."

So they did. Pilar said: "He told me I never gave him an hour's chance. He was married at breakfast, divorced at lunch and remarried at dinner. He'd always kid me about that."

This third plunge into matrimony completed Wayne's hat-trick of Latin American wives, a matter of good taste according to Pilar but a simple coincidence according to her husband. A month after the wedding he told an agency reporter that he had never been conscious of going for a particular type of woman. "They say a man follows a pattern but I haven't been aware of it myself . . . I certainly don't have anything against American women."

He remained married to Pilar for the rest of his life, though they separated in 1973, and by her he had three more children—Aissa, John Ethan and Marisa. By the strictest standards (or even by not very strict standards at all) he may have fallen some way short of being the ideal husband but he was certainly a devoted family man, co-existing with all his seven children in an atmosphere of mutual adoration.

As a father he could be strict. Michael Wayne said: "He just wanted you to do what was right. As long as you kept your nose clean you never heard from him; he wasn't constantly preaching. But the minute something went wrong the punishment was swift. You always knew where you stood. He'd just have to start to reach for his belt and we knew we were in trouble; he didn't have to hit us." He didn't have to but he would occasionally—"just a few taps, to let you know you'd done something bad."

George Sherman remembered an occasion when Wayne's eldest daughter, Toni, then a teenager, was smoking at the dinner table. "He walked up to her and said, 'Do you like to smoke?' and she said, 'Yeah, I'm enjoying it.' He said, 'Well, that's good' and he took the cigarette and shoved it right in her mouth. So that finished her smoking."

On the other hand this image of Wayne, the stern disciplinarian, is not truly representative. Claire Trevor said: "His whole family went with him everywhere. He was the most demonstrative father you could imagine. He loved his children with a passion; he was always putting his arms around them and hugging and kissing them."

Marisa, the youngest of the seven junior Waynes, summed him

up thus: "He was the best father I could ever have had. I loved him more than anything. He was caring and he was loving and giving and he was strict but in a good way. He disciplined me well and taught me always to be nice to everybody and to respect other people."

For Wayne the family man Christmas was the best time of the year. He would spray artificial snow all over the house, install Christmas trees in every room and cover them with tinsel and myriads of coloured light bulbs. "You couldn't walk into our living room," Marisa said, "because there were so many presents for everybody. And he'd have reindeer up at the house." They lived then on the bay at Newport Beach and every year out on the water there was a Christmas procession of yachts. "He'd get his big megaphone out and stand there on the porch booming 'Merry Christmas!' to all the boats going round. He was just like Santa Claus."

Without wishing to detract from the obviously genuine festive spirit with which Wayne was imbued it should be pointed out that he could, of course, well afford to play Santa Claus in such a lavish style. In 1956 he announced to the press that he had become the highest paid movie star in the world with a fee of 666,666 dollars a picture, a strange sort of sum but nonetheless welcome for that. By modern standards it is not a great deal of money (Dustin Hoffman, for instance, was paid more than four million dollars for starring in *Tootsie*) but when you consider that as recently as 1953 Clark Gable had left MGM because the studio could no longer afford to pay him 520,000 dollars a *year*, Wayne's salary appears almost astronomical.

Thus the 1950s ended with Wayne on yet another pinnacle. But the movie business is such that the only thing one can predict with any certainty about it is that it will always prove unpredictable and, true to form, the 1960s began with the biggest disappointment of Wayne's career—*The Alamo*.

The Alamo incident took place in 1836 when a band of eighty-seven Texans fought an heroic but inevitably losing battle against 3,000 Mexican soldiers. In American history it stands almost as a kind of nineteenth-century Dunkirk and for all manner of reasons —among which his intense patriotism was by no means the least significant—Wayne had been planning for ten years to produce and direct a film version of it. In the event he also starred in it, as Davy Crockett, with Richard Widmark as that other legendary backwoodsman, Jim Bowie.

It turned out to be a very expensive enterprise, costing Batjac twelve million dollars and obliging Wayne himself to mortgage his home and draw on all his business interests to raise the cash. (The party after the Hollywood premiere alone cost 50,000 dollars.) But Wayne justified the financial risks he was taking by saying: "This is the big American story that I don't think anyone could do better than I. It's the first time in my life that I've been able to express what I feel about people." More than that, it seemed to him that the story of the Alamo summed up everything he felt about America and American values.

The film's initial reception was good; the battle scenes were much praised and the picture was nominated for a number of Academy Awards, among them best film and best supporting actor (Chill Wills). But interest in it died away fast and in the end it won only one minor award, the Oscar for best sound, despite a costly and clamorous publicity campaign to influence the Academy voters—a campaign that backfired rather badly when Wayne was sufficiently ill advised to permit a slogan suggesting that "a vote for *The Alamo* is a vote for the United States", a notion that rather turned the voters' stomachs.

Eventually *The Alamo* did recoup its money and even returned a profit but it took a long time and meanwhile Wayne was obliged to mend both his reputation, which had taken a small knock, and his bank balance, which had taken a large one. *The Man Who Shot Liberty Valance* (directed yet again by his mentor, John Ford) did much to restore the former while a constant round of work, including cameo roles in the likes of *The Longest Day* and *How the West was Won*, helped take care of the latter.

(One of his cameo roles was in *The Greatest Story Ever Told* in which, as a Roman centurion looking on at the Crucifixion he was required to utter the line: "Truly this man is the Son of God." There is a popular, though no doubt apocryphal, Hollywood story that after the first take of that scene George Stevens, the director, approached him and said: "Duke that was . . . that was great, Duke, but see, this is Christ up here on the cross. What that line needs is awe. Do you think you could do it again and this time give it just a little awe?" Wayne said: "Sure, George." So they set the scene up again and Stevens said, "Action!" and Wayne said: "Aw, truly this man is the Son of God.")

By 1964 Wayne's career and finances were once more in a flourishing state but now his health began to trouble him. He was fifty-seven years old and smoked four packets of cigarettes a day and he suffered from pains in his chest. So in September he went into the Scripps Clinic in La Jolla, California, for tests. The diagnosis was cancer of the lung. At the time this was revealed Wayne was preparing to film *The Sons of Katie Elder* for the director Henry Hathaway and he broke the news of his illness and his impending operation to Hathaway and to his son Michael in somewhat tragi-comic circumstances.

Michael Wayne said: "I remember he came into the office and said, 'Sit down, I want to tell you something.' I didn't know what he wanted to tell us but he said, 'I've got the Big C' and I think Henry thought he meant the clap, if you'll excuse the expression, because he said, 'Well, you know, they've got penicillin and things like that.' My father said, 'Look, I've got cancer, Henry, I've got cancer in my lung and I've got to have the lung removed.' Well, he was talking to the right guy because Henry Hathaway had also had cancer and Henry said, 'Well, we'll just postpone the picture for a few weeks', and that's exactly what they did. They postponed it for maybe four weeks. My father went into hospital, had the lung removed and then Henry Hathaway had him up at 6,000 feet in Durango, Mexico, in freezing weather, jumping in and out of rivers. And my father said, 'That Henry is a mean old son of a gun but I think he really got me through this thing.' "

The four-week postponement is perhaps something of an exaggeration; Pilar Wayne said it was closer to four months, but Michael Wayne's story illustrates the apparent bravado with which his father treated his illness. He showed no fear, though he must have felt some (as Michael said, "he wasn't dumb so I know he had to be worried about it") and when he came out of hospital he made his now famous pronouncement: "I've licked the Big C."

This, it should be remembered, was before people talked so openly about cancer as they do now and for a star of Wayne's status to admit that he had had it was remarkable to say the least. For him then to add that he had "licked" it, as if it were Geronimo or some similar marauding redskin, served only to add yet another facet to the Wayne legend.

Once recovered from the operation he continued to work as hard as ever, making four films in three years before embarking on his second, and final, attempt at direction with *The Green Berets*, a story set in Vietnam and prompted, just as *The Alamo* had been, by his fervid patriotism. This was in 1967, a time when the Vietnam War was becoming increasingly unpopular in America and even the Pentagon advised him that it would be a mistake to make the picture.

But Wayne went ahead anyway, largely because he conceived the film as a tribute to the troops.

Michael Wayne said: "He didn't necessarily support the Vietnam War. He supported the fact that we should be there but I don't think he supported the conduct of the war. But he did support the soldiers who were fighting there. He felt that they were the bravest and best soldiers we ever fielded and he felt that they didn't get a fair shake. So what he did in *The Green Berets*—what *we* did because I was part of it as producer—was to show them as heroes. And I guess that was the terrible thing because the criticism of the film took the form of a review of my father's politics."

Whether that was the case or not the picture received a terrible pasting when it opened in June 1968. The *New York Times* critic wrote: "It is so full of its own caricature of patriotism that it cannot even find the right things to falsify . . . No acting, no direction, no writing, no authenticity, of course." Viewed now, some fifteen years later, it doesn't seem quite that bad—no worse anyway than many another gung-ho war movie—and certainly Wayne believed until he died that it was a true and honest film.

The way *The Green Berets* was received by the critics and his peers in the industry (though not by the public who rather enjoyed it) hurt Wayne deeply but, as ever, he swiftly bounced back. In July 1969, hardly more than a year after the disastrous opening of *The Green Berets*, he was hailed enthusiastically for his performance in *True Grit* in which, under the direction of Henry Hathaway, he played the fat, one-eyed, bellicose and elderly US marshal, Rooster Cogburn. His portrayal may well have been, as many people claimed, the best he ever gave and certainly it was good enough to win him, at last, the Academy Award for best actor. He received the Oscar in April 1970, at the age of sixty-three and after making 141 films in forty-two years.

Looking back it does seem remarkable that it should have taken him so long because among those 141 films there were several other performances—in a great many of the Ford movies alone, for example—which would not have been over-rewarded with an Oscar, especially when you consider that a number of other actors of lesser stature and not noticeably greater ability had won Academy Awards long before he did.

Michael Wayne's explanation for the fact that his father had been so long ignored in this: "He wasn't really a part of Hollywood in the strictest sense. He wasn't a part of the Bel Air circuit; he was an individual. He didn't live in Los Angeles; he lived in Newport

Beach and for a long time he wasn't even a member of the Motion Picture Academy. So he wasn't really the fair-haired boy. He was quite outspoken and he had a completely different political point of view from most of the people in town."

There may well be a good deal of truth in this because, although Oscars are supposed to be awarded on a straightforward assessment of a man or woman's performance, who is to say what kind of prejudices the voters bring to bear when they make their choice?

Until 1970, however, Wayne professed not to care very much about Academy Awards, possibly because he had only once before been in the reckoning. "But when he got nominated," Michael said, "he wanted to win. He was a fierce competitor. And when he won he was a happy, happy man."

With the Oscar behind him Wayne was once again No. 1 at the box office in 1971 and, despite his age, as much in demand as ever. Important as his family was to him, it was never as important as his career and as a consequence his third marriage suffered much as the other two had done. In 1973 he and Pilar agreed, amicably, to separate, having discovered gradually and over a longish period of time that they had less and less in common.

When the children were younger the family was constantly together; Wayne would hire tutors for them and take them with him on location. But as John Ethan and the two girls grew older it became more difficult to take them out of school for two or three months at a time. So Wayne, busy as he was, spent lengthy periods of the year away from home and on those occasions when he did return for a few weeks between pictures it was hard to re-establish any kind of normal life. Furthermore, while he was absent Pilar quite naturally developed her own interests. "I fell madly in love with tennis," she said, "and we decided to build a tennis club. And so I was very busy and kind of doing my own thing. Maybe, too, I was searching for my own identity. I don't know . . . But I do blame myself because I think it was partly my fault that we separated."

Repeating the pattern of his first marriage and divorce, Wayne remained on friendly terms with Pilar for the rest of his life and, as before, ensured that he stayed as close to the children as possible.

Meanwhile, the films kept coming his way—more Westerns, such as *Rio Lobo*, *Cowboys*, *Cahill, US Marshall* and *Rooster Cogburn*, a disappointing sequel to *True Grit*, in which he co-starred with Katharine Hepburn. But by this time cops and robbers had taken over from cowboys and Indians at the box office and Wayne, fearful of being left behind by the changing times, duly played cops in *McQ* and *Brannigan*.

By then he was in his late sixties, not in the best of health and hardly needed to work any more. Once Pat Stacy, his secretary and lover, asked him why he carried on at such a frenetic pace and Wayne replied: "A man never really grows old while he's still got a project."

Pat Stacy was the last woman in his life. She joined him in June 1972, as his secretary and became his lover one year later when, with a considerable degree of macho arrogance—he, after all, was sixty-six and she was only thirty-two—he swept her away to his bed. It happened one night in Seattle where they were staying on Wayne's yacht, the *Wild Goose*, while he filmed *McQ*.

"We'd been out to the opening of a movie one night," Miss Stacy said, "and we went back to the *Wild Goose*. I started to go to my state room, other people started to go to theirs, and he put his arm around me and it just seemed the most natural thing in the world to go with him."

After that . . . "He told me I was the only woman in his life," and that's the way it remained, although those last few years with Wayne cannot have been easy for her because he was frequently ill. The trouble really began soon after he made his last film *The Shootist* in 1976. On the face of it there seems to be a considerable irony attached to that film because in it Wayne played an ageing gun-fighter dying of cancer. But the irony was more apparent than real because he had, as he claimed, "licked the Big C" and had been free of it for a dozen years.

But now his heart began to trouble him and in 1977 he went into the Massachusetts General Hospital in Boston for open-heart surgery. The operation lasted three hours and aroused so much public interest and anxiety that, in Pat Stacy's estimation, at least 200,000 letters, gifts and get-well cards flooded into the hospital.

The operation, which involved replacing a defective heart valve with one taken from a pig, was a success and Wayne went back to his home at Newport Beach to recuperate. But the reprieve was short-lived.

Pat Stacy said: "We thought everything was going to be fine again and he was planning on making another picture. And then one morning he said, 'Pat, my stomach hurts. It's been hurting for a few days.' I really thought, 'Oh, Duke, you've become a hypochondriac; you know, you've had so many problems, you just *think* something else is wrong.' " But her diagnosis, though understandable, was incorrect: the pains became worse and in January 1979 Wayne was back in hospital for what was expected to be a comparatively minor gall-bladder operation. Tests, however, revealed a malignant tumour and he underwent a nine-hour operation for the removal of his stomach.

Once again the hospital was inundated with phone calls and letters from his fans and once again Wayne bounced indomitably back.

Three months after the surgery he appeared at the Academy Awards celebrations to present the Oscar for best picture to *The Deer Hunter*, a film which he actually disliked because it showed America and the American troops in Vietnam in an unfavourable light. He looked thin and haggard (he had lost three stone in weight during his illness) but he said: "Oscar and I have something in common. Oscar first came to the Hollywood scene in 1928; so did I. We're both a little weather-beaten but we're still here and we plan to be around for a whole lot longer."

In the circumstances it was a brave and defiant statement, because by this time the cancer was spreading throughout his body. Soon after that Academy Awards night he was back in hospital where, for the first time, he was overcome by despair and seriously contemplated suicide.

Pat Stacy said: "He asked me, he ordered me, to get his gun because he wanted to kill himself. He said I'd be better off, everybody would be better off and he would be better off because he'd gotten to a point where he couldn't eat any more."

She disobeyed the order and . . . "He seemed resigned to the fact that he had to fight it. He told the doctors, 'We have to do what we have to do because Pat and the kids have talked me out of killing myself.' "

Early in June 1979, Ben Johnson went to visit him. "Duke says, 'Ben, I don't know if I can make it or not but I'm giving it a helluva try.' Then about four days later they called and said he was gone. But he . . . he fought it right to the last, you know."

John Wayne died on June 11th, 1979, at the age of seventy-two. Just before his death he was received into the Roman Catholic Church, at least partly, Michael Wayne thinks, to please his children, who were all Catholics. And about the same time, around his birthday on May 26th, Congress authorised the minting of a special gold medal as a tribute to him. At the urging of his friend and frequent co-star Maureen O'Hara, the inscription on it read simply: "John Wayne—American."

Wayne himself could hardly have wished to improve on that and the public, which has since bought many thousands of copies of the medal, appears to accept it as a natural and fitting description of the man. But again one wonders why John Wayne should be regarded as typifying America.

One time, between our more heated political discussions, when we were talking about his career, he said: "I found a way of selling integrity in the movies." Well, it's a moot point whether integrity, once sold, remains integrity but I think I can see what he meant. In his screen persona there was a great quality of sincerity and dependability. Wayne was the man you would like to have with you on a cattle round-up or when you hit the beaches of Normandy; the man who could be relied on to protect you from the back-shooters. He was always honourable and fair, a man of his word. Those who knew and liked him maintain that as you saw him in the films, so he was in life and Wayne lent currency to this belief with his frequent assertion that, "I've spent my whole career playing myself." This was perhaps an arrogant and, at the same time, an over-modest claim: arrogant in that it asks us to assume that the man on the screen, a man of towering moral and physical strength and exceptional courage was merely a reflection of himself; and over-modest in that it belittled his own acting ability.

He was not a particularly versatile actor—nobody, for example, could have cast him in Shakespeare or a Noel Coward comedy— but he was a great deal better than most people gave him credit for, because he had the rare gift of making acting look easy and natural. And what tended to hide this not inconsiderable talent from sight was the sheer size of the man's own personality, which was such that whether he played a rancher or a marshal, an army officer or an ex-boxer seeking his roots in Ireland, he always seemed to come out John Wayne.

Kirk Douglas, who starred with him in *Cast a Giant Shadow* and *The War Wagon*, said: "He was the type of star that doesn't really exist any more and I think he began to believe his image. He developed that one macho character and he believed in it sincerely. When I played Van Gogh in *Lust for Life*, they had a special showing of it and Wayne was there. After a few drinks he motioned me out to the terrace and we had a talk and he was furious. He said, 'Kirk, how can you play a weak character like that? Fellows like us, we're the tough guys.' He thought I was not being true to my class."

Wayne was always true to his class—or rather to the class he adopted as his own. The public knew little or nothing of his avid reading, his love of Shelley, his collection of Red Indian dolls, his interest in art and antiques or his passion for chess, for these things hardly went along with the image.

To his fans he was the common man, writ large: Everyman, if you like, but greater than that. He was Super-Everyman. All the characteristics that Americans in particular admire in a man, Wayne possessed. He liked pretty women but was never dominated by them; he played poker for fairly high stakes; he loved the sea and deep-sea fishing; he preferred the company of men and was known to enjoy settling a "friendly" dispute with a fist fight; and he drank.

His drinking indeed was legendary in itself. He was not, by all accounts, an alcoholic, but when the mood was upon him his consumption of alcohol was formidable and occasionally—not very often—he had the endearing habit of appearing in public with perhaps a slug too many of "who-hit-John" under his belt.

Michael Wayne said: "They say he drank enough to float a battleship. Well, he did. I've seen him drink a bottle of brandy after dinner—and that's after consuming maybe a bottle of tequila or a bottle of gin *before* dinner. But he would only drink when he wanted to drink. In other words, he didn't *have* to drink and he didn't drink most of the time. But if he had a weekend clear, he might drink the whole weekend."

All these qualities, along with the fact that he looked larger than life and faced his personal adversities with considerable bravery played their part in forming the legend of John Wayne. And then, too, as Mark Rydell, his director on *Cowboys*, put it, "there was a sense of the individual in him. He felt that the group was by nature weak and that the individual was the most important element in our society. And he felt that he represented the individual—individual thinking, individual courage."

The result of all this was that he became, in the words of his son, Michael: "The symbol of the American man. I guess it's kind of like England. There you have knighthood and chivalry; here it's cowboys and the West. He became the symbol of the cowboy and all those virtues that were ascribed to the cowboy, he had."

That America, during the last knockings of the twentieth century should still be looking for a cowboy to admire, is not quite as curious as it sounds. Harry Carey Jr. said: "He was just the perfect guy at a time of so much doubt and fear. He seemed to be the epitome of what our country should be. I don't know whether he could have been elected president or anything like that but he was our hero. He was the kind of figure that our country needed."

On a similar theme Andrew McLaglen said: "He's part of the

American scene, as American as apple pie. And he stood for this country—on a nationalistic level, on a personal level, on a father image level, on a hero level. He was a lot of things to a lot of people."

To a certain extent, of course, what all these men said is true—except that, whether they realised it consciously or not, they weren't really talking about John Wayne but about the *image* of John Wayne.

There is an element of make-believe, even perhaps of self-deception, in what they saw in the man and I think Wayne himself helped to foster that. In his home he had one room—a room, Claire Trevor said, that was bigger than her entire apartment in New York—full of awards and tributes and medals and God-knows-what that had been sent to him over the years. He was very proud of them all, naturally. But the danger in keeping mementoes of that kind is that, after a while, it becomes easy to convince yourself that all this adulation is for you, personally, and not for the character you have projected in the cinema.

What happens is that a movie star creates an illusion; the audience believes it and eventually the star can come to believe what the audience believes. And that, I think, is what happened with John Wayne.

The fact of the matter is that he never actually did anything heroic in his life. It's true that he faced illness and great pain with much fortitude but that's a different kind of courage; it isn't heroism.

Through no fault of his own he did not fight in the Second World War; he never won the West, rescued a damsel in distress, foiled a villain or tracked down a murderer. Well, the opportunity to do any of those things is given to very few of us.

But to the American public he *was* a hero: he was all the American heroes rolled into one. It's difficult to think of any other country in which an actor can come to represent all that is finest in his nation. Perhaps it could only happen in America where the difference between dreams and reality is often blurred around the edges and it's easy to mistake the shadow for the substance.

Wayne's shadow, cast huge on the screen, looked like the epitome of the all-American male and so the legend arose that the substance was the same. That's why they have put up all those statues—not to a man, not to an actor, but to a legend.

John Wayne would surely have approved; because in the end I think he, too, came to believe the legend.

Cecil B. de Mille

De Mille, the founder of Hollywood (or so
he claimed), after making *The Squaw Man*
for the first time.

With the one and only
Mrs de Mille, to whom
he remained
married—but not
faithful—unto death.

Movie mogul, helpmeet
and assorted
grandchildren.

With Jeannie MacPherson, his collaborator and mistress and, centre, brother William. Male de Milles never did run to much hair.

With Julia Faye, whose feet took his fancy, silent star Rod La Rocque and Jeannie MacPherson.

At home in de Mille Drive with Mrs de Mille, Cecilia and John. . .

. . . and on set with niece Agnes, left (presumably before he required her
to dance on a bull), and adopted daughter Katherine.

Cecil B. de Mille,
Much against his will,
Was persuaded to keep Moses
Out of the Wars of the Roses.

In that popular Hollywood clerihew there speaks the voice of envy and, to some extent, of ignorance. Whoever wrote the lines didn't know his subject. If de Mille had made a film about the Wars of the Roses and felt that a brief appearance by Moses would help the plot along, he would have gone immediately into flashback and introduced Moses holding forth to whichever of the leading characters might be thought to benefit most from such an encounter.

De Mille was a virtuoso of the flashback. In *Male and Female*, a contemporary story set and made in 1919, he flashed Gloria Swanson back to the most decadent days of the Roman Empire and had her appear, in a previous incarnation, as a Christian sacrifice hurled into the arena to be all but raped by a lion. There was no particular reason for this—the plot could very well have done without it—except that it added to the titillation of the audience and, most of all, to the sheer spectacle. And de Mille was the acknowledged master of the spectacle.

In Hollywood's comparatively brief history there have been many finer directors than Cecil Blount de Mille but there has never been one who could gauge more accurately what the cinema-going public wanted or could give it to them more lavishly. For all his faults—and vulgarity held a prominent place among them—he was a giant in an industry that spawns a multitude of self-inflated pygmies; he was a man who thought big—not often deeply, but big—and in his career as a director he destroyed the Temple at Gaza, burnt Rome and parted the Red Sea, not once but twice. Even God can't beat that.

At the Gates of Heaven a newly arrived psychiatrist was greeted with warmth and relief by St. Peter, who said: "Boy, are we glad you're here, doc! We're very worried about God—he thinks he's Cecil B. de Mille."

Hollywood abounds in jokes about God and de Mille and in all of them de Mille turns out to be the more powerful and influential. The root of such stories is not simply the fact that de Mille exploited the Bible as a source of grandiose movie plots more comprehensively than anyone else but that for three decades he simply was more powerful than anyone else, or certainly than any other director, in Hollywood. Even in the 1920s when it was star names that sold pictures and the likes of Chaplin and Mary Pickford were already earning a million dollars a year, de Mille rarely felt the need to use stars at all, being confidently aware that his own name above the title was sufficient in itself to attract an audience.

At Paramount, where—except for a brief period in the late twenties and early thirties—he made all his films, he ran a little empire within an empire. The director Robert Parrish, who had begun in films as a child actor and extra, said: "Many wonderful directors were working at Paramount at the time—Von Sternberg was there, Lubitsch and others—and they all drove in the main gate, the Paramount Gate. But de Mille had his own gate, the de Mille Gate and if you were called to work for him, you went to the de Mille Gate, not to the regular gate."

Such an arrangement was unusual, if not unique, but de Mille would have felt it to be no more than his due for, according to legend, it was he who had created Hollywood. And if he did not invent the legend himself he never saw any reason to deny it. Towards the end of his life in an interview with Derek Bond for BBC television he was asked: "Were you influenced by the earlier film-makers?"

De Mille smiled indulgently: "The earlier film-makers? Well, there really weren't any earlier film-makers."

A nice reply but not exactly true because a certain David Wark Griffith, to take only one example, had already made forty films (two or three-reelers, admittedly) before de Mille even got started. Nevertheless, there is some substance to the legend for de Mille did indeed turn up one day in a small Californian settlement that consisted largely of a few orange trees and a barn and said something to the effect of, "Let there be Hollywood", and lo, there was Hollywood and he looked upon his work and found it good. Some films had been made there before but, coincidentally or not, Hollywood's reputation as the film capital of the world really began after de Mille turned up there in 1913.

At that time he was thirty-two and by common consent, or anyway the common consent of disinterested bystanders, something of a failure in life. He had been born on August 12th, 1881, in Ashfield, Massachusetts, the son of Henry de Mille, an Episcopalian lay preacher, who was also a playwright and thus torn between the church and the theatre. Bearing in mind Cecil's later predilection for biblical epics, this would appear to be irrefutable proof of the power of genetics.

Henry's career as a playwright was not unpromising. He worked for some time in collaboration with the famous theatrical impresario, David Belasco, before striking out, with some success, on his own.

But in 1893, at the age of forty-nine, he died of typhoid, at which point the widow de Mille, née Beatrice Samuels, took over as the dominant influence in Cecil's life. The family had never had much money; now they were poor indeed. But with great resourcefulness Beatrice turned her home into a girls' school and from her earnings managed to send her elder son, William, to be educated at Wiesbaden, in Germany, and then at Columbia University.

For Cecil, however, she had other plans. Presumably on the assumption that some kind of military career would be best for him she enrolled him at the Pennsylvania Military College from which, at the outbreak of the Spanish-American War, he zealously and patriotically ran away in order to enlist in the army. Being under age he was turned down, whereupon he left the American armed forces to muddle along as best they could without him and signed on at New York's Academy of Dramatic Art.

In those early days, according to William's daughter, the dancer Agnes de Mille, Cecil was much influenced by, and slightly resentful of, his elder brother, although the resentment only became manifest later when Cecil was climbing fast in Californian society and regretted bitterly that he, unlike William, had not had the advantage of an education at a good university.

Back at the turn of the century, however, the younger sibling was impelled by a desire to emulate his brother who had taken to writing plays and, although still in his early twenties, was doing rather well. By now, in fact, the whole family was in show business because after its initial success Beatrice's school had gone into decline, wherefore, as resourceful as ever, she set herself up as a theatrical agent in New York and also founded her own theatre company. With such maternal and fraternal examples to influence him Cecil, aged nineteen, made an unremarkable debut as an actor on Broadway in 1900.

Clearly he came early to the conclusion that performing was not for him and though during the next twelve years he acted with his mother's company he also took over as its general manager and began to collaborate with William on a number of reasonably successful plays. Like their father before them the brothers, too, worked closely with David Belasco who, inadvertently, may well have been responsible for Cecil's departure from the Broadway scene and subsequent arrival in California.

In 1913 Beatrice introduced her younger son to a vaudeville

musician and drama producer named Jesse L. Lasky, who in turn introduced him to his brother-in-law, one Samuel Goldfish, later to be known less amusingly as Samuel Goldwyn. And together the three men set up a company to film stage plays. It was called the Jesse L. Lasky Feature Play Company and Cecil assumed the grand title of director-general.

Agnes de Mille believed that her uncle chose to make this career switch out of desperation. "He hadn't been a real success at anything at all. He'd written several plays with my father and he'd acted in many plays. But he was also sort of an adjunct to David Belasco. They had a kind of father and son relationship but Belasco was a very strange old man. Cecil claimed to have written the better part of a play that was quite a success around 1906 or 1907 but Belasco had put his own name on it—I suppose because he wanted the royalties. And that embittered Cecil." Furthermore, if it were not bad enough that—at least in his own opinion—he had been screwed by his surrogate father, Agnes believed that Cecil had another cause for bitterness: he was quite overshadowed by his big brother. "Father was a great success as a young man; Cecil was not. Cecil was a failure. I think he was hell bent to show father and the world that he could do better."

Whether or not this was his motivation de Mille set out in 1913, on behalf of the Lasky company, to make a Western movie called *The Squaw Man*, the story of an Indian maiden who saves the life of a British aristocrat and, after bearing his child, commits suicide. The reasons for this latter act are somewhat complicated but probably they had much to do with the fact that in America in 1913, miscegenation was thought to be extremely bad form. Now the story was actually set in Wyoming, so de Mille decided to film it in Flagstaff, Arizona, thus becoming if not the father of the film industry then at least the father of the glorious illogicality of the film industry. What on earth was wrong with Wyoming that made it unsuitable as the location for a film whose action took place in Wyoming? Nobody has ever properly explained. In any event de Mille set out for Arizona and, no doubt, if all had gone according to plan Flagstaff might easily have become the capital of the movie industry. That it did not is due, depending on which version of the story you believe, to the fact that it was raining in Flagstaff when de Mille turned up or—and this is de Mille's own version—that the terrain didn't actually look like Wyoming. Possibly people could have told him that before he even set out but anyway he gave Flagstaff the elbow and carried on to Hollywood, which again didn't look a whole lot like Wyoming but at least the sun was shining.

A few days later the Lasky company in New York received a cable from de Mille in Hollywood saying, "We have rented a barn for 200 dollars a month . . ." This bewildered the men at head office rather for they, naturally, thought he was in Arizona but it was too late for them to do anything about it because shooting had already started. (Incidentally, de Mille was only the co-producer and co-director of that first version of *The Squaw Man*—he was later to make two others—in collaboration with Oscar Apfel. But Apfel is more or less overlooked now, probably because there is only room for one father of Hollywood.)

Those were parlous times in the movie industry, the days of the Patents War. The Motion Picture Patents Company was seeking a monopoly and was trying to stop independent producers such as de Mille from operating at all. Its method of doing so ranged from personal threats and violence (de Mille himself received anonymous letters warning him that his life would be worth little if he did not cease production at once) to stealing and attempting to destroy the negatives of independent pictures. One copy of the negative of *The Squaw Man* was in fact seized and so scratched and torn as to be worthless.

To counteract the desperados of the Patents Company, de Mille carried a revolver and kept a wolf at his home to frighten off marauders. These precautions clearly worked for the film was duly finished and became an immediate success. Being six reels long it was an epic by the standards of the day and its enthusiastic reception by both critics and audiences instantly established de Mille as one of the most important figures in the youthful film industry.

Much encouraged by such a response de Mille immediately set out to make himself a noticeable figure around town. For a start there was his dress: he affected billowing flannel shirts, tailored riding breeches, puttees and high leather boots. The boots (later adopted by other early directors such as Von Sternberg) were a wise precaution on account of the snakes that were common in the area. (The original snakes have been pretty well exterminated now; there was hardly enough room for both them and the two-legged, Gucci-sneakered variety that has since taken over.) For a while, de Mille continued to carry a revolver as well, though he did discard the wolf, possibly feeling that to be accompanied everywhere by a wolf might smack of the ostentatious.

More significantly, perhaps, when he settled down in the house that he had built on a street which, in honour of its most famous resident, was named De Mille Drive, he aped the style of his erstwhile father figure and possible betrayer, David Belasco. His office was furnished with an enormous desk, guns and swords all over the walls, lionskins on the floor and a huge, cathedral-like window. He remained in that house for four decades and in his autobiography he wrote: "Since I came to California in 1913, I have never lived anywhere but in Hollywood. There I have done my work; there I hope to die; and my last earthly home is waiting for me there, in Hollywood Cemetery." And so indeed it turned out.

The house itself, big and rambling, reflected its owner's personality and his nineteenth-century childhood—heavy, Victorian furniture, Bibles in profusion and an almost monastic simplicity in his own living quarters. His bedroom, dominated by a large, high bed, was extremely plain and his bathroom, which was white, cold and impersonal, would not have looked out of place in an old-fashioned hospital.

However, *The Squaw Man* having floated him straight to the top, de Mille at once set about consolidating his position among the leading figures of the new film colony. In his first two years in Hollywood he made twenty films, sometimes working on two at a time. He made comedies, Westerns, dramas and in *The Cheat*—a little masterpiece of the silent cinema—he daringly broke new ground by showing a relationship between a white woman, Fanny Ward, and a Japanese, Sessue Hayakawa. In this, too, he introduced the touches of explicit sadism which became rather a feature of de Mille movies. Furthermore, with great commercial success, he made a version of *Carmen*, starring the opera singer Geraldine Farrar. It was silent, of course, and thus it might be thought that Miss Farrar's talents were somewhat wasted but the punters enjoyed it.

Meanwhile, thanks almost exclusively to de Mille, the Lasky studios rapidly became *the* place to work. Before long the company expanded into Paramount and as such one of the most important and powerful organisations in Hollywood. De Mille, immensely prolific, was without doubt the studio's creative force. In 1918, he remade *The Squaw Man*—something he was inclined to do in moments of uncertainty or whenever nothing more attractive to him was in the offing—and the following year he discovered Gloria Swanson. De Mille had little use for established stars but he did occasionally create new ones, Miss Swanson and Charlton Heston being perhaps the outstanding examples.

A little before her death, Gloria Swanson recalled for me her first meeting with the great man. In those days, she said, Paramount was "the Garden of Eden. That's where everybody dreamed dreams and everyone wanted to be inside that studio. I used to look at it and wonder if I could ever get in there. Then I got The Call . . ." The Call, of course, came from de Mille himself who had seen her in a few small films she had made for lesser studios. Miss Swanson was twenty-two when she was summoned and . . . "It was like going to see God. I can remember, with my heart pounding away, I went to the studio and the door was opened for me and I walked in and I could see somebody, like a silhouette against this big, enormous, cathedral-like window . . . and I took a little look to see where the door was that I'd come in by because I'd heard some things about Mr. de Mille and I wanted to know where the exit was . . ."

At which point it seems appropriate to pause and examine what those things were that were said, not just then but almost throughout his life, about Mr. de Mille and women. To begin with he was married only once—to Constance Adams, a young actress whom he met and who became his wife in 1902 and who remained his wife until death did them part. This is not, however, to say that he was by any means faithful to her. There were two notable mistresses in his life and if rumour is to be believed—and it was rumour that prompted Miss Swanson's caution on that initial meeting—numerous more casual affairs. What she had heard was that he maintained a harem but since, later, she heard it whispered about—quite erroneously—that she herself was part of that harem, she was inclined to think that the stories were greatly exaggerated. No doubt they were but it is nevertheless true that de Mille always surrounded himself with what the screenwriter, Jesse Lasky Jr., described as "a court of women", all of whom doted on him. It was also firmly believed that he was in the habit of entertaining these women, individually, at his ranch in southern California, a ranch that, in keeping with his Godlike image, he had named "Paradise". My own impression is that while he was probably not averse to the occasional light dalliance, he was not a promiscuous man. He was also one with a great respect for the proprieties and even when he took his acknowledged mistresses away for a brief holiday he usually took their mothers along as well to act, if not as chaperones exactly, then certainly as "beards".

In any case, whatever his personal inclinations, he would not have gone short of offers from women. Despite being prematurely bald (the result perhaps of frustration, or jealousy of his brother, or rage at the perfidity of Belasco) he was by all accounts an attractive man in his own right and, besides, power is probably the greatest aphrodisiac of them all.

The cinematographer William O'Connell, who worked with de Mille from the early days, said there were always women in the background wherever de Mille was to be found. "Nobody ever went near one of his women. You didn't dare even talk to them. They were his." To discover whether de Mille was protecting these women paternally, to save them from sexual harassment, or possessively, it was a useful wheeze to look at their feet. "He was crazy about women's feet," said Agnes de Mille. "He was a foot fetishist. Julia Faye had the most beautiful feet in Los Angeles, he said; he thought they were superb. And they were pretty, I must say."

Julia Faye, an actress, was one of the two women with whom de Mille certainly had more than a passing relationship. The writer, De Witt Bodeen said: "She was in every production practically of a de Mille picture. Sometimes he gave her a big part—a very large part—and sometimes she was just a maid. At one time he even tried to star her in a picture called *Turkish Delight* but it didn't come off: it had a very limited release."

Julia Faye's rival and the partner in de Mille's other long-running extra-marital relationship was Jeannie MacPherson, about whose feet little is known. What is certain, however, is that she was an established writer, actress and film producer before joining de Mille, again in the early days of his success, as his chief scriptwriter and eventually his mistress. In many ways she was also the chief influence in his life—William O'Connell went so far as to describe her as "the main part of his life; the whole of his life. He relied on her for everything. There was something about her that he thought more of than he found in anyone else, family or anything. She was a demure little person—I think she wore the same clothes every day; she always looked the same—but she always sat right next to him on the set and his attention was always with her. She was the one who could tell him yes or no." In that she was surely unique because, despite his own protestations, de Mille usually found himself surrounded by people who only said yes.

Yet while both Julia Faye and Jeannie MacPherson were taken care of by de Mille and remained on his payroll throughout their lives there was never any question that he would marry them because always in the background and ultimately more powerful than either of her husband's mistresses was Constance de Mille. De Witt Bodeen is sure she knew of the other women but "she was very obliging and understanding. She never created a scene. She was a lady, a great lady." There is usually, however, a reason for a wife's complaisance when she turns a blind eye to her husband's philandering and in Constance's case it did not stem from a lack of affection for him or a desire to cling on to her position of privilege and social influence as Mrs. de Mille. Rather was it due to the fact that the physical part of marriage had little meaning for her.

The relationship between husband and wife, said Agnes de Mille, was complex. "Obviously they'd been very much in love as young people. But she said to me once, 'Sex has nothing to do with love', which I thought was an astonishing and very sad remark. But she had come to accept that in her life." Constance never indicated whether or not she resented her husband's other women but Agnes de Mille said: "In a moment of great privacy she said to my mother, 'As long as I live there will never be another Mrs. Cecil de Mille.' She had trained herself in some remarkable way to accept what he could give her and exactly how he lived and what he needed. I think Cecil adored his wife and respected her deeply but I don't think she enticed him sexually."

The marital situation was further complicated by the fact that after the birth of her daughter Cecilia in October 1908, Mrs. de Mille was unable to have any more children, although she and Cecil later adopted two boys, John and Richard, and another girl, Katherine. Of them all, Katherine, an actress who played many leading roles in the 1930s, was the only one who followed her father into the film business.

Generally speaking de Mille kept his private and professional lives apart. Constance took care of the social side of things while Jeannie MacPherson helped him build his reputation in the 1920s.

By the end of the First World War in 1918, de Mille had made thirty-three films, including nearly all the important ones that Paramount turned out. And he had been among the first to anticipate a public appetite for a new kind of social drama and comedy which fed and reflected the dreams of America. Films like *Old Wives for New*, *Don't Change Your Husband* and, especially, *Male and Female* (a loose adaptation of J. M. Barrie's *The Admirable Crichton*) were glossy and opulent, suggesting a glamorous, if somewhat improbable, lifestyle to which post-war America could aspire. In particular, de Mille created the bathroom. Now bathrooms had, of course, existed before he began to take an interest but never in the cinema had they appeared so lavish and downright sensuous as in his films. And along with fashions in bathrooms he created fashions in dress, jewellery and interior design, and what made the accoutrements of de Mille's pictures so alluring to the audiences was their association with sex. De Mille's silent films were amazingly sexy, never overtly explicit but boldly and enticingly suggestive.

One of the most common criticisms of de Mille is that his movies were hypocritical, that stern retribution was visited upon his errant characters in the last reel only after they had been seen indulging happily in all kinds of promiscuity and infidelity for the previous eighty minutes or so. By this means, it is argued, de Mille pretended to be righteous while really enjoying all the naughtiness. There is no doubt a great deal of truth in that and indeed de Mille, outwardly the upright family man but secretly the lover and keeper of other women, was a hypocrite himself, though hardly more so than many another man in his position. Nevertheless, the public enjoyed his films immensely, especially the half dozen that starred Gloria Swanson, whose small, beautiful and sexy body he clothed—or rather semi-clothed—to its utmost advantage. The two of them came together at exactly the right time, a time as she said when "the kind of pictures he was making were important because until then films weren't very attractive to look at. He brought a certain . . . I hate the word 'glamour', which is why I'm hesitating to use it but . . . he brought a certain glamour to the cinema. He showed a style of life that really didn't exist in most places in the United States and presented it as just ordinary life."

Once the public had accepted de Mille's fantasies as "just ordinary life", however, its appetite was becoming sated. Even his sophisticated and suggestive social comedies and melodramas were beginning to pall as the audience felt a craving for something new and different. So, ever mindful of the advantages of publicity, he decided in 1922 to ask the populace to suggest a theme for his next film. And by overwhelming public demand the choice was *The Ten Commandments*.

Probably de Mille had intended to make it anyway; if so the response of the cinemagoers merely underlined his determination and, in any case, with this film he found his own imperishable niche in the annals of the movies. He had in fact made a "spectacular" as long ago as 1916 with *Joan the Woman*, his version of the story of Joan of Arc. The idea of sheer size on the screen had excited him even then but it was not until that first, silent version of *The Ten Commandments* when he could reinforce size with those other two bestselling ingredients, sex and religion, that he found the jackpot-winning combination. In de Mille's hands the story became part-biblical, part-modern, the modern bit being a moral and philosophical allegory. In every way it was an exciting and innovative production, even using experimental Technicolor in places, but most of all it was memorable for the truly epic grandeur of its conception and execution.

For its time *The Ten Commandments* was a monumentally expensive film. The original budget stood at 700,000 dollars, which was breathtaking enough, but the final cost was one and a half million and although the eventual box-office take was more than four million dollars, de Mille's extravagance had sowed the seeds of disagreement with Paramount and its head, Adolf Zukor, which led to his leaving the studio.

The astounding success of *The Ten Commandments* caused de Mille to reflect on the fact that the Bible had enjoyed the best part of 2,000 years of free publicity which it would be positively criminal to waste and so, three years and five not very memorable films later he embarked upon an even more ambitious project, *King of Kings*, which was, of course, no less than the story of Christ.

By now, having parted from Paramount, he was an independent producer but finding financial backers was no problem. The only real difficulty was in deciding how to treat the delicate subject he had chosen. At that time portraying Christ on the cinema screen was a most hazardous business, the slightest lapse in taste being guaranteed to bring down the wrath of all America's multitudinous Christian churches on the head of the offending director. With great care de Mille selected for the role H. B. Warner, an actor of spotless reputation and apparently blameless habits. Spotless and blameless, that is, until he fell victim to an enterprising, though unscrupulous, young extra, an actress of tantalising physical attributes who seduced him quite comprehensively in his dressing room and then, thinking to benefit financially from her deed, dragged de Mille to the scene of this sinful action.

Jesse Lasky Jr., screenwriter and son of de Mille's erstwhile partner, takes up the story . . . "There on the floor, debauched, his clothes off, lip-rouge all over him, a wreck, drunk, lay H. B. Warner. And de Mille knew that the film would be finished if one breath of this got out, so he said, 'How much do you want?' and the girl named an astounding figure and he said, 'We will consider this' . . ."

There are two alternative endings to this story of attempted blackmail, both curiously enough presented by Jesse Lasky Jr. In his book *Whatever Happened to Hollywood?*, published by W. H. Allen in 1973, he says that de Mille paid up and the girl prudently

left Hollywood. But to me, several years later, he said: ''As I know it, de Mille called the district attorney's office and suddenly the little extra girl found herself on the way to Mexico City, never, never to return.''

The latter, and probably more up-to-date version is the one I'm inclined to believe. By 1926 the forty-five-year-old de Mille had far too much social and political muscle to succumb easily to blackmail. So, for that matter, did the film industry in general. Hollywood and the movies were so important financially to Los Angeles and its environs that the law tended to do what the studios and important independents like de Mille told it to do. Certainly, not a murmur of scandal leaked out to the press and the filming of *King of Kings* proceeded on its way as though nothing had happened.

Was this, though, yet another example of the hypocrisy of de Mille? Maybe. From childhood onwards he read the Bible, or at least a part of it, every night of his life before he went to sleep. Some may say that all he was looking for was another movie plot but this would be too cynical, for he was a true believer. But on the other hand it could reasonably be suggested that anyone as devout as de Mille appeared and claimed to be would have dismissed the reprobate Warner on the spot once he had been found in flagrante delicto. De Mille himself, however, might well have retorted that turning the other cheek and giving Warner another chance was merely his Christian duty.

Besides, the filming was already well advanced; to stop it and start again with a new star would have been prohibitively expensive. And anyway, according to his adopted daughter Katherine, *King of Kings* was not just de Mille's own favourite film but the project in which he had the most passionate interest.

''He was a man of great faith and it was a longing of his to bring that story to the screen. I think he did a magnificent job; I think it stands out as the finest thing he ever did. I was still a young girl but I lived on the set wherever I was home on holiday and I was there when they completed the filming of the Crucifixion. Everybody was tired but as they started to go off home father called out to them and said, 'I wish everyone would stand still a moment; I have something more to say to you.' '' This was Christmas Eve and all the cast and crew were interested in doing was getting back to their homes and wrapping presents. But de Mille stopped them and said: ''I want to remind you of what you have just filmed, of what you have just seen. I would like you to pause before you go

home, so that we can have five minutes of absolute silence while you think in your hearts of what you've seen and what it means to you."

At his behest the organist—in the days of silent films there was always a musician of some kind on the set to provide the required mood music—began to play a hymn or carol and, said Katherine, "people stood there and some turned back and walked up towards the Cross and knelt. And some just stood quietly and some wept and some prayed. It was very moving . . ."

No doubt it was and perhaps de Mille was inspired by true religious devotion. And yet . . . One can't help remembering that later, on another biblical epic when he felt the extras were not showing sufficient religious awe, de Mille called them all together and told them that the wife or child or whatever of someone whom they all knew and liked had been killed in a terrible accident and he wanted everybody to stand still for a moment and think of the bereaved. And they did and he filmed them and the shot was very effective indeed and there had not been a word of truth in anything he had said. De Mille was always a master manipulator.

But that being so, what kind of a man was he to work for? Well, by all accounts he seems to have been both loyal and cruel, an egotist and an autocrat and yet a man who was saved from galloping megalomania by a streak of kindness.

Robert Parrish dismissed him in one, telling sentence: "My impression, having worked as an extra in several pictures with him, was that he was cruel, sadistic, sarcastic and other adjectives like that that make you love a man."

Gloria Swanson said: "People were in awe of him. He scared the wits out of everybody. He was a disciplinarian and very exacting, no nonsense whatsoever with him. The only person that he never said an unkind word to was me."

One of de Mille's idiosyncrasies—possibly even an indication of his delusions of grandeur—was that he always employed a "chair-boy", a role that was filled for a time by Henry Hathaway, later to become a most distinguished director himself. The role of the chairboy was to walk behind the Great Man, carrying his chair. Chico Day, who was de Mille's principal assistant for many years, said: "If Mr. de Mille got up and walked anyplace the chair had to go right behind him. You never knew when Mr. de Mille was going to stop and want to sit down and if he did and the chair wasn't there, God help the guy who was carrying it. Well, that's a job I wouldn't want to have but there are a lot of people in the world who

CECIL B. DE MILLE

want to get on in the film business and to each his own . . .'

To employ anyone in the humiliating job of chairboy is a misuse of power; so, too, was de Mille's habit of stopping production and publicly bawling out those who had incurred his displeasure. William O'Connell said: 'He had the most cutting tongue and a sarcastic way of insulting people out in the open that would make you want to go and cry your eyes out—or knock hell out of him. Insulting someone is a terrible thing to do in front of other people.' But if you're an employer in an employer's market you can get away with it and nobody ever knocked hell out of de Mille. So . . . 'A lovable man? Not that I know of.'

And yet there was that loyalty, that unexpected streak of generosity. Chico Day recalled that 'one of his assistants went sick and Mr. de Mille called me into his office and made me responsible for seeing that all the man's expenses were paid—the food, the rent, the doctors' bills, everything. He had a tremendous loyalty to the people who worked for him. Another incident—one day he was stopped by a man who'd been an extra in several of his pictures and Mr. de Mille realised the guy needed money. So he gave him a 100-dollar bill and said, "Don't worry. You can pay me back when you're working again." '

This loyalty extended, too, to Jeannie MacPherson and Julia Faye long after each of them had ceased to be his mistress or indeed to be of any practical use in his business. He was not always personally kind to them in their late years, frequently showing the irritation of a man who is being given devotion that he no longer wants or appreciates; but at least he ensured that they were financially comfortable and never in need.

King of Kings cost two million dollars and by the time it opened early in 1927 de Mille was much in need of a hit, for his previous independent productions had not amounted to much at the box office. The critical reception was mixed but, fortunately, the public seemed to like the film. Indeed, in his autobiography published in 1959 de Mille reckoned it must have been seen through-out the world by at least 800,000,000 people, though precisely how he arrived at that figure is not revealed. Even so, the picture's popular success was not enough to save him from losing control of his own production company. Just before he finished his next picture, *The Godless Girl*, sound was introduced to the movies in *The Jazz Singer*. De Mille, like many others admittedly, thought it was a passing gimmick; his partners did not—and to his chagrin they brought in another director to add a few sound scenes.

174

So, in 1929, de Mille went off to join MGM, where his arrival was greeted with much pomp and excitement although, alas, the same could not be said of *Dynamite*, the first film he made there. It was an inferior melodrama notable only for the fact that it was the first time de Mille himself had made a talkie. His next production, *Madam Satan*, was even worse, whereupon in some desperation he fell back on his trusty old standby and remade *The Squaw Man* again. That didn't work either and since by now it had become obvious that even MGM was not big enough to contain two such giant egos as de Mille and Louis B. Mayer, he did a passing impersonation of the prodigal son and returned to Paramount.

By the time he arrived there he was fifty, his reputation was in rapid decline and he had reached just about the lowest point in his career. But at once he hauled himself straight back to the top with *Sign of the Cross*, an epic of ancient Rome that contained all the classic de Mille ingredients of sex, sadism, Christians-in-the-arena, orgies and imperilled virgins. Paramount loved it and so did the cinemagoers, wherefore he stayed in Rome for his next, and even bigger, success *Cleopatra*.

For this he hired his niece Agnes for one particular, and to him important, scene. She said: ''He asked me to do a dance on Cleopatra's barge to charm Antony. I was to be naked dancing on the back of a bull, a live bull. And that took me aback because there's very little you can do on the back of a bull except cling. So I got off and I started doing a dance and then Cecil said: 'Oh no, no, this won't do, there's no sex, there's nothing, there's no excitement. This wouldn't seduce anybody.' Then he turned to the censor, who was there to see that he wouldn't do anything so dirty it couldn't be allowed on the screen, and he said, 'Would that arouse you?' and the man said, 'Hell, no' and that's when everything broke and I lost my temper . . .''

This humiliating scene, incidentally, was witnessed by the entire cast. As Agnes de Mille recalled it her uncle was sitting on a chair that was at least first cousin to a throne with Claudette Colbert at his feet and the rest gathered behind him. ''I can handle an audience,'' said Miss de Mille. ''If it's human I can get something out of it. But this was not an audience; this was one man in a royal position and the whole cast waited. Their faces were . . . well, Hitler couldn't have had a court with more attention and more silence and I looked around the faces and there was nothing—it was like a row of eggs . . .''

In front of these assembled eggs de Mille said: "I want the kind of dance we had in *Sign of the Cross*."

Agnes said: "That was a lesbian dance. I thought it was one of the funniest things I ever saw."

To which Uncle Cecil retorted: "Well, baby, that's the kind of humour we're looking for," and walked away, leaving instructions with his assistant to "take over this dance and make something of it". At which point Miss de Mille's brother-in-law arrived and seeing her dressed in little more than a few bangles and a pleated skirt, said: "Good God, Agnes, if your father could see you now he'd horsewhip Cecil." Miss de Mille was never quite sure whether she resigned or was fired but that was the first and last day she worked for her uncle.

By this time, firmly back at the top, de Mille was giving free reign to the autocratic side of his nature. A few privileged people were permitted to address him as C. B., others—a touch less privileged —could call him Chief but from most he demanded far greater reverence. One day during the shooting of *Cleopatra*, Henry Wilcoxon, the English actor whom he had imported to play Mark Antony, approached him saying: "Would you prefer it if I were to call you C. B. or, as I do now, 'Mr. de Mille' or 'Sir'?" And de Mille said: "Well, Harry, I think you'd be more comfortable calling me 'Mr. de Mille' and 'Sir'. And, frankly, I rather like it."

Like the little emperor he had now become, with his own private gate into his own private part of the studio, he had also taken to distributing largesse. He always carried round a pocketful of specially minted gold half-dollar pieces and these he would graciously bestow on such minions as came up with ideas that he felt he might use. Generally speaking the minions, duly grateful, would keep them as prized possessions to the end of their days.

This feudal atmosphere was maintained throughout the working day. In the studio restaurant a special table was reserved for him and, said Robert Parrish, "De Mille would eat lunch with his crew —his own people, his film family—every day. He had a long table and the writers and quite often the cameraman, though not always the cameraman, and usually ten or fifteen other people were invited to lunch with him. But it was a command, not an invitation. And de Mille sat at the head of the table and a large Bible was placed on his right and the script of the film was placed on his left and he then humiliated the people at the table as much as he could and as often as he could because they were all employees." Reflectively, Mr. Parrish added: "He was running as a bully—no question about that.

He was very important in American films and made wonderful pictures that millions of people saw—maybe more than any other single director. But he was a bully."

Chico Day, whose affection for de Mille was far greater than that of Robert Parrish—not difficult really since Mr. Parrish was never likely to put himself forward as a candidate for the de Mille fan club —explained his employer's attitude thus: "He paid good money to his crew, his actors—everybody. So he demanded perfection and everyone thought he was a tyrant. If somebody did something on the set that he didn't like—that's when he became a tyrant. Every time anything did go wrong the man who carried his megaphone would come over and give it to Mr. de Mille and, boy, believe me everything just broke loose. He would immediately start belittling the individual who was at fault. He would *really* give them a tongue lashing."

On the other hand the autocrat, the tyrant and the bully all vanished as soon as de Mille got home. His daughter Katherine said: "People don't understand the qualities he had, the warm, loving personality who made you feel important. Sometimes when he walked in the front door he was tired from the long hours he'd worked and the troubled times he had had but he really made an effort to relate to us."

Neither to her nor to his grandchildren, Cecelia Presley and Jody Harper—the children of his daughter Cecilia—was de Mille even remotely a tyrant. Jody Harper remembered him as "someone you loved, someone you kissed when he came back from the studio, someone whose lap you sat in". He doubted whether many people were in the habit of kissing de Mille or sitting in his lap but "to me he was always grandfather first and Mr. de Mille very much second".

Katherine de Mille explained the Jekyll and Hyde qualities of the man (qualities which, to be fair, are probably shared by many another tycoon or captain of industry) like this: "The de Mille at the studio had to be thinking of cost, delays, what had to be accomplished that day—I mean it's a very pressured job, being producer and director combined. He was a disciplinarian when you got on that set, no matter who you were. You were there to earn your living, to do your job; you weren't there to play around. He expected you to be concentrating on the work, not dilly-dallying in the corner, or whispering, or interrupting the take. He enjoyed coming home. I think the moment he walked in that front door he breathed a sigh of relief, because his family was there and he was eager to hear what we had done. The de Mille who came home was a father. As a young girl I remember the excitement of waiting for father to come in. Mother would say, 'Go upstairs, get into your pyjamas, get ready for bed and then come down and wait for your father.' And the man who came in the front door had cold cheeks and we'd kiss him and he was tired and you were concerned for him. Then he would have his dinner in front of the fireplace in the living room and we would sit around and hear about his day. He'd share with us and that's what we wanted. And then he'd ask a little bit about what we were doing before we kissed him and went off to bed. But it was a *father* who came home—a tired and interesting father."

This cosy domestic scene would certainly have come as a surprise to Robert Parrish and all those who were humiliated around the studio lunch table or insulted on the set. But perhaps it's hard to be an ogre all the time and no doubt even the toughest of movie moguls needs to relax somewhere, especially if his tyrannical image is really but a front, as Cecelia Presley believed was the case with her grandfather.

"He was a hard man to know," she said, "because he was a very shy man. To overcome that he became an actor on the set at work. It's difficult for a shy man, I think, to be a director of thousands of extras or to walk into financial situations where you're asking for millions of dollars for a picture that other people don't think should be made. So he adopted a way in which he could cope, in which a shy man could cope. At home the mask went and he was a gentle, lovely, delightful man."

Putting it another way, a slightly less flattering way, Jesse Lasky Jr. said: "In this lies the whole key to the de Mille character: the actor who believed totally in the role he was playing at the moment he was playing it. When he sat in the bosom of his family he suddenly became the very pillar of the American family. That was *one* important role; the other was the rather flamboyant figure, the showman."

Or the tyrant, the ogre, the man who could never be gainsaid. And yet . . . there was a paradox in the character even of the hard, dictatorial, public de Mille. Henry Wilcoxon said that people treated him with respect and "some treated him with a certain amount of fear. There were two sets of people—those who hated him and those who loved him. I happened to be one of those who loved the old buzzard. Sometimes he'd be a little rough on somebody who might be alibi-ing or not doing his best and he might go overboard and ham it up a little. He was never an easy man to work for. But contrary to the popular conception he did not like yes-men. He always said, 'I don't want people agreeing with me, agreeing with me, agreeing with me all the time. I don't want fifty little de Milles running around the set; it's bad enough to have one, let alone fifty.' But by the same token he didn't like 'no-men'."

Agnes de Mille put that, too, another way: "You didn't contradict Cecil later in life, ever. If he said at the dinner table, 'The greatest poem in the English language is Kipling's *If*,' and my jaw dropped, it dropped silently."

Like Robert Parrish, Agnes de Mille was never very fond of her uncle and yet twenty years and more after his death she had developed an understanding of him, perhaps even a certain sympathy, for she said: "I'd like to say something about the way Cecil lived. You think of him as sort of lolling around on satin beds with gorgeous women and leopards and that sort of thing. He certainly had them on the set but his life was quite austere within the family range. He slept only about five hours a night, never more, and read the Bible before he fell asleep. He read very little, I would say, except Holy Writ and he knew that by heart. He woke up early in the morning and had breakfast with his wife, and the grandchildren came in and they would climb around him, because he loved them. And then he took his car and went off to the studio and there he had a terrible day. In the morning he would look at sets and costume designs and so forth; he'd be on the set by nine o'clock, maybe earlier, and he'd keep working all day long with an hour's break for lunch—but working hard and sometimes with great mobs of people and this takes an animal strength. A lot of the time he got quite rough with them: he whipped them into what he wanted. And then when the shooting was over he would see all the rushes of the day before—and that's a tedious business—and then he would have interviews about costumes and that sort of thing. If he had a business meeting of any kind he never allowed himself to smoke or drink or even chew gum because he said he had to keep alert. And after all that was over he drove himself home where his wife had kept his dinner hot for him and she served it to him, personally, in front of a fire on a beautiful little table with Belgian lace and he'd have one glass of German wine. And he'd talk to her and they'd go up to bed and he'd read his Bible and go to sleep. And that's a very stern life. The weekends he took off at his ranch, Paradise, and what went on there I have no idea."

Few of de Mille's immediate family knew what went on at Paradise because they were only allowed to go there on his invitation. Sometimes, perhaps, he did entertain women like Jeannie MacPherson or Julia Faye there. But at other times he would throw parties for people in the film industry where all the men had to wear Russian cossack shirts which their host provided for them, making sure that he alone had a white one. And he would play games with his guests, laying before them a tray of precious stones mixed with imitation jewellery and challenge the company to pick the piece they liked best. Those who selected a genuine diamond or ruby or sapphire won his admiration; those who opted out of ignorance for an impressive-looking piece of glass won his contempt.

A curious man, Mr. de Mille; as William O'Connell said, not exactly lovable, except to those bound to him by ties of blood or adoption. What is particularly curious is that for one who was inclined to treat his fellowman with such contumely he had an amazingly direct line to the public taste, to which he pandered successfully first with his sexy melodramas and comedies, then with his biblical and ancient Roman epics and later, in the 1930s, with a series of films such as *The Plainsman*, *Union Pacific* and *Northwest Mounted Police*, which exploited the pioneering spirit that lies, usually dormant, within every American breast. De Mille was a great student of his country's history and was much given to extolling the virtues of the pioneers. As De Witt Bodeen said: "He, more than anybody else I think, really believed in this country and he didn't care whether people called it over-patriotism or what. He believed in this country and he wanted to show it."

Politically de Mille was a rigid conservative, perching on the end of the extreme right wing of the Republican Party, of which he was an active and influential member. And in 1944 his politics brought him into sharp and dramatic conflict with the American Federation of Radio Artists (AFRA). Since 1936 he had been presenting a weekly radio programme, the Lux Theatre of the Air, which featured most of the star names of Hollywood and drew an audience of up to thirty million people. But in August 1944 he received a letter from AFRA imposing a one dollar a head levy on all its members (of whom de Mille was one) to establish a political fighting fund. The object of this was to oppose a piece of Californian state legislation, which would have abolished the closed shop. Now de Mille, who would most likely have regarded Genghis Khan as a left-wing pinko, was opposed to the closed shop and therefore in favour of the legislation. He was even more violently opposed to the idea that any union had the right to demand a compulsory political levy from its members. So he refused to pay his dollar.

The union extended the final date of payment to October, then to November and even December but de Mille still refused to pay up. When he was told that unless he produced his dollar he would be banned from the airwaves he took the dispute to law. Cecelia Presley said that before he finally lost his case it had gone as far as the Supreme Court. "They told him before he started the fight that he could lose everything and he said that, well, he'd think about it. I remember he came down to breakfast one day and said, 'I've made a decision: we're going to fight it.' I said, 'Why did you elect to do that, grandfather?' And he said, 'Because I have to shave every morning and look at myself in the mirror.' "

Thus on a point of principle de Mille was ejected from both his union and his radio show. The decision cost him at least 100,000 dollars a year in lost fees but just as significantly, perhaps, it foreshadowed the extreme right-wing stance he was to adopt a few years later, slightly pre-dating even Senator Joe McCarthy and his House Un-American Activities Committee.

De Mille was always fiercely anti-Communist and after the war when public opinion in America turned violently against the Russians and the brilliant theory of "premature anti-fascism" was conceived, thus making it possible to prosecute as a potential traitor anyone who had remarked, let us say, a little before Pearl Harbor, that the Russians were putting up rather a good fight against the Nazis, he brought his fears strongly into the open. "He was very worried," said Cecelia Presley, "that Communists were infiltrating the motion picture business and he wanted to stop that."

Robert Parrish put it even more strongly. "Anyone he suspected of being left-wing, or Communist, or socialist in any way, he abhorred. He wouldn't hire them. He formed an organisation of his own called the Cecil B. de Mille Foundation for Political Freedom and he asked people to join it."

The Foundation was formed in September 1945, and under its auspices de Mille went about warning against the evils of Communism and again pre-dating McCarthy by naming at least one so-called red infiltrator. What it all amounted to, in effect, was a foundation to give people the political freedom to think exactly the same way as Cecil B. de Mille did. Among those who failed to avail themselves of this kind offer was Joseph L. Mankiewicz, one of the wisest of all Hollywood denizens, a liberal in the true sense of the word and, at the time he incurred de Mille's wrath, the president of the Screen Directors' Guild.

De Mille came to the conclusion that Mankiewicz was a dangerous leftie and, according to Robert Parrish (by this time a member of the Directors' Guild himself), determined to have him removed. In the president's absence abroad, de Mille pushed through the Screen Directors' board a resolution that all members must sign a loyalty oath declaring that they were not in any way Communists. Parrish said that the members themselves, and even Mankiewicz, were not consulted on this and that Mankiewicz refused to sign.

"Actually," Parrish said, "he had already signed the loyalty oath because the Constitution of the United States says that all officers of unions must sign it. Mankiewicz had done that—no problem there. He didn't mind being told by the Constitution of the United States to sign a loyalty oath; what he didn't like was for anybody to be told by Cecil B. de Mille to sign a loyalty oath." Mankiewicz therefore took the matter before a meeting of the Guild membership on the grounds that what de Mille was demanding was anti-American—and a bitter verbal battle ensued.

The meeting was actually convened as a result of a petition drawn up on Mankiewicz's behalf and signed by twenty-five of the most famous directors in America, among them Billy Wilder, Robert Wise, William Wyler, Reuben Mamoulian and Joseph Losey. Soon after the meeting began, Wyler declared that he was sick and tired of being told what to think politically by Cecil B. de Mille, adding that the next time *anybody* told him what to think politically he, William Wyler, would punch that person on the nose. Since Wyler was looking directly at de Mille at the time, Parrish said: "We all thought we might see one of the best directors in the world punch the nose of the most successful director in the world."

Nothing so unseemly, however, came to pass. Instead Reuben Mamoulian rose to complain about de Mille's suggestion that some of the twenty-five who had signed the petition were politically suspect because they were of foreign origin. Mamoulian, himself Armenian by birth, asked whether Mr. de Mille might care to withdraw that remark. Mr. de Mille failed to reply, whereupon Mamoulian declared that for the first time in his life being an American made him feel afraid.

At this tense moment in the proceedings John Ford stood up and declared dramatically, if unnecessarily: "My name's John Ford; I make Westerns."

He then addressed the gathering, saying: "There isn't one person in this room who knows as much about what the public wants as Cecil B. de Mille and he knows how to give it to them and for that I respect him." Then he turned to de Mille, who was about twenty feet away from him, and said: "But I don't like you, C. B., and I don't like what you've been saying here. Joe Mankiewicz has been vilified and I think he deserves an apology and I think you should give it to him."

The direct result of this was that de Mille found himself totally defeated—even humiliated, as Robert Parrish described it—by his fellow directors. "It was quite sad," Parrish said. "When we all left the room, instead of feeling exultation we all felt sadness for him."

This is not, curiously enough, an episode that de Mille even mentioned in his own autobiography. No doubt he simply put it out of his mind on the basis of win some, lose some. In any case he had other matters to occupy him including, in 1949, yet another biblical epic in *Samson and Delilah*, which though again successful at the box office was certainly the worst and most absurd of all his films in that genre.

As Samson he cast the massive Victor Mature, an actor about whom the best that can be said is that he looked impressive in G-string and sandals; and as Delilah he chose the beautiful but less than sparkling Hedy Lamarr. Critical opinion was universally unkind and was encapsulated most succinctly by Groucho Marx, who said: "I didn't like it. Samson had bigger tits than Delilah."

By now de Mille was beginning to slow up, as a man of sixty-nine had every right to do. But in 1950 he made a rare screen appearance, as himself, in Billy Wilder's *Sunset Boulevard*. In this Gloria Swanson made her comeback, as an ageing actress trying to make a comeback, and in one scene she visits the set of her erstwhile director Cecil B. de Mille, played of course by Cecil B. de Mille. It was the now famous scene, in fact, in which she informs him that she's ready for her close-up.

Miss Swanson said: "I heard such a darling story about him when we were doing that. His secretary said she couldn't get any work out of him because whenever he came into the office he wanted her to cue him; he wanted to be sure he'd know his lines. He would have been cross with any actors who didn't know theirs and he wasn't going to be found wanting in any possible way. So for days and days, every time he saw his secretary he wanted her to give him a cue so that he could get the line right. It was easy working with him because he was very sincere and the way that scene was written it was all very natural."

In the early and middle years of the 1950s Hollywood began to crumble under the onslaught of television (a process that has never really been halted) and at that time it was largely de Mille's films that kept Paramount in business. Whatever their artistic merits, or lack of same, they made money and *The Greatest Show on Earth*, a circus spectacular, was no exception. To play the circus boss he cast a young and comparatively unknown actor named Charlton Heston, who arrived in awe of him and remained so. "He was already, to use the classic phrase, 'a legend in his own lifetime'," Heston said. "He was the major attraction on the Paramount set as well as their major asset. With the single exception of Alfred Hitchcock he was the only director whose name was put on the marquees ahead of those of the actors."

Heston found him courtly and courteous to actors but . . . "He had a justified reputation for tearing strips off prop men and wardrobe people and assistant directors but those targets were chosen so carefully that I couldn't but feel that it was something of a performance. I remember once we were on location at the circus' winter headquarters in Florida and we were shooting a formidable scene with trains, animal cages and so forth and something had gone badly wrong with one of the shots. So he assembled the eleven assistant directors, lined them all up and in front of not only the whole company but of the maybe 500 civilian spectators who had been watching he introduced these men by name and said: 'Ladies and gentlemen, I want you to meet these men because while they have been hired specifically to help us make this film as expeditiously and creatively and excitingly as possible, I must confess to you that instead they are obstructing our every move and doing nothing more than get in the way and I would like you to meet them all.' And each man had to step forward and respond to his name. It was a painfully embarrassing experience but it involved no obscenities and no shouting and it was a salutary object lesson to the rest of the company . . . Nobody ever came late onto de Mille's set."

In 1952 *The Greatest Show on Earth* won the Academy Award for best picture of the year. It was presented, naturally, to de Mille and it was the only Oscar he ever won. Of that film, and of its successor, he once said that what appeared on screen came closer to the concept that he had had in his mind than was the case with any of his other works. Interestingly, they were the last two films he made, suggesting perhaps that it had taken him fifty years and seventy-one pictures to get it right.

De Mille's final production was his remake of *The Ten Command-ments*, which cost more than thirteen million dollars—a colossal figure in 1956—and which was three years in the writing alone. The role of Moses went to Charlton Heston because de Mille had asked someone to make a sketch of Heston in a white beard and was struck by its similarity to Michelangelo's statue of Moses. This didn't necessarily mean that Heston looked like Moses himself, for it was reasonable to assume that neither de Mille nor Michelangelo had actually seen him, but it was good enough for de Mille.

So Heston was called in for an interview. He said: "This seems to have been his casting method. You never got to read a script for de Mille: he called you in and told you the story of the film. His whole office was covered with sketches and models of sets and he would show you these things and tell you about the character he was thinking of having you play. He never actually said, 'I'm seriously considering you for this part'; that was never touched on, he just told you the story. I went through this experience about five times in the case of Moses, the interviews separated by weeks or months. My agent would call me up and say that Mr. de Mille would like me to call on him at my convenience and, of course, my convenience was his convenience and I would go in and we'd go through exactly the same procedure as before, almost as if this was the first time we'd ever talked about it. The only appropriate response seemed to be, 'Well, yes, that certainly sounds like an interesting film—good part, too.' That seemed to be about all he wanted you to say. I think in some way he was working out your role as he told it to you and watching you listening to him." Heston must have listened very attentively because finally he was given the part.

During the making of the film in Egypt, de Mille suffered a heart attack while running up a 200-foot ladder in order to look down upon the crowd scene that he had assembled. Doctors advised him to stay in bed and rest; he ignored them. Amazingly, he seemed to suffer hardly any ill effects. When the filming was finished on August 13th, 1955—the day after his seventy-fourth birthday—he was still being given electrocardiograms every month and his heart appeared to be in perfect condition.

The Ten Commandments opened in New York in November 1956 to respectful reviews, even though it is not in fact as good a film as its silent predecessor. After the American première he went on a triumphal world tour with it. His future plans, he said, as he always did now, being seventy-six years old, involved either "another picture or another world". In the event it was to be the other world because although he produced a film called *The Buccaneer* in 1958, he did so only as a favour to his son-in-law, Anthony Quinn—at that time married to Katherine de Mille—who badly wanted to direct it and indeed directed it pretty badly.

By the time that opened de Mille himself was in precarious health. In June 1958 he had another heart attack and though he recovered enough to make what was to be his last visit to Paramount Studios early the following January and was still indomitable enough to declare that, "We have a lot to do in the next three years", it was fairly obvious that the end was near.

Less than two weeks later, in the early hours of January 21st, 1959, he died at his home. And among his papers in his room, his daughter Cecilia found a handwritten note predicting that, soon, the words of the Episcopalian funeral service would be spoken over his own body and asking: "After these words are spoken, what am I? I am only what I have accomplished. How much good have I spread? How much evil have I spread?. . ."

As to the good, even his enemies must admit that he spread some of that. Anyone whose work can enthral, thrill, entertain and amuse millions of people or which can—as he claimed repeatedly in his autobiography—cause men and women to think again about God, religion and their own relationships with others, must be said to have spread some good.

As to the evil, I doubt if there was much of that. Nobody could seriously claim to have been corrupted or in any way defiled by being exposed to a Cecil B. de Mille picture.

If ruthlessness is a sin—and I believe there's a case for arguing that it is—then almost certainly he was guilty of that. He could be loyal, he could be kind, he could be generous but he was not often benevolent. In the words of Robert Parrish: "Benevolent is not a word I would have chosen; I'm not jumping at that. He used to get what he wanted and if he had to step on a few throats on the way, he did what he felt he had to do. But he wasn't running as somebody who wanted to be liked. I never heard anybody say, 'I like Cecil B. de Mille.' "

Well, that's a chilling comment to make about anybody but on the other hand, I imagine Robert Parrish hadn't spoken to de Mille's family, or to Chico Day or to Henry Wilcoxon, all of whom claimed affection for him. It must be a unique man who is disliked by everyone he has ever met but sometimes it seems that de Mille, despite the awe and respect he evoked from others, had a remarkable lack of capacity to inspire genuine liking.

His niece, Agnes, said that he had no friends. "His daughter told me that as he grew older there was nobody. He had business acquaintances, lots, and of course business rivals and all that but no friends, nobody to talk to. There was only his wife, I think."

Anthony Quinn said: "Undoubtedly he was the epitome of success. But let me say that the last man I would want to be is Cecil B. de Mille because I'm sure he was a very lonely man. In spite of all the show I don't think he was a happy man because he was so many personalities. Shakespeare said we all must play many parts in our lives and, I don't mean this deprecatingly at all, but de Mille was only playing a part when he was at home and he was the father. And then he played the part of the patriot, of the boss, of the genius —it must have been terribly exhausting. I don't know how much time was left for him, for himself. I know he loved his boat but even then he had to play the captain, the admiral, and at Paradise he had to play Count Tolstoi. The man was of such power that he had to be in control of everything. I think of all that wasted energy. He could have done something so wonderful, so humane with all that talent and all that energy . . ."

De Mille, the man, seemed to combine the public image of a despot with private benevolence or, if that is too strong a word, then with sensitivity; to combine devout Christianity with more than a touch of hypocrisy. Professionally, he used the Bible to uplift the spirit, to titillate the flesh and to keep the box office happy. If his films were a mixture of Victorian morality, piety, sex and retribution, then much the same might be said of his own life, if you take away the retribution which never did seem to be visited upon him. Agnes de Mille described him as "only a partial person" on the grounds that nobody who had no friends could be a complete man. He could never relax, she said, and he kept strange objects around his house—shrunken heads and a cup modelled on Madame du Barry's breast—to serve as conversation pieces. And his already complex nature was made even more so by the fact that his mother was of Jewish extraction, a fact he never liked to admit because somehow he thought it sat uneasily with his reputation as a devout Episcopalian.

What makes de Mille's foibles, idiosyncrasies and eccentricities important, however, is the extent to which they affected and infected his work. And every facet of the man comes across in all his films —the vulgarity, the hypocrisy, the religiosity, the showmanship. Even Robert Parrish who, generally speaking, could take Cecil B. de Mille or leave him alone and who, given his choice, would rather have left him alone, said: "Making a movie is having a white wall in front of you with nothing on it and you, as the movie maker, have got to put something there that makes people look at it. It's that simple. Now, if you put something there that makes your mother-in-law and your children look, it's kind of fun but it's not terribly important. Cecil B. de Mille knew how to put something there that had more people look at it than did all the members of the Screen Directors' Guild. Call it what you will—spectacle, mass entertainment. Other people could do it, too—Eisenstein wasn't too bad at it—but in the long run de Mille knew more about it than anybody else. Therefore as a movie director I was much impressed with what he did and in that sense I respect him and feel that he was immensely important to the film industry."

The reference to Eisenstein is well chosen because, in fact, de Mille was closer in spirit to the great Russian director than to any of his American contemporaries. He could not hope to compete with, say, Frank Capra or William Wyler in composing an intimate scene of great emotional intensity but equally they were not in his class when it came to handling and manipulating great hordes of people and filling the screen with incident.

Grahame Greene once said of him: "His evangelical films are the nearest equivalent today of the glossy German colour prints which sometimes decorated mid-Victorian Bibles. There is the same complete lack of a period sense, the same stuffy, horsehair atmosphere of beards and whiskers and, their best quality, a childlike eye for details . . ." Other people, more brusquely, dismissed him as being more of a salesman than a director or, in the case of the critic Pauline Kael, accused him of making small-minded pictures on a large scale. Well, towards the end of his career when the old breathtaking flamboyance had degenerated somewhat into the crude and garish such criticisms may perhaps have been true. But they do little justice to his early work and particularly to the remarkable versatility he showed in his silent pictures when, I believe, he was at his best.

Certainly the films were coarsened rather than refined by time and for this Agnes de Mille offered an interesting explanation. "I think he got seduced by his own sexual dreams," she said. "I think he just went soft and became corrupted by them. He was driven by thoughts of power—power and sex. He even combined sex and religion because that seemed to be the magic box-office formula. I think it was rather disgusting and along with that went a degree of sadism that developed over the years."

Indeed all those elements were there in de Mille's most successful talkies but the true hallmark of his films was size—no great depth perhaps but width and breadth. Now it's simple enough to decry a movie that runs fast and shallow like a river in spate that has overflowed its banks. But it would be stupid to ignore the fact that such a film, like such a river, can be impressive and even awe-inspiring. Again Grahame Greene recognised that when he wrote of de Mille: "There has always been a touch of genius as well as absurdity in this warm-hearted, sentimental salvationist."

It's not at all a bad summing-up—genius, absurdity, sentimentality, salvationism. De Mille juggled all these things together because, as Jesse Lasky Jr. said: "He was terrified that the audience would go to sleep, that he couldn't hold them, that he'd lose their interest. Perhaps that's why he over-cluttered his films and why he kept bringing in every kind of thing happening every minute."

To over-clutter, to over-elaborate, was certainly one of de Mille's faults but it was a fault on the right side, the fault of a man who realised that films—like any other medium of creation—could sometimes aspire to being art but that mostly they were mass entertainment and there is nothing at all wrong with that. I don't believe de Mille ever created art, certainly not consistently throughout a whole film, although there were flashes of it, again in the earlier work, in occasional scenes. But I do believe he would have liked to be regarded as an artist and he undoubtedly had a vision of the potential of motion pictures when he said: "Films are the new literature."

Well, literature comes in all shapes and sizes and all degrees of quality. De Mille was the master specialist in the cinema equivalent of the long, sprawling, bestselling novel, a superior Harold Robbins perhaps with laudable ambitions to become a Dickens. Of course, he never realised those ambitions; he had not enough subtlety and he was too often guilty of monumental bad taste. But while it is easy to deride much of what he did, only a fool would dismiss him or attempt to belittle the impact he made upon Hollywood and the movies. As John Ford said: Nobody knew better than de Mille what the public wanted and nobody knew better how to give it to them.

Bing Crosby

Young Bing carrying both banjo and
puppy fat.

top left: The budding baseball star, before he discovered he could sing.

above: A fine focus on the ears that won him his nickname.

left: With his first wife, Dixie. As he drank less, she drank more.

The ideal Hollywood family? Bing and Dixie with (l to r) Lindsay, Gary and the twins, Philip and Dennis.

With his son Gary in 1958 when they seemed to be on good terms.

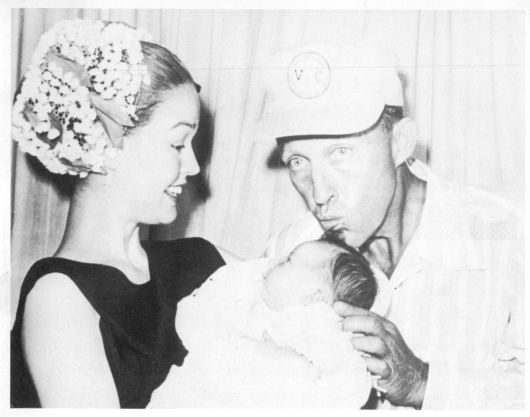

opposite page: The start of a second family—Bing with Kathryn
(wife No. 2) and Harry Lillis Jr. . .

. . . and, with the addition of Nathaniel and Mary Frances, the second
family complete and on stage for Bing's Christmas TV special.

As Father O'Malley with Barry Fitzgerald and Rise Stevens in *Going My
Way*, Crosby's only Oscar-winning performance.

One of the tricks that journalists resort to when they can't think of any more sensible questions is to ask celebrated interviewees to suggest their own epitaphs. Sometimes the answer can be quite revealing. Clark Gable, for example, said: "He was lucky and he knew it," which serves quite neatly as a summary of his career. But at other times the answer can be almost breathtaking in its inaccuracy. Consider this suggestion from Bing Crosby: "He was an average guy who could carry a tune." And now let us look more closely at the component parts of that sentence.

An average guy? Bing Crosby? No, no. Bing Crosby was a most complex guy, a sharply contrasting mixture of light and shade, which meant that he presented different, sometimes apparently contradictory, aspects of himself to different people. He could appear warm and affable or hard and cold and all these things were part of his nature.

And what about the self-effacing claim that he "could carry a tune"? Well, yes, he could certainly do that but to leave it there as the last word on his talents is about as revealing as to say that Cole Porter could compose rhyming lyrics or that the Beatles made a few records. Crosby was very probably the most influential popular singer of this century and if that fact is widely overlooked these days it is not because anyone else has totally surpassed him but because his own activities in other areas have attracted more attention.

At this point devotees of Frank Sinatra may well be leaping angrily about, crying "Of *course* Crosby was surpassed!" Well, to this I have an answer but for the moment it can wait. First, let me establish the background of this "average guy who could carry a tune".

The story begins in confusion with some doubt about the date of his birth. Crosby himself declared confidently that it was May 2nd, 1904, but other sources have it as early as May 2nd, 1901, or as late as May 3rd, 1910. The one person who could have cleared the matter up, having been the most active participant in the birth, was of course Crosby's mother but she always declined to do so on the grounds that her son's age was his own business. As it turns out, however, even Crosby was wrong for the actual date, gleaned from a baptismal certificate discovered after his death, makes it clear that the birth occurred on May 3rd, 1903. Crosby therefore went to his grave firmly believing himself to be a year younger than he actually was.

In that peculiar way Americans have the Crosbys claimed to be Irish. It's very difficult to find any American who admits simply to being an American: they all seem to need some other ethnic origin to establish their identities and with the Crosbys that origin was Irish on the strength of the fact that, according to family lore, the earliest known Crosby was the descendant of a Viking who had settled in Ireland. Why they didn't go right back to source and claim to be Vikings, far more dashing and romantic, I have no idea.

In any event the Crosbys were well established in the USA when Bing's father, Harry Lowe Crosby, a book-keeper, married Kate Harrigan. And by the time Bing was born—and baptised Harry Lillis Crosby—the fourth of seven children, the family was living at Tacoma in Washington State. A few years later they moved to Spokane near the Idaho border where Crosby Senior found work as a book-keeper in a brewery and where eventually young Harry Lillis and his siblings went to school. It was there, too, that Harry Lillis acquired his famous nickname. He was a devoted reader of a comic called *The Bingville Bugle*, which featured a character named Bingo, who was noted for his protuberant ears. Since Harry Lillis' ears protruded so far that later in life Hollywood attempted to stick them back with plaster and Bob Hope was wont to refer to him as "Dumbo", the nickname Bingo (soon to be abbreviated to Bing) attached itself to him rather neatly.

The dominant figure in the Crosby household was not the father, who appears to have been an easy-going, gregarious sort of character, but the mother, Kate, a devoutly religious Roman Catholic, who had insisted on her husband becoming a convert, and who believed in firm discipline and corporal punishment. "My grandfather on my dad's side was a kind of little leprechaun of a guy," said Gary Crosby, Bing's eldest son. "He enjoyed a drink now and then and played the mandolin and sang funny songs and told funny stories. He was a happy-go-lucky type of little Irish guy. But my grandmother was very stern. I could tell just by their attitude (i.e. that of Bing and his brothers and sisters) when she walked into a room how she was the disciplinarian and the real head of the household as far as they were concerned. To her dying day they would all straighten up when she walked in."

Obviously Kate Crosby was a powerful influence on Bing in all manner of ways but in particular in his religious upbringing: she had always wanted one of her sons to become a priest and since Bing was her favourite and, until the birth of his brother Bob ten years later, the youngest, he was her chief candidate for clerical office. Though in fact the closest he came to the priesthood was in serving as an altar boy at the local church his belief in God and

Roman Catholicism was unshakeable and possibly and perversely it helps to account for some of his more wild behaviour later on.

In those early years, however, Harry Lillis was a better than average student, a fair athlete and earned himself pocket money in various jobs from washing cucumbers in a pickle factory to helping out in the props department at the local theatre. Briefly, too, at his mother's instigation he took music lessons but, becoming rapidly bored with practising the scales and not being permitted to sing the popular songs of the day, he soon gave that up. As a result he never did learn how to read music.

The Crosby family itself would, I suppose, be designated as lower middle class. It was not poverty stricken but there was a constant need to watch expenditure. It was also extremely musical: father Crosby played both the mandolin and the four-string guitar and Kate was a talented contralto, while Harry Lillis had a good enough voice to give his first public concert at the age of twelve in the parish hall. But neither then, nor for some years after, did the idea of becoming a professional singer, or indeed any kind of musician, occur to him; in fact, in September 1922 he went to college with the intention of studying law. True, he joined the college band, the Juicy Seven, in the role of drummer but this was purely for diversion.

But one day he received a telephone call that was literally to change his life. In fiction such telephone calls are a familiar and useful device; in reality they are not particularly common but one of them was received late in 1922 by Harry Lillis Crosby.

The call was made by Al Rinker, a pianist and college acquaintance of young Crosby, who had formed and led a five-piece band called the Musicaladers. Rinker's problem was that he wished to convert it into a six-piece band but was desperately short of a drummer. And then it was brought to his attention that Bing Crosby was not only a drummer of sorts but, best of all, even had his own drums.

Hence the phone call and the invitation, promptly accepted, to join the band which, in truth, was very successful locally despite the inability of any of them to read music. What each of them had instead was a good ear and considerable skill at copying the latest hit arrangements. In any event, they were sufficiently in demand and earning enough for Crosby to decide to drop out of college altogether and make his living from music. And though the Musicaladers split up fairly quickly, Crosby and Al Rinker stayed together as a singing duet with Rinker on piano.

This duet proved to be rather less popular than the band but they scraped along, filling in the idle hours by learning to play golf, until in October 1925, having amassed 100 dollars between them, they set off to seek their fortune in Los Angeles where Rinker's sister, Mildred Bailey, was already pretty well established as a blues singer.

This, of course, was the age of Prohibition, not that it affected Crosby and Rinker much because Miss Bailey, who gladly put them up, was married to a bootlegger. She also had a certain amount of influence around town and thanks to her good offices the Rinker-Crosby double act was taken on, at a salary of seventy-five dollars a week each, by a touring company called the Syncopation Idea, which featured the Tiller Girls, a troupe of sixteen beautiful English dancers.

It was around this time that Crosby met William Randolph Hearst Jr, the son of the newspaper publisher, cum-lover of Marion Davies, cum-owner of San Simeon and eventual model for Orson Welles' Citizen Kane. "He was playing at this itty-bitty theatre down in Hollywood, or maybe lower Los Angeles, when I first met him," said Hearst, "and we just hit it off. He was very gentle and unprepossessing—not pushy at all. You'd never know he was a show person —always smiling and grinning and very easy to get along with."

Since it *was* the time of Prohibition, Hearst said, booze was particularly attractive and "nobody went out after dark without having had a few snorts. Bing was never caught napping, never caught with an empty glass for very long. We all had a good time and drank up more than our share, I should think." As a student at Berkeley, Hearst invited Crosby, Rinker and the Tiller Girls to a party in his fraternity house and "I'm not so sure we didn't get run off the campus for making too much noise. There was supposed to be some decorum observed." As he remembered it the popular drink of that evening was gin, not because of the taste but because it was less of a health hazard than bootleg whisky. "Whisky, having a colour, you never knew who the hell had coloured it or with what, whereas with gin you could see them making it if you wanted to. They'd take distilled water and good alcohol, which you knew was good alcohol and not rubbing alcohol or wood alcohol. And so gin was the favourite campus drink, because it was cheaper than whisky, which if it was any good was imported."

Now all of this sounds fairly trivial but it does have some significance because this was the period, when he was in his early twenties, when Crosby embarked on his brief career as a notorious drinker, although his taste for the bottle had not yet become a serious problem.

Professionally, indeed, Crosby and Rinker were advancing steadily. From the Syncopation Idea they moved on to Morrissy's Music Hall Revue in Los Angeles (billed as "Two Boys and a Piano") and from there (billed as "Crosby and Rinker") they joined a troupe that put on shows between the movies in cinemas. And while they were so engaged they came to the attention of Paul Whiteman, who ran one of the most famous and popular jazz bands of the era. They joined the Whiteman Band in Chicago in late 1926, having earlier cut their first record—a vocal duet called "I've Got the Girl"—in Los Angeles. Very soon afterwards, with the Whiteman outfit, they cut their second, "Wistful and Blue", which turned out to be a hit.

Thus regularly employed, already quite successful and earning good money, Crosby set out to explore speakeasies wherever they were to be found, which was in most places. Unfortunately, however, his appetite for liquor was not matched by his ability to hold it and he was frequently rescued, drunk, from some gin-sodden back room. But still there was no great problem and indeed when trouble arose it had nothing to do with drink. After minor triumphs in Chicago and elsewhere Crosby and Rinker opened with the Whiteman Band at the Paramount Theatre in New York in January 1927—and were an instant flop. Either the audience couldn't hear them in the huge auditorium or, if they could hear them, were unimpressed by their style—whatever the reason they died right there on stage. The band was popular; the singers were not and Whiteman dropped them from the show.

But at this low point a mutual friend suggested that they should team up with a singer-songwriter-pianist named Harry Barris and, having nothing much to lose, they did. Thus the Rhythm Boys were formed and instantly achieved the success which of late had so signally eluded Crosby and Rinker. Records followed swiftly— "Muddy Water" (a Crosby solo with the Whiteman Orchestra), "Side by Side", "Mississippi Mud" (still a classic of the period) and "From Monday On". By this time the three of them were earning upwards of 150 dollars a week each, excellent pay for the time, but it could hardly be said that they worked hard for their money. They spent much of their time in urgent pursuit of alcohol, women and golfballs and they only had a repertoire of about a dozen songs.

Even so when Whiteman sent them out on a tour of the vaudeville circuit they did so well that in 1929 he invited them to rejoin the band for a trip across America in a private train, which stopped at various places en route so that the occupants could give concerts and make radio broadcasts. The journey culminated in Hollywood where the band and the Rhythm Boys were to film *The King of Jazz*. It was to be Crosby's first appearance in a feature movie but his contribution turned out to be smaller than it should have been.

Unfortunately, the film—which took its title from Whiteman's own soubriquet—was not ready to start when the entourage arrived early in 1930, which left Crosby and the others plenty of time for golf and drink. It also gave Crosby, who had already decided that the future lay in moving pictures, time to present himself at studios other than Universal (where *The King of Jazz* was to be made) and ask for screen tests. He was given several but the protruding ears caused him, in every case, to be turned down. (At much the same time Clark Gable was suffering a similar fate for exactly the same reason, which shows how much people who organised screen tests knew.)

By the time Universal was ready to start shooting *The King of Jazz*, the Rhythm Boys had played a short but popular season at the Montmartre Café on Hollywood Boulevard and had also discovered the delights of Hollywood parties. And it was when he was returning one night from one of these that Crosby was involved in a minor motoring accident, arrested by the police and sentenced to thirty days for defying the Prohibition Law. Although, thanks to Whiteman, he was allowed out of jail during the daytime to attend the studio, the bandleader punished him by giving his designated solo spot, "Song of the Dawn", to John Boles; Crosby's contribution to the music track was consequently reduced to joining the Rhythm Boys in performing "A Bench in the Park".

When the film was over, the band went on tour again but had gone no further than Seattle when the Rhythm Boys finally parted company with Whiteman. Al Rinker maintained that they left by mutual consent; Crosby, on the other hand, said that the parting came about because a bootlegger tried to charge him for a bottle of scotch that he had never received; that he refused to pay; that the bootlegger went to Whiteman, who gave him the money and then deducted it from Crosby's salary; that this led to an altercation which culminated with the bandleader informing Crosby that he was more trouble than he was worth and firing the whole group.

Whatever the facts the Rhythm Boys were now on their own. They returned to Los Angeles and were hired to appear at the Coconut Grove, a celebrated night spot in the Ambassador Hotel on Wilshire Boulevard and it was there that at last Crosby became a solo singer. It was also while they were there that their act was broadcast live over the radio, that the group appeared in a couple of two-reel shorts and that Crosby made his first screen appearance without Rinker and Barris in the feature film *Reaching for the Moon*, which starred Douglas Fairbanks and Bebe Daniels. Furthermore it was while he was appearing at the Coconut Grove that he met Dixie Lee.

What, though, was Crosby like at this stage in his career? Artie Shaw, one of the greatest of jazz musicians, remembers him vividly. Shaw, then aged about twenty-six, a year or so younger than Crosby, was working with the Irving Aaronson Band at the Roosevelt Hotel on Hollywood Boulevard. The Roosevelt at that time was an extremely smart place, much frequented by the stars.

"Bing used to come down once in a while and ask us to let him sing in the little floor show the band put on, in the hope of attracting the attention of some producer or whatever. I remember him singing 'Ol' Man River'; he didn't sing it in the classical way, he sang it like Bing would sing it, with a peculiar sense of dramatics. Not very many jazz singers were able to do that. He had his own thumbprint even then and it's not easy to do that, you know, in any art form— to find out who you are and go with it."

Despite the success of the Coconut Grove show and the radio broadcasts, however, Shaw didn't remember him as an especially popular singer of the time. "He wasn't too well known. That's why he'd come and sing with us, just to get a hearing, and it took quite a while before he made it." Nevertheless, he was on his way and already impressing jazz musicians.

Another who met him around that time and became not merely a friend but a lifelong admirer was Phil Harris, who was initially drawn to Crosby because both of them had started out as drummers before becoming singers and who, more than fifty years later, could still remember the first time he heard Crosby sing. "It was in the Montmartre and there was just him and Rinker. Bing sang 'I Kiss Your Hand, Madame' and I was amazed because it was so beautiful. And when he finished you could almost hear a pin drop." It was Crosby's style, he said, that made him so special and "the tone he produced that was so warm and quite different from anything else before". And as a man at that time? "Well, he was like all young musicians; naturally he'd take a drink. He was just a guy, a regular guy. I mean everybody likes to have a girl and maybe go out and have a few snorts."

That being so, it was perhaps understandable that Crosby would find himself deeply attracted to a pretty girl who also liked a few snorts. Dixie Lee was born Wilma Winifred Wyatt on November 1st, 1911, in Harriman, Tennessee. She studied singing and dancing and showed such talent that by the time she was seventeen she was already in Hollywood with a new name and a movie contract. Two years later when she met Crosby she was the better established of the two and when, very swiftly, they decided to marry her friends felt she was making a grave mistake. Crosby, they said, was irresponsible—a drinker and womaniser; she would almost certainly have to support him for the rest of her life.

Undeterred, she married him anyway—at the Blessed Sacrament Church on Sunset Boulevard on September 29th, 1930. They had very little money and no home of their own and after a brief honeymoon they moved into a house in the Hollywood Hills that was lent to them by a friend of Dixie's. They did not, however, stay there very long for within three months they had separated.

In those early days, it seems, Crosby was not about to let the trifling inconvenience of marriage interfere with his way of life. He was still inclined to spend his days playing golf and his nights carousing with his friends, sometimes returning home drunk or not even bothering to return home at all. In the report of the separation in one of the Los Angeles papers, Dixie was quoted as saying: "We have already found out that we are not suited to each other. Our separation is an amicable one and the only reason for it is that we just cannot get along. Bing is a fine boy as a friend but married he and I cannot be happy."

But as it turned out the parting was brief. For several reasons (not least the fact that he was a devout Catholic who, throughout his life, never failed to go to Mass on Sunday no matter how frightful his hangover) Crosby could not contemplate divorce. Besides, in those days a divorce could have had a most harmful effect upon his career. So with those two arguments in mind as well, let us charitably assume, as a genuine desire to be reconciled with the woman he had loved enough to marry only a few months previously, he promised Dixie that he would reform and thus persuaded her to return to him.

Yes, but how much reforming needed to be done? Well, by all accounts quite a bit. First, let us take his drinking habits. On the one hand there is the testimony of friends such as Bob Hope who regarded Crosby's youthful bibulousness as a joke or, at worst, a mild though oft-repeated indiscretion. "That was where the boo-ba-de-boo feature of his singing came from," said Hope. "When he started down at the Coconut Grove he used to love to take a little nip now and then and if he'd had a few too many nips he'd forget the lyrics and then . . . boo-ba-de-boo."

But against that there is Carroll Carroll who later on and for many years wrote the script for Crosby's radio show and who said: "He was an alcoholic, although he did stop drinking. I don't think he took any cures or anything: he just controlled it."

Crosby's eldest son Gary disagrees with that diagnosis. "When he first got married Dad was doing a lot of drinking and fooling around, falling down, getting thrown in jail—everybody was, you know. It was the thing to do. You went to jail for the night and they bailed you out in the morning and everybody had a big laugh. He continued like this after he got married and Mom evidently left him and went down to Mexico and he followed her there and I think she said something like, 'if we're gonna stay married this has got to cease.' Whereupon it ceased. He was not an alcoholic ever. From that day on as far as I know he controlled his drinking; he did what no alcoholic can do and that is he would drink normally. He would have maybe one or two drinks at a party. I saw him high maybe three times in my life."

All of which, given that this *was* the age of Prohibition when people who probably wouldn't touch alcohol if it was freely available felt morally obliged to get smashed as often as possible, sounds fairly reasonable, although Crosby's drinking affected his work as well as his marriage. "I've heard stories about him in those early days," said Gary Crosby. "There was a little old lady who called into a talk show I was on and she said she played piano for him and at one place the only real reason the piano was out there was so he could hang on to it. Because that's how ripped he'd get."

Artie Shaw, too, remembered the drunken Crosby from the early years. "I was playing on CBS radio when I was a staff musician and he'd come in to sing and somebody was holding him up at the mike. He couldn't enunciate, his words were slurred. He had a bad drinking problem at that time. You don't speak badly of the dead but it's a fact; everybody knew it."

A bad drinking problem, yes—but on balance an alcoholic, no. And clearly he did control it, as he promised Dixie he would. The womanising, though, seems to have been a different matter. There are many rumours that he continued that practice long after he was married. Gary Crosby said: "Mom knew about his affairs. I mean, she heard about them; she had a pretty good idea of what was going on and when she would get loaded and forget that I was in the room some names would slip out. I'm not going to mention them because

I don't *know* if they were true. I didn't know anything until one time a couple of his friends were sitting around the house and forgot I was in the room again and they told a story that concerned him and a certain lady. It was a humorous story but I thought, 'Ah-ha', and then it came to me that maybe those times I was listening to my mother with the names, maybe they weren't so far-fetched as I thought, maybe it wasn't all alcohol talking."

A lot of maybes in there and not much evidence, though the indications are that Dixie at least believed her husband was having affairs with other women. But perhaps the most significant point in what Gary Crosby said was the reference to his mother drinking, for Dixie was certainly an alcoholic.

Her drinking began long before she married Crosby and started because she was unusually shy and unselfconfident, a handicap for anyone but especially so for a girl in show business. She could only perform when bolstered by a few drinks. Gary Crosby again . . . "Mom was great, a really warm, wonderful but very shy person, too shy to be in show business. She was a good singer and a good dancer and actress but she hated every minute. It just scared her to death every time she went out on stage. I can remember seeing movies of her singing and the voice is great but you look at her hands and her hands are at her sides and she's got both fists clenched."

After marriage Dixie gave up her career, probably with some relief, but by then the drink habit was too well established and she was unable to give that up, too. So, ironically, as Crosby began to drink less, she began to drink more.

At the time of the reconciliation, however, this was no particular handicap. What was, briefly, a problem was the fact that Crosby had lost his job at the Coconut Grove. As to how this came about there are conflicting explanations. Crosby's own version is that he had missed a number of shows because of what he called his "bibulous behaviour" and that the manager of the Grove planned to fine him every time it happened in future. But the first time he attempted this, Crosby walked out taking Al Rinker and Harry Barris with him. A later explanation claims that Crosby had been wanting to get out of his contract for some time and used the proposed fine as an excuse to break it. What is clear is that Rinker and Barris did go with him and that their joint walk-out also brought about the end of the Rhythm Boys, probably because the irate boss of the Coconut Grove managed to persuade the Musicians' Union to "black" them. Rinker went into radio, and later television, production; Barris remained a songwriter (with hits like "I Surrender,

Dear" and "Wrap Your Troubles in Dreams") and Crosby became a solo performer.

The union ban did not last long, thanks apparently to a show business attorney named Roger Marchetti. By August 1931, according to the trade paper, *The Hollywood Reporter*, Crosby had a contract with Brunswick Records and Marchetti had also secured him 4,000 dollars a week to appear on CBS Radio plus 35,000 dollars to play the lead in a film called *The Big Broadcast* in 1932.

Crosby family records never mention Marchetti, whose connection with the singer lasted only a year or so. The final reference to the relationship appeared thus in *The Hollywood Reporter*: "Roger Marchetti dug Bing Crosby out of the Ambassador (the site of the Coconut Grove), fought his union battles through to victory, took him to New York and secured one of the best salaries a crooner ever received for broadcasting. Then his troubles began, with Marchetti finally selling out his interest to the crooner himself. Now the crooner is telling the world that he is sick of paying 'twenty per cent' to the man who made most of his success possible."

If all this is true (and Crosby is said to have bought out Marchetti for the ludicrously small sum of 40,000 dollars) it indicates either deep ingratitude or cold business sense on Crosby's part. Either way Marchetti was out and most of Crosby's financial affairs were handled from then on by his brother Everett.

By now, in any case, thanks to records and radio the singer was fast becoming something of a national celebrity. *The Big Broadcast* was the thirteenth film in which he had appeared. Indeed, he was offered top billing in it but declined—as he did throughout his film career—on the grounds that if the picture flopped he didn't want to take all the blame. Even so, he did play the leading role and, just as importantly, sang "The Blue of the Night", which was destined to become his signature tune. And Paramount liked the film and Crosby enough to sign him to a long-term contract.

There were, however, two obstacles to Crosby becoming a movie star: in the first place there was his hair, or rather the lack of it, for he had begun to go bald very early. A well designed toupee coped with that, leaving one more problem—actually two more problems, his ears. They stuck out; they stuck out almost at right angles. And received opinion in Hollywood declared that a leading man with ears like wind sails was never going to be taken seriously. The studio's solution to this was to stick his ears back with glue and adhesive tape but even that was not infallible.

Mary Carlisle, who appeared with him in two films—*College*

Humour in 1933 and *Double or Nothing* four years later—said: "The heat of the studio lights affected the glue and I remember, when we were making *College Humour* we were doing a scene and suddenly one of his ears popped out. We were all hysterical."

By the time they made the second film in 1937, Crosby had thirty-one pictures behind him and was so popular that Hollywood had given up trying to control his ears and was content to let them flap free. As early as 1934 he had begun to feature in the annual list of the ten most popular stars at the cinema box office and by 1937 he had risen to fourth place. The critics, though, were not always as kind to him as the public. In 1933 *Picturegoer* magazine said his "screen personality and histrionics were negligible" and Graham Greene described him in *Two for Tonight* in 1935 as "attractively commonplace" and in *Rhythm on the Range* in 1936 as "like Walt Disney's Cock Robin".

Crosby, however, cannot have been too concerned by such luke-warm reviews, for he was not simply a star of film, radio and records, he was a business, employing his entire family—except his youngest brother, Bob, who was to become a famous bandleader—in his financial empire. Furthermore, by 1934 he was receiving 10,000 fan letters a month and eighty-five Crosby fan clubs had been set up around the world.

In addition, he was rapidly acquiring a family of his own. His son Gary (named after Crosby's great friend Gary Cooper) was born in January, 1933; the twins, Philip and Dennis, followed in July 1934 and the last son, Lindsay, arrived in January 1938.

To the world at large the Crosbys were, indeed, the ideal Hollywood family, a happy, self-contained little unit. But the facts were rather different.

In the first place there was the matter of Dixie's alcoholism. "I would never in any way, shape or form say that my father made my mother an alcoholic," said Gary Crosby. "That can't be done. But my mother, as I said, was a tremendously shy person who needed a great amount of demonstrative affection and she was married to a guy who couldn't show a *normal* amount. So there was that chasm. When people ask me about it, I liken it to looking down to the end of the hall and seeing him come home after a day's work and he'd say: 'Honey, there's a great party tonight. Do you want to go?' And she'd say: 'No, I can't. My hair's not fixed. I haven't got a dress. I don't have the right shoes . . .' Now he was supposed to say: 'Okay, I'll get your hair fixed; I'll get you a dress; I'll get you some shoes.' Whatever the objection he was supposed to coax her so they could go to the party and have a good time. That was her version: she wanted him to coax her; she wanted to go. His version was that he'd say: 'Honey, there's a great party tonight. Do you want to go?' And she'd say: 'No', and he'd say: 'Well, okay, I'm going. I'll talk to you in the morning.' To him, he'd fulfilled his obligation, he'd asked her did she wanna go and she'd said no. But then, when he'd gone, I'd sit and watch her turn inward on herself and eat herself up for not being able to just say: 'Yes, sure, I'd like to go.' And she'd put herself down and she'd have this low, low self image and then she'd start to drink."

But the family set-up was even more complex than that. Crosby was a repressive father, inflicting harsh rules and even harsher punishment on his four sons, particularly Gary, the eldest.

"When I'd hear his voice coming from the end of the hall, I knew it was trouble," Gary Crosby said. "If I heard: Gary, get in here! I knew I'd done something. I never knew what the hell it was. He always thought corporal punishment would work . . . all sorts of punishment, withdrawal of privileges, being sent to bed without dinner. Everything was punishment, punishment, punishment. It made me and my brothers very defensive cats growing up because I can never remember concentrating on trying to do something right. I spent my whole time trying to keep from doing anything wrong. I think he just misread me. I think Dad always thought that all kids are the same and you treat 'em all the same. But you've got to know which ones you kick in the tail to get the best out of and which ones you slap on the back. I happened to be one that you could get a lot out of by slapping on the back but I got kicked in the tail instead."

In his book, *Going My Own Way*, Gary Crosby has listed in some detail the misdeeds that he perpetrated and the punishments that ensued. Taken individually none of the "crimes" nor the punishments was particularly remarkable. But taken over a period of years with each misdeed leading to more punishment and each act of punishment bringing about another misdeed and with Crosby never apparently inclined to take his son to one side and ask him what the hell was going on in an effort to find a less traumatic basis for their relationship it becomes easier to understand the distrust and even fear that Gary felt for his father. He said: "After going to the Catholic school for a while I kind of started getting the same feelings about God and my father. They seemed to me to be the same person. My religious upbringing had me looking at the just side of God but not the merciful; I saw the strict side rather than the loving. And that's the way it was with my father. When I was little everybody knew two people—God and Dad. The guy at the gas station, the teacher at school, the fellow walking down the street would all yell, 'Hey, how's your father?' It was like they all knew him. You know, one reason I never ran away from home was because I figured everybody knew him and they'd bring me back and then he'd really kick the hell out of me."

According to Gary therefore—and I must stress that he spoke to me without rancour and without any sign that he was attempting to gain some sort of posthumous revenge on a cruel father—Crosby was a man who showed little sensitivity towards his wife and no real affection towards his sons. Some kind of monster then? Gary thought not.

"His motives were all good. He wanted to raise kids that weren't typical Hollywood kids. It scared the hell out of him when he saw kids around who were banging up cars and getting in trouble and all their dads were doing was handing them more money and another new car. He used to say: I don't want any Hollywood kids around here. And I think he did a 180 degree turn from that when maybe ninety degrees would have been enough. He got way overboard into discipline and too many rules and regulations. So you couldn't ever win. There was no way you could get through a week without breaking some of the rules. And when you did, you got it."

But perhaps even that would have been sufferable if Crosby had been the kind of man who could take his sons in his arms and say "I love you". But when I asked Gary if his father had been capable of that, he simply laughed. "Oh no," he said. "No, no, no. That wasn't how he was raised. If we did wrong we got a shot in the head, if we did right maybe a pat on the back. Dad was to be left alone, you know. Dad wasn't to be messed with. He could, kiddingly, in a joking, bantering kind of way make you feel you were all right for the moment but that's as close as he ever got to saying 'I love you'."

Probably the significant words there were "the way he was raised". Crosby's mother (the dominant influence in his life until the day she died) was a firm believer, after all, in discipline and punishment. So it's interesting that Crosby reacted to this background first by rejecting it and becoming a boozer and a womaniser and then, as it were, by repenting and embracing his mother's stern Victorian principles, which in turn he tried to impose on his own children. His sons resented and rejected this aspect of him but it's reasonable to assume, as Gary appears to have done, that he believed he was acting in their own best interests. The fact that his over-strict methods had the very opposite effect from the one intended and caused the four boys of his marriage to Dixie to behave, when they grew up, as wildly as he had done in his own youth is sad and ironic but by no means unique.

Nevertheless, within the Crosby household there emerged another—and to the public, had they known about it, unbelievable—side to the familiar good-natured crooner: that of the apparently cold pater familias. Neither side alone but both sides together seem to have represented the real Crosby.

Gary said: "The Bing Crosby that everybody knows and loves, the easy-going, casual guy who made singing seem so easy that we all believe we can do it in the shower, that was part of his personality. We're all made up of different sides and he was different when he came home. But he was still the same man; he wasn't putting on an act either in public or at home."

But while all this private Sturm und Drang was going on behind the locked doors and curtained windows of the family home, the well-known Crosby—he of the affable charm—was becoming ever more successful. In late 1939, teamed with Bob Hope and Dorothy Lamour, he began filming on *The Road to Singapore*, the first of a series of seven pictures which, with the singular exception of *Going My Way*, were to bring him greater fame, popularity and kudos than any of his other movies.

Oddly enough, this one was not originally conceived as a vehicle for him at all. Under the title *Road to Mandalay* it was offered first to Jack Oakie and Fred MacMurray and, when they turned it down, to George Burns and Gracie Allen, who likewise declined. It was only as an afterthought that somebody came up with the idea of teaming Hope and Crosby—who had long been engaged in a good-natured feud on their respective radio shows—with Lamour as the perennial glamour girl.

By now, thanks to films, records and radio Crosby was already one of the richest stars in America as well as being undoubtedly the most popular crooner of the past decade—a position he was to continue to hold virtually unchallenged until the rise of Frank Sinatra. True, Sinatra might not like to be called a crooner but then neither did Crosby but the word does serve as a loosely fitting label for singers of a certain kind, a kind epitomised by Crosby. Indeed, his career as a singer alone is amazing: by the time of his death he had sold more than 400 million records, more than anyone else in history; the sales of "White Christmas" alone were more than thirty million.

Crosby first recorded "White Christmas" in 1942 when he sang it in the film *Holiday Inn*. Ironically, he was reluctant to sing or record the number at all, since his religious convictions told him that it would be wrong to commercialise the most important date in the church calendar. But when, finally, he was persuaded it took him only eighteen minutes to put it on record, proving that the nickname "One-Take Crosby" that he had acquired back in the days when he sang with the Whiteman Band had not been bestowed upon him lightly.

The coming of the war to America hardly cut into Crosby's activities at all. Between the beginning of 1942 and the end of 1944, for example, he cut well over 100 records, as well as making ten films and doing his bit—fund-raising and entertaining the troops —towards the war effort.

Two of the films he made in that time were part of the *Road . . .* series (to Zanzibar and Morocco) but the most significant of them was *Going My Way*. And again, ironically, he took against the idea at the start.

In May 1943, the producers of his radio show suggested that he should play a priest in one of the sketches, a send-up of gangster movies with James Cagney making a guest appearance as a mobster. Crosby refused for the same reason that he had earlier refused to record "White Christmas"—the whole idea offended his religious beliefs.

Thus when, a few weeks later, the director Leo McCarey approached him to play the leading role of the priest in a film then to be called *The Padre*, Crosby's initial reaction was vaguely hostile. Crosby said: "I told him the church wouldn't stand for that kind of casting. Priests in pictures were usually dramatic actors and I'd been a crooner, a sportsman, a racetrack habitué and one thing and another." (Not only a racetrack habitué either—he'd actually owned a racetrack, Del Mar in California, at one time as well as owning a baseball club.)

He was, however, impressed by the story and in the end McCarey managed to talk him into playing the part whereupon, according to his co-star, Rise Stevens, the opera singer, Crosby hurled himself into the character and the enterprise so wholeheartedly that she became convinced that he would in fact have liked to be a priest himself.

"He had a tremendous love for this particular part," she said. "I do believe that in his heart and perhaps as a young man he had wanted to be a priest. Had he not had a voice I think he might have become one and he would have made a very good priest, too." Which, after all, is what his mother had thought, though it's interesting that Rise Stevens was not aware of the early maternal plans for Bing.

In any event, Crosby approached the film devoutly. "He never touched one drink throughout the whole production, neither did Leo McCarey. After every other picture they did together both of them used to go out and carouse or whatever. Not on this film. It was a very serious situation for Bing. Which makes me believe that in essence he really imagined himself as that particular priest."

Crosby's faith in both the part and the film was not, however, shared by Paramount, the studio to which he was under contract for most of his career. Having elected to make the picture, Paramount promptly lost interest in it and even had it shelved for a while. Such a lack of judgment is by no means unusual in Hollywood; a few years earlier, after all, MGM had come very close to cutting the song "Somewhere Over the Rainbow" out of *The Wizard of Oz* on the grounds that it wasn't much of a song and didn't do a lot for anybody.

Paramount's reluctance to show *Going My Way* arose from the belief held by one of the studio executives, Buddy de Sylva, that the public would never accept Crosby as a priest. Eventually, though, they agreed to show the picture to a church dignitary— "an archbishop or someone"—in the presence of the cast and the director.

Rise Stevens said: "We all sat there and we watched it and there was total silence when it was all over. The archbishop got up, with all the other priests he had with him, and they walked out. The rest of us sat there, petrified. And suddenly Bing said, 'I don't know. I have a feeling they didn't like it.' And then in comes Buddy de Sylva saying, 'He was *ecstatic*, absolutely ecstatic! It never occurred to him that Bing could do this but now he's all for the film.'"

And so with this blessing from on high *Going My Way* was released, cleaned up a fortune at the box office and won seven Academy Awards, including the Oscar for best actor, which went of course to Bing Crosby. Miss Stevens said she was not at all surprised that Crosby won. "For the first time in his life he was so sure of himself in that film; he was portraying someone he believed in and he almost transported that priest within himself—he thought like him, he behaved like him."

As an incidental bonus, quite apart from all the awards it collected, the film and Crosby's role as Father O'Malley made him the most popular star at the box office for the fifth consecutive year.

Soon after he collected the Oscar—and indeed within a couple of months of D-Day, a rather more significant event for the world at large—Crosby made a short tour of Britain to cheer up the troops. It was a measure of his popularity at that time that one night, when it became known that he was dining at a certain restaurant in London, such a crowd gathered outside, despite the blackout, that he was obliged to sit on a first-floor windowsill and sing before the people would agree to disperse. It was also at that time that he broadcast to the German troops, more or less exhorting them between songs to give in at once. And he promptly became known to the enemy forces as "Der Bingle".

By the beginning of November 1944 Crosby was back in Holly-wood to make the fourth Road film, *Road to Utopia*. Bob Hope remembered the making of those films as "nothing but fun", though there seems to have been a good deal of organised chaos involved. Certainly there was always a script to begin with but Hope and Crosby (aided and abetted by Hope's large and private team of writers) would hurl much of it out and introduce gags of their own. "We'd go on set," Hope said, "and throw in these extra things and the director would look with his eyes wide open and say, 'What was that? What was that?' And we'd say, 'Well, did you like it?' and usually he did because there was a feeling of spontaneity on the set which was marvellous. But it bothered the writers because they'd heard we were adlibbing and one day they walked on the set and I said, 'If you hear one of your lines, yell Bingo!' And it bothered the hell out of them until the picture was released and was a smash and from then on it was smiles all round."

In theory, of course, Hope and Crosby should not have been allowed to behave in such a way; each was under contract to the studio and technically could be forced to do precisely what the director wanted. But Melvin Frank, who co-wrote *Road to Utopia* with Norman Panama, said: "In those days they were enormous stars. It's impossible to imagine the prestige of those people."

What sort of a man, though, was Crosby the enormous star of that era? One who knew him pretty well was Carroll Carroll, the chief writer on Crosby's radio show. The relationship, however, was solely professional. "In the whole time I worked for Bing I was only in his house three times and each time it was to use the bathroom. I was never a friend. I was a business associate. I never saw him from Thursday to Thursday and then we would have lunch together to discuss the script." It was Carroll who always paid for the lunch—"Crosby never carried money".

Carroll admits that he did not like Crosby. "I liked him the way I liked Al Jolson, whom I didn't like at all. I admired tremendously what Crosby did and what he could do. I'm basically a shy person and I could appreciate that he was, too, but nobody could be that shy without being rude. And he was rude to people, though I don't think he knew it. I don't think he ever learned how to react to people, because before he could do so he was getting rich and I think he was very scared of people trying to take advantage of him. He was one of those people you run into every once in a while who doesn't know how to be gracious. I think he was a selfish man and a very considered person, by which I mean that he categorised people.

"He had friends for golf, friends for fishing and friends for hunting. Phil Harris was one of his hunting friends, Bob Hope was one of his golfing friends, Jock Whitney was one of his horseracing friends. And then he had business friends, generally lawyers. And they never crossed, they never met. I don't think anybody was ever really close to him, certainly not for long. He was a loner to the extent that he kept you at arm's length. If anybody ever made the faux pas of calling up and saying, 'Hey, Bing, I'd like to come over and swim in your pool this afternoon', they never made that mistake again."

Was he, though, a happy man? "Well, I don't know what a happy man is . . . No, I don't think so really. People who worked in his house said that after an evening of whatever it was that kept him at his desk, they'd find a whole pile of broken pencils. I don't know what made him break them—anger, maybe. But people don't break pencils for fun."

That aloofness, the desire to be close to people only when it suited Crosby, was noticed, too, even by the people who knew him best and liked him most. Phil Harris, for example, who said: "One of the greatest things that ever happened to me, one of the highlights of my life, was that just before Bing passed away somebody asked him who was his best friend and he said, 'Phil Harris' and that was a big thing for me, because I loved him."

But equally Harris said: "Bing was hard to know; he was more or less a loner and he was tough—he was a *tough* guy! Well, I'll tell you how tough he was: you could make one wrong move and he'd never speak to you again. And he'd never let you know why. He cut more people off and broke more hearts than you can ever imagine, because they'd made one little mistake."

The fact that he and Crosby remained friends for fifty years probably owed much to Phil Harris' ability to read the signs and know when not to push. One year, for instance, they went to the US Masters golf tournament together and . . . "Bing was having a little trouble with his first four boys. Philip had wrecked a car in Washington, Gary was having a little trouble at Stanford, Dennis had some trouble with a girl and all these things came at once. So Bing locked himself in a room for a couple of days. But we just let him go, you know. I wouldn't bother him; I'd let him go till he was ready."

In all manner of ways Crosby seems to have been a demanding sort of friend, one who expected more than he himself was prepared to give. To bear out what Carroll Carroll had said about there being no cross-fertilisation of Crosby's friends, Phil Harris remarked that if he and Crosby went, perhaps to Florida on a trip "there were a lot of parties that he would go to where I couldn't go because I wasn't in that clique. He ran with some gold-plated people, you know." (These gold-plated people who, apparently wouldn't accept Phil Harris, were Crosby's wealthy business associates.)

As he grew older he seems to have become no more amenable. "In later years," Harris said, "he had a couple of problems with kidney stones and he had to have two or three operations. And then he'd want his breakfast at a certain time, his lunch at a certain time, his dinner at a certain time." Not too unreasonable, perhaps, but he was by no means an invalid and one might therefore have expected him to show a certain amount of flexibility in his routine when he was, let us say, dining with a friend. Apparently, however, he did not. Dinner, even at the friend's home, had to be at the precise time when Crosby wanted it otherwise he would not bother to come. Maybe wealth and fame makes people like that or maybe it was just part of the personal aloofness that contrasted so sharply with the relaxed, laidback manner that made him such a public favourite.

And indeed throughout the 1940s and most of the 1950s he remained a public favourite with a popularity that was rarely surpassed by anyone else and with an income to match. In the late 1940s, for example, he was earning 150,000 dollars a film and making two or three films a year; on radio he was taking home 7,500 dollars a week for hardly more than an hour's work; and, choosing one year at random, in 1945 his record royalties, with eight million discs sold, came to 400,000 dollars. His income therefore in most years was at least one million dollars, a sum on which the average person could scrape by quite happily even now but a quite remarkable amount at that time. Furthermore, those figures don't take into account what he earned from his various business enterprises, such as his investments in land, property, oil and the very lucrative orange juice company that he had set up.

And so, securely established at the top in whatever enterprise he undertook (even collecting one year the Dwight D. Eisenhower Medal for "Father of the Year", which must have mystified his son Gary) Crosby moved on towards his fifties. Before he reached that landmark, however, the rumours of trouble in his marriage, which had cropped up earlier from time to time, began to spread again. In 1950 Crosby took part in the British amateur golf championship at St Andrews and then went on to spend time at the races in Paris, where he was usually escorted by some good-looking young woman.

And it was while he was away that the *Los Angeles Times* quoted his lawyer as intimating that "the singer's twenty-year-long marriage was headed for the rocks". In Paris Crosby denied it; in California Dixie refused to comment. Unabashed, the gossip columnists pursued the rumour with some vigour, mostly suggesting that any trouble there might be in the marriage was due to Crosby's habit of going off by himself for long periods of time.

Phil Harris maintains that there was never any scandal attached to Bing and, generally speaking, that was true. Neither was there very much criticism levelled at him, at least not personal criticism. But in the midst of all the speculation about his relationship with Dixie, the newspaper columnist Florabelle Muir took the opportunity to deliver the following observation: "Bing has an amazing capacity for ignoring all criticism. He just doesn't hear it. He is so indifferent to the opinions, good and bad, of those with whom he comes into contact that it is surprising that he has so long kept such good public relations."

This could, of course, have been prompted by the disgruntlement of a journalist who had been denied an exclusive interview. It could even be taken as a sign of strength and great self-confidence on Crosby's part, in which case the implied criticism might be interpreted as praise. But Miss Muir's contention also seems to underline what Carroll Carroll and Phil Harris had said about his indifference to other people.

However, all the rumours notwithstanding, the marriage remained intact. Of his mother, Gary Crosby said: "She was always supportive of him, always. She was going to be the best wife she knew how to be and you'd better not open your mouth about him or say anything bad about him or even look as if you didn't like what he told you to do—because if you did you'd get the back of her hand. She was real loyal, dog-loyal."

In 1952, Crosby went to Paris again, this time to play a straight role in *Little Boy Lost*, the screen version of a novel by Marghanita Laski. And at that time Dixie was seriously ill with cancer.

The illness and the gravity of it were diagnosed just before he left for Europe. Crosby was given the facts, Dixie was not and indeed the doctor advised that she should not be told, which faced Crosby with quite a dilemma . . .

"The way I got the story," said Gary Crosby, "was that he knew she was dying and he didn't want to go to Paris. But the doctor said, 'If you don't go, *she'll* know she's dying.' So he had to go and pretend that everything was okay. If he'd wavered for one second she'd have known, because she was as sharp as a razor, that something was wrong."

For the same reason, to keep Dixie believing that whatever ailed her was not serious, Crosby returned from France the slow way, by boat, just as he had planned before the cancer was diagnosed. When he reached Los Angeles Dixie, although by now extremely ill, went to meet him at the airport and a few days later arranged a surprise party for him. That was in October of 1952; on November 1st, the day of her forty-first birthday, Dixie died.

"I believe," said Gary Crosby, "that she was still in love with my father right up to the day she died. I feel that it was pretty torturous for her—but she still was."

As for Crosby himself, Carroll Carroll said: "He felt terrible when she died. But I think he was more involved with his own career than he was with being tender and thoughtful and considerate of any wife. And because he was so involved in his work, I think Dixie really felt lost."

With Dixie gone, Crosby too seems to have felt lost. He finished the film he had been making but apart from a brief cameo appearance with Bob Hope in *Scared Stiff*, which starred Dean Martin and Jerry Lewis, he made no more pictures that year. He spent a great deal of time at home, where his mother had moved in to look after him and Lindsay, the other three boys being away at school. Indeed, he appeared so little that there was much speculation about his impending retirement. It appears unlikely that he himself ever seriously contemplated it: after all, he was only just fifty or, by his own reckoning forty-nine.

Towards the end of the year he was tempted back to the studios to begin work on *White Christmas*, a movie inspired by his—and, credit where it's due, Irving Berlin's—hit song. And it was while he was so engaged that he met a nineteen-year-old starlet and former beauty queen named Olive Grandstaff. Or, rather, she had begun life as Olive Grandstaff but this, though a serviceable enough name for most purposes, was not considered to have quite sufficient glamour for a beauty queen and starlet. So by the time Crosby met her she was growing accustomed to being known as Kathryn Grant.

Quite soon they were going out together and within a few months a love affair had developed, even though Kathryn was actually five months younger than Bing's eldest son. But the romance was a long time coming to fruition. He proposed to her, and was accepted, on October 30th, 1954—two years almost to the day after Dixie's death—and the wedding date was set for February 7th, 1955. Unfortunately, Crosby had to go into hospital for an operation for kidney stones and so the marriage was postponed until May.

But by May perhaps doubts were setting in because another postponement was announced—September 10th this time, definitely. But September 10th came and went and so did Kathryn and they still weren't married. A little later another date was set. Kathryn showed up—and so did the press, TV and radio. Crosby made an excuse and left. "Bing had a very private feeling about life and marriage and death," said Kathryn. "He hated having to share certain things." This, of course, is perfectly understandable but it began to look as if he didn't even want to share his wedding day with his prospective bride. In any case after this latest debacle, Kathryn would seem to have had enough because not only would she not discuss another wedding date, she refused even to speak to Crosby for a whole year.

This policy of silence obviously concentrated Crosby's mind, for now he began to woo her afresh both through intermediaries and letters, none of which she answered until in one "he actually came out and said he loved me."

I find this astonishing. What on earth had he been saying to her hitherto? He'd known the girl for nearly four years and had come close to marrying her on four different occasions and yet not until this moment, apparently, had he found it necessary to inform her that he loved her. Such behaviour ties in, of course, with his inability to tell his sons that he loved them but nevertheless you would think he might have dropped at least a hint to that effect to his bride-to-be.

Still, this passionate (for Crosby) declaration did the trick. Swept off her feet by his silvery tongue, Kathryn went with him to Las Vegas where, at last, they were married—in church and not in one of those joke marriage parlours that proliferate in that ghastly town —on October 24th, 1957.

The outsiders' view of why it had taken the couple so long to do the deed ranges from Carroll Carroll's contention that "Bing chased her and chased her until she caught him", to Phil Harris' more serious belief that the proposed Crosby rules of marriage had caused Kathryn to consider for a long time before she decided to accept them. Bing, the loner, had frequently spent long periods away from home throughout his marriage to Dixie and, according to Harris, intended to carry on in much the same way after his marriage to Kathryn. "I think," Harris said, "and this is only my opinion, that Bing must have sat down and had a talk to her and said: 'Now look, I love you and I want to get married but when I want to go someplace I go.' After they were married, Bing would take off and a lot of the times he wouldn't even tell her he was leaving. He'd just pack up and go. And I think that was the understanding—that he had said to her, 'Now go home and think about it.' Bing was always in demand; he'd go anywhere for a shooting trip or a golf game on a new course and I'd say he was gone three-quarters of the time without her."

But finally, and whatever the house rules, the marriage took place and the new Mr and Mrs Crosby spent their wedding night at the home near Palm Springs of Phil Harris and his wife, Alice Faye.

Meanwhile, in between not getting married umpteen times, Crosby had completed six films, two of them among his very best. The first of these was *The Country Girl* in which, co-starring with Grace Kelly and William Holden, he played an alcoholic actor struggling to make a comeback. Once again, because this role was different and called for a great deal more acting ability than was usually demanded of him, he was initially reluctant to play it. But again, as so often happened when he found the nerve to step out of character, the result was excellent. And it did take nerve for a star of Crosby's magnitude to present his public with an image so drastically different from what they knew and wanted. A movie audience can be painfully fickle and Crosby in his fifties looking fifty and playing a drunk could easily have alienated a vast proportion of them.

Instead, he gained some of the best reviews of his career and was nominated for best actor in the Academy Awards, losing out in the end to Marlon Brando who took the Oscar, deservedly, for his performance in *On the Waterfront*.

The other notable picture Crosby made during this period was *High Society*, the musical remake of *The Philadelphia Story*, in which his co-stars were Grace Kelly and Frank Sinatra. It was beautifully made and beautifully played and in some of the musical numbers with Louis Armstrong Crosby showed more than in almost any of his other films why jazz musicians thought so highly of him. What's more in the duet *Did You Ever*, which could easily have become a sort of championship bout between the two best popular singers in the world, he and Sinatra held each other to an honourable draw.

High Society was released in 1956 and though Crosby went on to make another fourteen pictures in the next sixteen years it was by a long way his last big success. Even the final Road film, *Road to Hong Kong*, which he and Hope made in England in 1961 (with Joan Collins replacing the now matronly Dorothy Lamour in the glamour role) was hardly more than a tired rerun of a lot of old gags.

By the time that film started Crosby was the father of two more children: by the time it finished he was the father of a third. Harry Lillis Crosby Jr was born in 1958, Mary Frances in 1959 and in October 1961 Kathryn left her husband cavorting on set with Hope and Collins (and, in what amounted to a cameo role, Dorothy Lamour) while she flew home to America to give birth to Nathaniel.

But during that spell in England Crosby acquired more than a third—or, counting his first family, seventh—child; he also acquired a butler, Alan Fisher, who had previously performed this office for the Duke of Windsor and was later to do the same for the Prince and Princess of Wales.

If no man is a hero to his valet he is probably even less so to his butler, especially if that butler is accustomed to calling his employer "Your Royal Highness" rather than merely "Sir", which being so Alan Fisher's view of the private, as opposed to public, Crosby during the last sixteen years of his life is probably more dispassionate than most.

In any case, when he joined the household butler Fisher was no great admirer of Crosby the performer and in the ensuing years saw no particular reason to change his stance. Indeed, it was Kathryn Crosby who persuaded him to take the job. "When I first met Mrs Crosby I thought how theatrical she was and I thought, My God,

I couldn't work for this woman. But after five minutes of sitting and talking with her I sort of fell in love with her. She was warm and friendly. At that point I wasn't interested in Bing Crosby and in fact all the time I was with him I was never a fan. I didn't like his singing and I didn't like his acting. But he was really a superb person to live with."

Alan Fisher joined the Crosbys when they and the Bob Hopes were sharing Cranbourne Court, a country mansion in Berkshire, and then went back with them to their own home near San Francisco. "It was almost monastic there," he said. "He lived a very quiet life, you know. The moment he came in from, say, the golf course at four o'clock he put the chain on the front door and basically we were indoors for the rest of the day. I can't think of anyone who lived a simpler, quieter life. They hardly ever entertained at all in their home. Bob Hope came for dinner once, Fred Astaire once, Phil Harris and Alice Faye once but they didn't really entertain the show business people at all. His closest friends were tycoons of industry."

A monastic life perhaps but not a reclusive one. Crosby, said Alan Fisher, was unfailingly accessible. If people telephoned him he would always talk to them. "But he was one of those men who never picked up the phone to call anybody himself: they called him. And, of course, part of that was because he was such a loner. He really didn't need anybody. He certainly didn't need a butler, nor the trappings of the great. It was a fairly opulent life we lived— they had three homes in Mexico, an enormous ranch, a home in Pebble Beach, a home in Palm Springs, this enormous house in San Francisco . . . He didn't like to stay in hotels; he loved to buy property and stay in his own house wherever he was. But at the same time you could have put him in a paddock with a gallon of water, a can of corned beef and a tin opener and he would have been quite happy."

The hub of this quiet, though opulent, domestic existence was Kathryn. "She was the perfect thing to have happened to him at his time of life. There was a great difference in their ages but she had the knack of rising to his level and when you saw her with his friends she almost seemed to be of their generation—this very attractive, very young woman blended in with every situation."

Amy Archard, one of America's most influential show business journalists, who had known Crosby for twenty-five years before he married Kathryn saw the marriage as "the rebirth of his life and a new impetus for him to continue in show business". In one of her columns she wrote: "I doubt whether he would really have gone on as successfully as he did in this second half of his life had he not married again . . . I think he got the urge to be Bing Crosby again."

That last part may be overstating matters a little. There is no evidence that he had ever tired of being Bing Crosby; he never stopped making films or records and although he had given up radio it was only to move, with equal success, into television.

But what does seem to have changed after his marriage to Kathryn and the arrival of his second family was his attitude to fatherhood. Once, in an interview with the writer Joe Hyams, he admitted that he had been too hard on his first four sons, had not spent enough time with them. He did not repeat that mistake with Harry, Mary and Nathaniel.

Indeed, if you listen to Gary Crosby and then Harry Crosby on the subject of Bing, the father, it's as if they were talking about two different men. "He was terrific to all of us," said Harry. "I think at that stage of his professional life he felt that he had pulled out all the stops in his career and what he really wanted was a family life. I was very fortunate to have come along at that time."

Thus Harry's childhood memories are very different from those of Gary. He remembered his father making an effort to spend time with him, to take him hunting and fishing. True, he also remembered discipline and strict rules about what time he had to be in at night but he didn't remember punishments. "The most he would say to me was, 'Okay, you're grounded for the weekend' and that was bad news, not because you had to stay in for the weekend but because you'd let him down. I think he was at a point in his life when he had mellowed and really wanted to enjoy his children and any discipline he imposed was out of affection for us."

A loving father then as, to be fair, he probably had been the first time round but now, though he was still not inclined to go about telling his children he loved them he was better able to show it. "He would say, 'Nice job', or 'Good work', and you had to be sensitive to that, to pick up on it and know that what he was really saying was, 'Yeah, I love you'."

Gary Crosby, whose relationship with his father had become a lot easier over the years, also noticed the difference. "When I'd go up to the house in San Francisco I saw kids who were allowed to get angry. They'd still have to do what he said but they were allowed to get angry about it and voice their displeasure. I saw kids who loved their father and weren't afraid of him as we had been. They were allowed to be themselves. Now he was still a strict parent but it was a more human relationship."

A more disinterested bystander, Alan Fisher, said: "He was a very concerned father and verbally a very strict one. His idea of chastising the children was to grab a rolled-up newspaper and walk around the house saying, 'My God, this has got to stop.' The children were not at all afraid of him; they were afraid of upsetting him because they desperately wanted to please him. Mind you, he was a hard taskmaster; he wanted them to excel in whatever they did."

Fisher was also in a position to observe Crosby's later relationship with his four older sons. "He was always accessible to them and what is so fascinating is that they all turned to their father in any crisis in their lives. The sad thing for him was that all the first four boys disappointed him because they broke the promises they made to him. He said to me, 'Alan, anybody can make a mistake, you can give somebody a second chance or a third chance but after that I begin to lose patience.' But when they did turn to him he solved their problems for them."

The influence of Kathryn in Crosby's changed attitude towards his second family appears to have been vital. The children, said Alan Fisher, "had to shape up because they had a mother who made them shape up". And Gary Crosby said that, from his observation, it was Kathryn who, far more than her husband, was responsible for discipline around the home.

Harry Crosby agreed with that. "She was the disciplinarian in the house but I think she was also the one who taught my father affection towards children. She's the most warm, affectionate and open person and thanks to her, perhaps, he became more open and quieter and . . . and sublime."

There is, however, a price to be paid for being, as it were, the "heavy" in a family. A number of Crosby's friends, who had been particularly close to him before his second marriage, said they saw far less of him afterwards and at least by implication seemed to suggest that Kathryn was responsible for alienating him from them. Thus they tended to speak of her with less warmth than they did of Dixie. But it's possible that Rosemary Clooney came close to the truth of the matter when she suggested that Kathryn deliberately and willingly took the blame for Bing's failure to go places, do things and see people that in fact he himself had decided that he didn't want to go, do or see.

And so Crosby the family man, less involved now with his old cronies and far more involved with hearth and home, moved into his sixties, still unquestionably one of the biggest stars in America and indeed the world and by now immensely rich. His fortune has been estimated at anything between 200 and 400 million dollars and of all his contemporaries it's probable that only Bob Hope was richer. The bulk of Crosby's fortune came, as did Hope's, less from fees and royalties than from exceedingly shrewd business investments. But although he had no need to work he continued to do so, mainly on TV and in recording studios. His film career virtually came to an end in 1965 when, for 20th Century-Fox, he co-starred in a remake of the old John Ford–John Wayne classic *Stagecoach*. The role Crosby played was that of the drunken doctor which, in the original version, had won Thomas Mitchell an Oscar for best supporting actor. Crosby did not enjoy anything like that success—indeed neither was the film at all comparable to its predecessor—but his was nevertheless a good performance and as a swansong it hit fewer duff notes than does the average swansong.

There were to be three more big screen appearances—in *Cinerama's Russian Adventure* (1966), *Bing Crosby's Washington State* (1968) and *Cancel My Reservation* (1972)—but none of them was of any account. This withdrawal from the cinema was probably voluntary and obligatory in equal measures. There aren't many light leading roles for a man well into his sixties and besides Crosby disliked the new permissiveness of the movies. As late as 1972 he said that he hadn't officially retired and would return to films if the right part came along—"one that wasn't dirty, pornographic, lascivious or full of smut". One has to assume therefore that no such part was offered to him and anyway his provisos were by no means unreasonable. Crosby's personal code remained to the end both Victorian and strictly religious. In a TV interview near the end of his life he said that if one of his sons (meaning, presumably, his two younger sons) announced that he was living with a girl without benefit of wedlock "I'd never speak to him again". And if Mary Frances was "having an affair" he would make her leave home. Quite clearly his new-found mellowness had its limits.

All things considered Crosby bowed out of the movie scene gracefully enough and slightly ahead of the time when ill health would probably have caused him to do so anyway. He suffered frequently from kidney stones and early in 1974 had about two-fifths of his left lung removed when doctors diagnosed an abscess "the size of a golf ball". It was not, fortunately malignant and it left his voice unaffected. So, over the next few years, he continued to appear in his TV specials and travelled frequently to London to make record albums and, in 1976, to star triumphantly at the Palladium.

The following year, during a gala performance in Pasadena to celebrate his golden jubilee in show business, he slipped and fell twenty-five feet from the stage onto a concrete floor, crushing a disc in his spine. Undeterred, he was back at the Palladium by September for another hugely successful two-week run. Rosemary Clooney appeared with him on that occasion and felt that reappearing at the Palladium was a kind of self-imposed test for him. He wanted to prove, she thought, that his first amazingly popular run had not been simply a fluke. That a man in his position should even have suspected that it might have been a fluke says quite a lot about either his humility or his lack of self-confidence. Humility probably; after all those years of almost unqualified success there's absolutely no reason why he should ever have suffered from a lack of self-confidence.

But whatever part of his personality needed a massage, it must have been amply satisfied by the enthusiastic reception he was given night after night at the Palladium. Miss Clooney said: "At one point at the end of a song they applauded so much that he said to them, 'I love you'. And it was the first time I'd ever heard him say that. He wasn't a demonstrative man. He'd punch you on the arm and say, 'You're looking good', but that was the extent of it; that was as much affection as he'd show. So when he said, 'I love you' at the Palladium that was the only time I ever heard him say anything like it."

When the Palladium season was over, Crosby stayed in Britain to fulfil a few more engagements while Kathryn went home to California. When she left him he was in good health and still appeared so when he flew to Spain for a golf match near Madrid. That was on October 13th, 1977. The following day he played the match and he and his partner, Manuel Pinero, the Spanish champion, duly won. He was joking happily about the game, and the victory, as he walked away from the eighteenth green when, suddenly, he fell forward—and died. A massive heart attack had, apparently, brought him down even as he was in the act of collecting his winnings from the side bets. For one as enamoured of golf as he was, there is probably no better way to go.

Alan Fisher and young Harry Crosby had the dolorous task of flying to Spain and collecting the body, before flying it home for burial in California. And a very strange burial it was. It took place

at 6 a.m. on October 18th at the Holy Cross Cemetery in Baldwin
Hills, Hollywood. Crosby was interred in a grave close to those of
his parents and his first wife, Dixie. His six sons were the pall-bearers
but apart from them the only people present were Kathryn, Mary
Frances, Crosby's brother Bob and sister Mary Rose, Rosemary
Clooney, Bob Hope and his wife, Phil Harris and his wife, Alan
Fisher and about three others. Even Dorothy Lamour, who had
very much wanted to attend, was not invited.

Once again Kathryn was blamed for the remarkable modesty of
the ceremony. But in fact the funeral was arranged according to
Crosby's own wishes.

He simply did not want the kind of mass turn-out that had
attended, for example, the funeral some three years earlier of Jack
Benny. He wanted to be buried quietly and with dignity. Phil Harris
said: "Mary Frances wanted to have an open casket, so that people
could walk by and pay their respects. Well, if that had happened,
they'd be walking through there yet."

Crosby would certainly have been embarrassed by any such overt
show of public emotion. "The first time Bing was ever caught up
in a public display of grief," said Rosemary Clooney, "was when
Dixie died. And he had a terrible memory of that. So evidently he
talked it over with Kathryn and she wanted his funeral to be as
quiet and private as possible, because that's what he wanted."

The media, therefore, were excluded from what would have
been a spectacular media event but even so, as Rosemary Clooney
remembered, it was a media man—one Geraldo Rivera of ABC
television—who summed the whole business up by reporting that
Crosby had been buried "when the blue of the night meets the gold
of the day".

You may well say "Ugh!" and throw up quietly in a corner but
corny though it might be, the remark was pretty apposite.

And in any case the fact remains that at the age of seventy-four
—or seventy-three or seventy-six or sixty-seven, depending on
which date of birth you prefer—Bing Crosby was dead, leaving
behind him a reputation as an entertainer that was quite unparalleled
and memories as a man that varied sharply according to the experiences of whoever recounted them.

Let's look at him first as an entertainer. If you take his film career
alone, his record is quite staggering. In one way or another and in
one role or another he appeared in 100 films and displayed a talent
that was good enough both to win him an Oscar and establish him
among America's most popular movie stars for two decades. As an

actor he once said of himself: "I've been described as a light comedian and that's just about what I am." On the whole this was probably true but it was also an over-simplification because it came about through his own choice. I believe he decided what his own limitations were and determined, wherever possible, to stay within them. Commercially this was probably a wise move—as it was also a wise move to insist on sharing top billing whenever he could, so that total blame for disaster was never likely to fall entirely upon him—but artistically it was limiting. When, reluctantly, he was persuaded to step out of character—as in *The Country Girl*—he displayed a versatility and depth of talent that probably surprised even himself. But, as he may well have argued, why take the risk of stepping out of character too often when the public revealed, time after time, that all it really wanted was the familiar, relaxed Bing Crosby. The public may not always be right but when it keeps insisting that you are among the few actors it loves best it can hardly be ignored.

So, as a movie star alone, he was—despite his self-imposed limitations—among the very greatest, so far as popular acclaim was concerned.

But then there is his music to consider. If you take him simply as a singer of popular ballads he was astonishing. I said earlier that he was unsurpassed and conceded that Sinatra fans might disagree with that. Well, let me now state my case: everyone I talked to from Artie Shaw to Rise Stevens to Rosemary Clooney agreed (no, more than agreed—volunteered) that without Crosby popular singing as we know it now would never have come about. To those who insist that Sinatra surpassed him I would simply present a literary analogy, namely that Crosby was to Sinatra what Dashiell Hammett was to Raymond Chandler. Without the one, the other could never even have aspired to the heights he later scaled.

Indeed Artie Shaw, who is certainly not given to paying idle compliments, said this: "Bing was seminal. He was the first guy who could sing a song in a popular way that could reach large masses of people—and at the same time did not offend jazz musicians. He started a whole new thing; he was all by himself and he had a host of imitators—Perry Como, Dean Martin (who sounds like him to this day). I'd say even Sinatra was influenced. He was an artist, as opposed to an entertainer. I don't think he owed anything to any singer I ever heard of. Like John Wayne, he became a kind of icon. I don't think you could have had a phenomenon like Sinatra without Bing, or a Tony Bennett or a Perry Como without Bing. They're not necessarily imitative of him but they are derivative—they followed him. Bing set the standard."

Thus Crosby the movie star and Crosby the popular singer par excellence. When, in the "Did You Ever" duet in *High Society* he says to Sinatra: "You must be one of these newer fellers", it's not patronising—it's simply the old master acknowledging the advent of a rising generation of pupils who have learned well. It has been said of him that on film and record, on radio and TV, he gave more pleasure to more people than any other entertainer—and that in itself is a better epitaph than any Crosby was ever moved to suggest for himself. But best of all, and this is something which his great commercial success as a light comedian and singer of ballads tended to obscure, he was by common consent the most innovative jazz singer of the twentieth century, the first whom even jazz musicians were inclined to treat with total respect. The word "great" is tossed around so casually these days that it has come to mean nothing much more than "not bad". But if you take it to mean "of surpassing excellence", then Crosby the singer was great indeed.

That leaves us then with Crosby the man. What sort of creature was this? Well, as I said at the very beginning, he appears to have been different things to different people. Carroll Carroll disliked him; Phil Harris loved him. That he was financially generous there appears to be common accord. Rosemary Clooney said that when she had a nervous breakdown in 1968 one of the first letters she received was from Crosby and it said simply, "If there's anything you need, just make one call and it will be done."

She also knew of another story—and Crosby never had any idea that she was aware of this—of Bing getting into a New York taxi one day and recognising the driver from the photograph that he was obliged to show in the cab, as a former producer he had once worked with in television. Crosby introduced himself, discovered that the man had fallen upon perilously hard times, took his address and sent him a cheque for 10,000 dollars with a note that said, "No repayment necessary".

Even Gary Crosby admitted that "he helped me at one point financially. He paid for a dry-out clinic that I went to, when I was trying to beat alcoholism. I didn't know about it at the time and I wouldn't have accepted it if I'd known." Well, perhaps a father could hardly do less for his son. Gary, looking back with hindsight, was grateful for his father's help. But he also remembered another, perhaps more chilling, occasion. At dinner with Bing and Kathryn one night, Gary was talking about one of his brothers who was having a psychiatric problem—"I called it a mental problem"—and as the evening ended and Gary and his wife were at the front door and Kathryn was fetching the coats, Bing turned to Gary and . . . "He said, 'Tell me something'—and he looked me dead in the eye and he wasn't faking—'Tell me something,' he said, 'how does anybody have a mental problem?' And I looked at him and I thought, Man, this guy must not know fear or anything. I said, 'Dad, some of us are not as strong as you are and life scares the hell out of us.' And he just looked at me and nodded his head and he didn't understand."

But then Gary and his father never understood each other either. Seven years after Bing died I said to Gary: "Can you think of him now with love?"

And Gary said: "Love's kind of a strong word. I respected him, I admired him as an entertainer, as a great singer, as a pretty good actor. He became a good father, he was always a good provider, he gave an awful lot of people an awful lot of happiness for a great number of years. When you're totalling it up that means a lot. But . . . I liked him. Towards the end I liked him and I kind of understood him a little better. But I can't say I loved him."

If that were all it would be the saddest possible comment on a man's life, no matter how materially successful he had been. But there were others—not always perhaps those who knew him so intimately as Gary—who had a different, warmer tale to tell. Phil Harris, for instance . . . "I miss him more than I can say. Bing was a special guy."

And Rosemary Clooney: "It was one of the joys of my life to know him personally."

And perhaps most significantly of all, Crosby's son, Harry, who knew him quite as well as Gary did and possibly better: "I grieved for him when he died and I still miss him now. I had such a special, such a very close relationship with him . . . It was unique. It's something that can't be taken away."

Many people can be all things to all men; many people can be whatever the person they are with would like them to be at any given moment. Bing Crosby seems to have been different: he seems to have been whatever *he* wanted to be at any particular time and in any particular company. It takes self-confidence, maybe arrogance, to behave like that and in his case there was very likely a mixture of both. Arrogance, in him as in anybody else, is an unattractive quality but self-confidence, especially in him, is easily acceptable. Crosby, the film actor, was no better and no worse than a score or so of others. But Crosby, the musical innovator, was a kind of genius and I believe that the more the history of popular music in the twentieth century is explored, the greater his contribution will be seen to be. He was small, on the whole he was affable, he wore a toupee, his ears stuck out, he won the love of many and the dislike of a few, in some cases an important few. But he bestrode the contemporary scene like a Colossus and, by God, he could carry a tune . . .

Scenes From
Hollywood Life

"There are three 'nevers' in Hollywood: never answer the phone on the first ring; never say 'I'll be right over'; and never let them see you sweat"—Actor Robert Woods on American TV.

Admittedly Mr. Woods was appearing on a commercial for some anti-perspirant but nevertheless the dicta he laid down had an uneasy ring of truth about them. Hollywood is a town governed by fear—predominantly the fear of failure but also physical fear, the fear of being kidnapped or mugged or of simply being blown away by some psycho who hates you merely because you exist. Of course all these fears afflict most profoundly the rich and famous, many of whom employ armed bodyguards to protect them and their families twenty-four hours a day. But the greatest of fears is the first—the fear of failure.

Maybe it was always so because Hollywood has always been an intensely competitive town, a place where it is firmly believed that God's final word of advice to Moses as he handed over the tablets was, "And remember, you're only as good as your last picture." From the 1920s to the 1950s, when the film industry was in its heyday, the fear of failure—of diminishing box-office returns, of being dropped by the studio, of offending one of the moguls— haunted its denizens. And today, when television dominates the town, that fear is perhaps even greater. At least the film studios were prepared to show patience, to allow talent a chance to establish itself. The television companies, however, are very short of patience. Promise and talent by themselves have no commercial value unless they are accompanied by success and success must be immediate; it must be reflected from the start in the ratings and if it is not there's no second chance.

But if the price of failure is inordinately high, so too are the rewards for success. When the film *E.T.* was breaking box-office records all over the world and its director, Steven Spielberg, was said to be earning one million dollars a day, there was a report in a Los Angeles newspaper that he had just bought a plot of land in Bel Air for six million dollars and was planning to erect upon it a seven million dollar mansion. And it occurred to me that the poor man had had to fork out nearly a fortnight's salary to pay for all that.

California, you see, is extremely rich. If it were to declare itself an independent nation it would be the eighth most powerful industrial country in the world, which is one reason why the advice "Go West, young man," is still regarded thereabouts as the best advice. Every day the new pioneers of the technological age climb aboard their covered 747s to make the long and arduous trek westwards across the land and for many of them Hollywood—that rather tacky suburb of Los Angeles—is the ultimate destination because Hollywood is still the centre of the TV, film and pop music industries, the home of the American Dream, where fame and fortune lie eagerly in wait for every enterprising newcomer. Or so the story goes.

On TV there one day a woman preacher was holding forth on the theme: prosperity is your divine right, and in Hollywood everyone says "Amen" to that. For some, of course, prosperity does appear but even when it does, even when the lucky ones have achieved celebrity and wealth and a Rolls-Royce and have built their mock-Spanish castles in Bel Air they can never be complacent or even content, for when you stop close to the American Dream and peer round the edges a murky and menacing side appears . . .

"I would say," said Jay Bernstein, "that terror is probably our biggest diet here. If you're an actor you're afraid you're not going to make it. And when you've made it, you're afraid you're not going to sustain it."

Jay Bernstein is a personal manager, a comparatively new kind of occupation in Hollywood and one that came into being because the old order had changed. The old order, the film studio order, looked after its own and its own were the actors, the stars. The studios may have exploited them but they also protected them. Today, according to Bernstein, the Hollywood establishment looks after itself and each other. Executives scratch the backs of other executives and none of them looks after the actors. "And that's why," he said, "I decided that that was what I wanted to do as my life's work."

Bernstein was the personal manager who boosted the blonde and toothy Farrah Fawcett into whatever it was Farrah Fawcett became and then moved on to do the same sort of thing for Linda Evans, the star of the TV series *Dynasty*, and, as such, one of Hollywood's hottest properties.

Unlike an agent a personal manager has only a handful of clients at a time and devotes himself to guiding them as swiftly as possible to the top. But he selects those clients carefully. Bernstein, for instance, uses what he calls a scale of one to ten. "If someone is a six, that means he or she has a vehicle. I started Farrah Fawcett when she was a six. What I do is, I take people from six and move them up to ten. Now how do I know that someone is a six? Well, I have to decide whether they have the three ingredients I need to make me interested. First and most important is a 'quality'. If they have a 'quality' and it appeals to me, then I'm interested. If they also have a very special look, then I have to make certain they have talent, or at least a talent that can be built upon."

Having satisfied himself that a potential client has the three ingredients what then can he do for them? Well, he said, in the few years when he was looking after Farrah Fawcett he helped her make seventeen million dollars. For instance . . . "Once she was asked to have her photograph taken with a certain item of jewellery. That's all she had to do. Now the offer started at 250,000 dollars. But by the time we were through negotiating it was a million dollars and she didn't even have to do any kind of promotion or anything. She just worked three and a half hours, which was the length of the photo session. Actually, the final fee was 1,150,000 dollars."

Oh, really? And what was the extra 150,000 for?

"That was for me," he said.

And very nice, too. But, he insisted, there was more to being a personal manager than negotiating tough deals and taking a fat commission . . . "You have to realise that what this is out here is a jungle and if you want to get from one end of it to the other—say the other is where Marilyn Monroe was, or Steve McQueen—you need a guide. The thing most people do, which is wrong, is to try the shortest distance between the two points, but that way they go right into the quicksand. Now the ones who are a little smarter, they say: 'Well, I know there's a quicksand but I've heard that if you go to the left you can get to superstardom.' So they go that way —to the left—but that's where the cannibal village is.

"So those who are *really* smart say: 'Okay, if that's the cannibal village and that's the quicksand, there's only one way to go and that's to the right.' But the right is where the crocodiles are. So they say: 'How, in heaven's name, do you get from one end to the other if all the trails are blocked?' Well, what you do is you get a professional guide—which is what I consider my job to be. I'm a professional guide through the Hollywood jungle. I know how to go a mile and a half this side of the quicksand, which takes me about seven kilometres that side of the cannibal village and three kilometres the other side of the crocodiles and around them all. To survive in Hollywood you don't necessarily have to be mean or tough or rude —you just have to know how to get from one end of the jungle to the other. But it's a very dangerous place and very few people last here very long, because usually they're swallowed up by the quicksand or eaten by the cannibals or dragged down by the crocodiles.

"What's bad about living here is that it's so competitive. Like, about two weeks ago there was a very nice story about me on the front page of one of the papers. Altogether I would say I know most of the people I ought to know in this town and I think I got four phone calls saying, 'How wonderful for you'. But I know that if I'd gone into bankruptcy or something I'd have gotten over 4,000 condolence calls. It's just that kind of town. People don't really want to wish you well, because it makes them feel that they should be where you are. But if you fall, that makes them feel better because then it's not so bad where they are. And I think that's sad."

Sometimes in a clearing in the Hollywood jungle you come across the young aspirant—an actor or actress, a singer or dancer—who has not yet attracted the attention of a personal manager but who has, nevertheless, managed to avoid the quicksands and is now trying to find a way past the cannibals. Annie Gaybis is one of these: a former beauty queen from Baltimore, a girl who can sing and dance and act and who came to Hollywood in search of the American Dream. She has not yet found it but she lives in hope and meantime she survives because she's a quick learner and at least she knows where the cannibals and the crocodiles lurk . . .

"There are three types of producer in this town," she said. "First there's the higher echelon producer. If you go up to see him for a film you don't have to worry because he gets all the action he can manage. I mean, he's either happily married or he's involved with someone he wants to be involved with because he's been in this town long enough to know his way around. Then there's the middle-line producer, a former actor or a former director of photography and with him you have to make a decision. Because if there's twenty-three girls and they're all equally talented and it's down to a choice between you and any of the others, what are you going to do to get the part? Well, if it's important enough you have to make a few personal decisions . . ."

Come, come. Not the casting couch, surely? Not that old myth?

"Oh yes. Oh, for sure. It's there. I don't know if it's really going to help or if it's really going to hurt someone. But it's there and if a girl can handle it, well, I say 'Good for you.' "

And the third type of producer?

"Oh, those are the guys with what I call Moonlight Productions or Miracle Productions. If the production comes off it's a miracle, because they've been around with the same script, the same ideas, for years. These people, they open up offices, put big notices in the

233

trade papers, they change their names and their locations and the big thing to remember, to warn you that you're dealing with a Miracle Production is when they say, 'No experience necessary'. Everyone else wants you to have tons of experience, to have films to show them and tapes to play them. But not these guys—'No experience necessary'. I fell for it, or nearly fell for it, once in my first year in Hollywood. The producer had an office in a reputable studio and I went to see him and he said, 'I want to see how you can improvise. Here's the improvisation: I'm the delivery man and you're the housewife and you and your husband have had this terrible fight and I come to do the deliveries and you want to get back at your husband. Now I've come every week to your house but this time I want you to look at me in a new way. I want you to absolutely ravish my body.' I said: 'You want *me* to ravish your body?' He said, 'Yes.' So I said, 'Do you mind if I go outside for five minutes and think about this?' And he said, 'Fine', so I left and didn't go back and I said to the people who'd sent me to him, 'Don't ever send anybody else down there because the guy's an animal.' "

The last time I saw Annie Gaybis she was wearing a short, frilly black nightdress while reclining on a perfectly ghastly pink and purple bed that looked as if it had seen active service in some low-grade bordello. The location was the Channel 11 TV studios in Hollywood; the occasion a press and TV conference for Annie and ten other young actresses who had been chosen as Channel 11's "Bed-time Movie Girls". Their task was to add extra titillation to the midnight movie by introducing it while thus attired and lying on that bed. Annie was one of 500 girls who had applied, such is the ferocity of competition in Hollywood, and she was delighted to have been chosen. Well, it wasn't a job that would win her an Oscar or an Emmy but at least it was a job. For the moment anyway the cannibals and the crocodiles were being held at bay. And she was surviving.

At the last count there were some 23,000 aspiring actors and actresses in Hollywood, nearly all of whom will be out of work most of the time and most of whom will be out of work all the time. Every waiter, waitress and car-park attendant in the place is not really a waiter or waitress or car-park attendant at all but an actor or actress waiting for the big break which, by the laws of probability, will never come. One day they'll all wake up to discover they are now forty and have hardly done a day's acting in their lives but such is the resilience of these people and such is their hunger for fame and fortune that they will carry on undeterred, the only difference being that they will now insist that they are *character* actors and actresses waiting for a break.

Why is it, though, that so many people should be prepared to waste their entire lives in pursuit of a dream that, except for a very few, is most unlikely to come true? Zsa Zsa Gabor, I think, provided the simplest and probably the truest answer.

"American people think about actors as royalty in their country," she said. "And they are."

Miss Gabor is, of course, an actress if you interpret the word with a certain amount of generosity. Certainly she has appeared in a number of films. But she is, most of all, a peculiarly Hollywood phenomenon, as famous for the number and variety of her husbands as for anything she has achieved on screen. She is a survivor, a self-made personality who, I ventured to suggest, was one of the most celebrated figures in Hollywood. She didn't take too kindly to this, feeling perhaps that I had understated the case.

"I am the *most* famous, maybe," she said.

"Well, yes," I said, accepting the reproof, "but you're much better known now as a personality, aren't you?"

"Oh, no," she said, not having that either. "I played Broadway for a year. I play every theatre in the world. I'm a very famous actress. But a personality I am because I have, thank God, personality and I am not a milktoast."

And at this point, just as I was reflecting that all this modesty must have been a handicap in her career, she proceeded to tell me how famous she was and—as a member of American royalty—how influential.

"I got Mr. Nixon in twice," she said. "I went with John Wayne and with Mr. Reagan and we campaigned for him. I still campaign for Mr. Nixon because I think he was the most intelligent president of our time. Well, you see, famous people are almost like presidents themselves. In one of my campaigning for Mr. Nixon—I campaign with Mr. Rockefeller, with Mr. Reagan and with John Wayne and Jimmy Stewart—all of a sudden the public all of a sudden screamed, 'We want Zsa Zsa Gabor as president!' And Mr. Rockefeller got up, he said, 'Now that we have our president, who is going to be our vice-president?' "

At the age of sixty-four, as celebrated as ever—president of the United States, apparently, by popular acclaim if not in fact—she says her true home is in Palm Beach, though she still has a house in Bel Air, which is where we met. By American standards it's a

mansion, an enormous place surrounded by high walls and elec-
tronically controlled gates. The wardrobe in her bedroom is huge,
a walk-in cupboard about the size of the average man's walk-in
semi-detached, housing 300, maybe 400 elaborate gowns.

A number of lissom young men, presumably on the payroll but
of indeterminate occupation, drifted about, looking decorative.

The room in which we conducted the interview—or more accurately, I suppose, she being royalty, in which the audience was
granted—was on the large side of vast and, as I remember, predominantly gold in colour. Upstairs was an equally vast games-room-
cum-bar where, as became apparent on the guided tour, one of her
dogs had crapped in the corner. I couldn't help feeling that this
rather marred the overall impression and wondered whether one of
the lissom young men might not usefully be delegated to serve as
an indoor pooper-scooper.

Miss Gabor had lately returned from a visit to England on behalf
of the World Wild Life Fund for which she is an enthusiastic worker,
arguing that, "I am not so interested in people. I am interested very
much in animals."

While in England she had, she felt, been unwarrantably snubbed
by various members of the aristocracy and grossly insulted by a
butler, so there was an acerbic, anti-British edge to her conversation.
What this butler had done, apparently, was to slide up to her while
she sat at a formal dinner and whisper in her ear: "You are just a
little bit of an actress. I should like to fuck you."

"I think," said Miss Gabor, "that he was drunk."

"I think," I said, "that he *must* have been."

Reverting, however, to that curious and essentially American
alliance of show business and politics, I enquired whether the
ultimate had been arrived at with the election of a Hollywood actor
as president of the USA.

"No," she said, "I have nothing to do with it." Nixon yes; Reagan
no. But she added magnanimously: "It just shows how wonderful
America is, how great America is that they do dare to elect an
ex-actor. America is the most wonderful country in the world. As
more as I travel, each time I come home I say to myself, 'Thank
God for America.' We have the answer how the world has to be.
We are not so snobbish—we don't have royalties. We have people
of achievement who become royalties, not people who are born to
it because the people who are born to it are too much inbred.
Achievement is the answer today. If you're a good cameraman, if
you're a good television star, if you're a good actor, a good actress,

then you achieve something. Just because you are born to the purple that doesn't make you brilliant. Napoleon's son, later on, was a nitwit."

(She didn't explain how he became a nitwit later on, having presumably not started out as one but never mind.)

Still, I said, surely there was a high price to pay for achievement, for becoming royalties. People like herself were obliged to live surrounded by a phenomenal amount of security.

"No worse than in England," she said, getting in a dig at what appeared to be currently her most unfavourite country. "Every place I go I can be robbed. I can be robbed in London. Listen, in London I was robbed by the people who rented me a car. Every time I rent a car it costs me more than for an English person. Every time I buy a Rolls-Royce—and I have three—it costs me more than for an Englishman just because I'm an American . . ."

Yes, okay, all right, already—but getting back to security . . .

"No. We have our security. When you are very famous everybody has it. Why, the Queen has security, doesn't she?"

"Indeed she does," I said. "But movie stars don't have that much security in England."

"Well," she said, triumphantly, "movie stars are not as famous in England than here . . ."

On that subject—not the comparative fame of American and English movie stars but security—exactly what kind of security are we talking about? Well, I'll give you an example.

One day I was doing some filming in Windsor Square, an area of about one square mile in old Hollywood. It's a residential district of eminently desirable properties, the houses bigger and the plots more expansive even than in Bel Air but in a way, and despite the fact that, among others, Tom Bradley, the mayor of Los Angeles, lives there, it has come down in the world because now it's surrounded on all sides by light industry and somewhat rundown commercial firms.

Just as we set the equipment up for the interview I was about to conduct a powerfully built black man, around five feet ten with a battered face and a terrifying expanse of muscle around the arms and shoulders, darted out from behind the tall metal gates of a property across the road and demanded to know, curtly and with deep suspicion, why we were filming Donna Summer's house.

I told him, truthfully, that we had no intention of filming Donna Summer's house, partly because I had no idea who Donna Summer was. (Well, pop music isn't my field.) The black man treated this explanation with much scepticism and said that if we knew what was good for us we'd go and do whatever it was we were doing someplace else.

I was inclined to tell him, loftily, that he couldn't threaten me but I knew it would be a lie. He was a very menacing figure indeed, running a little to fat around the middle perhaps but clearly a man who was quite capable of stamping on faces. He was, I noticed, wearing a T-shirt that said "Sugar Ray Leonard" across the chest. Now I knew (because I have some knowledge of boxing) that he was not himself Sugar Ray Leonard but assumed that at some time he had served as one of that great man's sparring partners. And it occurred to me to wonder, if the sparring partner was so terrifying, what on earth Sugar Ray Leonard must have been like in his prime.

Anyway, discretion prevailed over any faint stirrings of valour, and we moved, and this bruiser went back to join a couple of identical bruisers who were lolling about among the Cadillacs in Ms. Summer's spacious driveway. They were none of them, as far as I could see, armed but they were certainly bodyguards and it struck me as both alarming and depressing that a popular and harmless singer, however talented and successful, should need this kind of protection.

Well, as it happened, Gabe Thierry—the man I had been about to interview when we were so brusquely interrupted—had the explanation. Gabe Thierry is an extremely fit young man who works as a patrolman for Westec, one of the numerous private security forces that make up what might well be the fastest growing industry in Los Angeles. He wears a tan uniform, carries both a handgun and a baton and Windsor Square is his beat.

In a sense Westec and its rival companies amount almost to private police forces, financed by the thousands of firms and private householders who subscribe to them, and it's widely accepted that their existence is absolutely necessary to protect the well-to-do of Hollywood, Beverly Hills and Bel Air. But if such outfits are indeed necessary what, you may ask, are the police doing?

Well, the answer is, I suppose, that they're doing their best. (Or at least most of them are, although at the time of which I write the main story in the *Los Angeles Times* claimed that the cops in the Hollywood Division of the LA Police Department were the best organised and most successful burglars in the whole city.) But even counting the bent coppers, the police force is hopelessly understaffed, so understaffed in fact that the Beverly Hills fuzz employed Burt Reynolds in a TV commercial begging for recruits; so understaffed that on a bad day an urgent complaint from a private citizen that even now a heavily armed burglar was chopping down his back door with every apparent intent of inflicting the maximum possible mayhem might not get a response for about half an hour. But with Westec, or a kindred outfit, an alarm call would, according to Gabe Thierry, produce a patrol car skidding to a halt at your front door within one to three minutes.

As we drove around Windsor Square—keeping an eye open for a reportedly suspicious character in a blue track suit who had been seen on one of the sidestreets, heading south—I asked Mr. Thierry whether celebrities actually needed more protection than other people.

"Sure they do," he said. "They're more vulnerable. They have a lot and everyone knows they do. Also, due to their profession, they're not around their houses that much, so during the time they're gone that's when they become particularly vulnerable. And that's where we come in, because we watch the houses by means of an intensive patrol and that keeps them safer."

(Mind you, the private security forces are only a part of the protection that many of the celebrities use. Apart from employing armed guards day and night, a great number of them also provide their chauffeurs with sawn-off shotguns and equip their cars with "panic buttons"—electronic devices that set up a piercing scream for help in the event of an attempted mugging or kidnapping. There are those who believe that such precautions are wildly excessive, that the danger is not really that great. But perhaps if you're a big celebrity in Hollywood, a touch of paranoia goes with the territory.)

The streets of Windsor Square are wide and spacious, adequately provided with sidewalks. But there, as in Beverly Hills and all the other posh residential areas in and around Hollywood, the only people who actually walked were gardeners, postmen and the like. (In Beverly Hills one day I even saw a jogging postman, track suit, training shoes—the lot—delivering the mail at a smart canter.) One of the reasons for the general absence of pedestrians is that people are, to say the least, strongly discouraged by the police forces and the private security patrols from walking anywhere, especially after dark. The attitude seems to be that anyone caught walking is presumably unable to afford a car and if you can't afford a car in the Hollywood area you must be a bum and a bum walking in, let us say, Beverly Hills, is clearly up to no good. The idea that some people walk simply because they enjoy it doesn't appear to have occurred to anyone.

I asked Gabe Thierry what would happen if he found me, shortly after dusk, strolling around Windsor Square, casually dressed in shirt and jeans. Would he stop me?

"Yes," he said, "you'd find yourself talking to us. We'd stop you and ask to see some kind of identification, ask what you were doing in the area and generally treat you very well but try to determine why you were there and identify you. Then if there was any crime reported in the area during that period you'd be called in as a suspect."

"Isn't it," I said, "an awful reflection on the times we live in that people can't go out for a walk even in their own neighbourhoods?"

"Absolutely," he said. "In this area and Beverly Hills you'll see people walking down the street with golf clubs and canes. And they don't use the canes because they limp or the clubs because they're going to practise putting—they're carrying these weapons for personal defence."

What though would be the difference, if any, in the kind of crime committed in Windsor Square and an equally affluent area such as Beverly Hills?

"Well," he said, "here you have the criminal element coming from outside—people who don't belong in the area, who stick out like a sore thumb. It's easy to detect them as being criminals. Here, if you see someone walking down the street and he doesn't look affluent and he's not a gardener, the chances are he's a burglar and if you watch him long enough you'll be able to catch him in the act. Now in Beverly Hills, it's a lot more difficult to detect the criminal because a lot of the time he lives in the area, belongs there, fades into the atmosphere. The kind of thing you would have, for example, would be a rich person's son who's a drug addict and can't go and ask daddy for 500 dollars for his daily fix, so instead he goes out burglarising his next-door neighbour or his best friend from school."

As we drove around Gabe Thierry's patch the streets were silent save for the buzz of lawn mowers and the tinkle of water sprinklers; his seemed rather a peaceful occupation. Well, he said, not all the time . . . In the last six months he had come close to being stabbed twice, had apprehended two armed intruders who, fortunately, had surrendered their guns on demand and had an alarming encounter with a girl high on angel dust, one of the most pernicious of drugs.

"It gives someone the strength of ten men," he said, "and allows them to do things that are phenomenal, such as breaking handcuffs. In the process they usually break their own wrists but they become extremely violent and extremely strong."

The girl in question, clad only in a swimsuit, had driven through the gate of a complete stranger at sixty-five miles an hour, broken into the house, taken over an upstairs bedroom, rolled in the ashes in the fireplace and taken to yelling obscenities from the window. When Gabe and his partner attempted to reason with her she had laid out the partner—an ex-policeman, a six-footer weighing about 200 pounds—with a crisp right hook. The woman herself was only about five feet eight inches tall.

"In the end," Gabe Thierry said, "it took five of us to get her into a police car. We had to use two sets of handcuffs on her arms, because she was so strong, and we also had to restrain her around the knees and ankles. Oh yes, we really see life around here, absolutely."

What we didn't see, though, was any sign of the man in the blue track suit, heading south. But he was probably only a jogger anyway.

At a garden party in Beverly Hills one lunch time, Henry Winkler, star of *Happy Days*, one of the longest-running shows on American TV, remarked: "In this town you don't get to make that many mistakes. Most of our entertainment is based on the dollar, so if a show doesn't make a lot of money then, 'It was nice to know you and goodbye and good luck.' And then the people you thought were such good friends won't return your calls."

Which brings us to the other prevailing fear in Hollywood—the fear of failure. Failure is regarded thereabouts as practically a contagious disease; people will literally cross the street to avoid greeting someone who is tainted with it, whose movie has just bombed or whose TV series has been pulled. If you're a failure in Hollywood, even if you're also a star name, people don't recognise you, you can't get a table in the smart restaurants, you aren't invited to the parties or the premières. You aren't even invited to the *funerals*, for God's sake.

One night I went to a party given in honour of Charlton Heston and in the course of the evening an old friend of his, an elderly actor who had once been a considerable star himself but who had not been in any kind of demand for some years, drifted in. Heston greeted him warmly and the two of them stood in the middle of the room chatting and reminiscing while the TV cameras and the press photographers recorded the meeting. After a few minutes one of

Heston's entourage, who had been watching the proceedings with increasing concern, summoned a minion. "Get that bum out of there," he muttered. "Get him away from Chuck. Get somebody else in."

"Yeah, right. Ah, who do you want in?"

"Anybody!"

So the elderly star was led firmly away in the direction of the bar and young Christopher Atkins was put alongside Heston in his place. Now the effects of this switch of personnel were twofold: Heston was no longer seen to be associating with failure but, and this was much more upbeat, was being projected as someone who, despite his seniority in Hollywood, was still in touch with youth and promise. And Atkins, who played opposite Brooke Shields in *The Blue Lagoon* and is one of the current crop of good-looking young Hollywood newcomers, was being presented as a kid who was already accepted by the Establishment in the person of Heston, the old lion.

The former star understood what had happened. He had one drink at the bar and then quietly, almost unnoticed, he left.

The question is: what can you do to insure yourself against this kind of humiliation ever being visited upon you? And the answer is: you can't. All you can do is surround yourself with the best help and advice available. Business managers, personal managers, public relations people—yes, all those. But first and most important of all you need an agent, a very, very good agent.

In Hollywood power is cyclical, depending on whether you have a buyer's market (when there are more actors available than jobs) or a seller's market. In a buyer's market obviously the employers, the producers, have the muscle and most people seem to agree that a buyer's market prevails right now. But whatever the state of the market the one group of people who never really lose power is the agents. "Most agents," said Jay Bernstein, "have larger egos than the actors they represent." And perhaps this is understandable: in a seller's market the agents dominate the producers; in a buyer's market they dominate the stars. Neither way can they lose.

Sue Mengers is one of the top agents in Hollywood. She lives in Bel Air in a bigger house than, I fancy, many of her clients can afford. Apart from negotiating the best terms she can possibly squeeze from a reluctant employer, she sees her job as that of adviser to her clients rather than arbiter. "I have clients who listen to my opinion but really do very much what they want and I have other clients who take my opinion more seriously. The artistes' instincts are usually pretty sound about what they can be good in and what they can't."

But if an actor finds himself in a real flop, does he ever go to her and say: "Why the hell did you let me do this?"

"Occasionally," she said, sweetly, "but they're not with us any more."

On the day I talked to Sue Mengers she was also visited by one of her clients, Ali MacGraw, one of the most intelligent and therefore attractive, actresses in Hollywood. She's had an up and down career, starting strongly with *Goodbye Columbus* and *Love Story*, establishing herself in *The Getaway* and then partially fading from sight during the time she was married to Steve McQueen, when she chose to work very little.

On this occasion she had been summoned by her agent to discuss a TV mini-series she had just completed and also a new film script that she had been offered. Both Miss MacGraw and Miss Mengers were optimistic about the TV series and doubtful about the film script.

Their conference, to which I was invited to listen, perhaps gives some indication of the adviser/arbiter side of an agent's work. They began by talking about the film script, which Miss MacGraw seemed inclined to turn down in the hope that the TV series would do so well that bigger and better offers would ensue. In part the discussion went like this . . .

Sue Mengers: Alice, I am so thrilled after seeing some of the rushes and stuff of the series and therefore I think you're right in waiting until it opens.

Ali MacGraw: It's a real gamble. I'd really rather—wouldn't we always?—find something wonderful, whatever it might be—television or film or whatever—than just work for work's sake. I mean, it's such a temptation to say, "Oh, I haven't worked in a *year*! I've got to do *something*." So I'm . . . I'm relieved you said what you did.

Sue M: And don't forget they're going to be wanting you for a lot of press interviews so for the few months before the series starts you're going to have to devote so much time to travelling and publicising it. I just don't think it makes a lot of sense for you to be rushing into a picture and from a picture into a publicity tour.

Ali Mac: It would be a pity to be in just an okay movie, which is what I really think this is. I wish I could tell you that I loved it . . .

(Up to this point they had been in agreement: the TV series—"several nights of saturation, prime-time television"—was a good thing; the movie was a bad thing. But now Miss Mengers, the agent, clearly felt obliged to point out the advantages of doing the film.)

Sue M: It's a lot of money. It's a *lot* of money . . .

Ali Mac: And I need to pay some bills, right? (She laughed.) What about a waitress job?

Sue M: I think we have a lot of time before we have to think about that.

Ali Mac: I hope you're right. But the thing I would love to find if it were possible and gosh, I know this is the worst time in the movies . . . what I'd love to find is either another extraordinary mini-series or—and this is what we always talk about—a good script, without which I might as well forget it, having done a couple of the all-time terrible scripts . . .

(The film script under review, whatever it was, seemed to fall somewhere in that vast chasm between good and all-time terrible, which is where most movie scripts are to be found. So should she do the picture or not? Miss Mengers said it would start shooting in September, which was a little early. Ideally, they wanted something to begin in January—when the TV series would be aired—so that nobody would be asking, "Okay, so what's she gonna do next?" There was a possible English film whose shooting dates seemed to fit in . . .)

Ali Mac: Perfect. It would be perfect. But (and here she harked back to the current offer) it's such a temptation . . .

Sue M: It's a very hard decision.

Ali Mac: It's such a temptation because there comes that moment when you say, "Oh, I *really* should be making money." You know that I've never been the sort of person who needs the ego reassurance of back-to-back commitments. But there's that moment of terror when you say, "Well, I haven't made any money in, what, six months," and I need you badly to say what you just said.

Sue M: Well, also it should be very flattering to your ego to know that you've gotten a sizeable money offer that you're turning down for the right reasons. So you know it's out there, it's not as though it doesn't exist. You've just chosen to turn it down, that's all.

Ali Mac: You know what I think? I hope you don't think it's silly but . . . as you know I did that documentary on lions and wild life conservation in Kenya for no money because they said, "Would you go to Kenya?" and I said, "Well, just so long as I can take my son with me." And I'd rather be doing something like that in the meantime and getting my head filled than being the girl in a man's movie.

Sue M: And that's what this is—there's no question about it.

Ali Mac: I know, I know.

Sue M: There's *no* question about it . . .

So Ali MacGraw turned down the movie and waited for the mini-series to open, because "I have a feeling it's going to be amazing. If I'm not good in it I should say it will be harder and harder for me to get work." She said: "I'm not quite in the position I was, say, right after *Love Story* or *The Getaway*." So she needed it to be amazing to re-establish her at the top.

Unfortunately the mini-series in question was *The Winds of War* which, though financially successful, was universally derided by the critics. And, alas, most unfairly and most unkindly the worst of the adverse reviews—in America at least, though not in Britain—were directed at Ali MacGraw.

It just shows that the instincts even of the best agents and most intelligent actresses are not always right and that there is no insurance against failure. The English picture didn't happen. Maybe Ali should have made that other movie after all . . .

The latest Hollywood diet, so they say, is a glass of Perrier water and a line of cocaine. Cocaine is the "in" drug of the 1980s. Here's Annie Gaybis on the subject . . .

"It's like passing the salt and pepper at a luncheonette, really. I've been offered a lot. I'm not on these things but I've been offered a lot of stuff when I've just been on readings where they had maybe run down a little bit—the casting director or producer—and they open up their little drawer, they take out a little bottle with some white powder in it and instead of saying, like they used to say, 'Would you like something to drink? Would you like a coffee?' they say, 'Would you like some?' and I see them take it right in front of me. Even though I say no they take it and they go on like nothing has happened."

The summer—particularly June and July—is "hiatus" time on TV, holiday time. It's also "renewal time", the time when the networks decide which shows to retain and which to drop and which new series to develop. There's a lot of panic on the streets around June and July, a lot of careers in the balance.

The three networks—ABC, NBC and CBS—will have commissioned between them around 500 scripts. Each script will have cost them perhaps 20,000 or 25,000 dollars—small beer to the networks. Of those 500 scripts 100 will be made into pilots and if the pilot is successful it will be developed into a series. Maybe twenty of those pilots will be deemed to have worked and so twenty new series hit the air in the autumn—and 480 scriptwriters, their dreams shattered, return to the storyboard.

Meanwhile, what of the people currently employed in series whose future is doubtful, series that may be dropped to make way for one of the new twenty?

"Yeah, well," said Angie Dickinson, "renewal time for TV series, when that show is maybe the only way you're known, that can be an awful time. And sometimes they wait until the last minute to tell you and that's tough. When you really don't know—and you don't know whether to buy the new house or the new car or go on a trip or have the baby's teeth fixed because you literally don't know if you're gonna be renewed, that's very tough."

Angie Dickinson has had the experience both of being renewed and not renewed. She starred for a long time in the very successful *Police Woman* series and then, for a much shorter time, in the awful *Cassie and Company*. Recovering from a flop and having your series dropped is much like being thrown from a horse—you have to remount swiftly or you might lose your nerve with the added danger, in TV, that if you don't remount swiftly you could vanish into oblivion. The man who said that in Hollywood you can be forgotten while you leave the room to go to the toilet was not entirely joking.

Miss Dickinson is in little danger of being forgotten; she's been a star of movies and television for thirty years but even for her there are no special dispensations. The competition is as tough for an Angie Dickinson as it is for anyone else.

She said: "They sent me a script last Thursday and I read it and it was wonderful and the producer was positive that they wanted me. But on Friday they called and they said, 'Oh, wait a minute, we're not sure now because ABC wants somebody else.' I said, you know 'That's okay, that's fine, there's nothing I can do about it and it's all right.' So it got pulled out from under me and so I'm not immune either."

What makes it worse is that there are no secrets in Hollywood, no shrouds under which a flop can be decently concealed. The two daily newspapers and the various trade papers and magazines publicise failure as prominently as success.

Bud Yorkin, a prominent producer/director in film and TV, said: "If you don't know what the other guy's doing it doesn't bother you as much, I guess. But when you look around and each day you're being fed the knowledge of someone else's success, well I think it does breed a certain desperation."

It sometimes seemed to me, I said, that nobody hates a loser as much as people in Hollywood do.

Bud Yorkin disagreed: "I think it's the other way round. I think people gain solace from other people's misery. Because if they're not doing well—their picture or their series didn't get made—they're looking to the other guy to fail, too, because that makes them feel better psychologically."

Charlton Heston had told me that Hollywood was a great town to be rich in but he would think—and he couldn't speak from experience because it had never happened to him—a very bad town to be poor in. Bud Yorkin agreed. "You know, it isn't apartment-house living here; primarily you have to have your own house and you have to be able to keep up with your friends. And sometimes your friends aren't your friends any more when you're not on the top of the ladder."

In Hollywood a man is what he owns. When the late Marty Feldman first arrived in town he drove everywhere in a Chevrolet. It was the biggest car he had ever possessed and he was extremely proud of it —until one day a senior executive at one of the studios took him aside and said: "Marty, you gotta get rid of that Chevvy. It's bad for your image. *Anyone* can have a Chevvy but a man in your position, you should be driving a Rolls."

My brother-in-law Bernard Williams, producer of *The Bounty*, moved to Hollywood from London a few years ago and bought a house at Encino in the San Fernando Valley. It's a very nice house indeed and he happily told all his friends and acquaintances about it. One of them, a top man in a film studio, listened anxiously.

"Bernie," he said, "this house—is it north or south of Ventura Boulevard?"

"Er, south," said Bernie.

The top man gave a little grunt of relief. "That's okay then," he said. Now the houses north of Ventura Boulevard are quite as nice as the houses south of Ventura Boulevard. But south of Ventura is socially acceptable, while north of Ventura—well, you might as well be dead.

Hollywood, you see, is an élite society without roots; it consists almost exclusively of immigrants from other places and has no historical perspective. So the philosophy of the good time and the fast buck prevails and everyone is judged on appearances. What you do is less important than how well you appear to be doing. If you can't afford to buy a Rolls-Royce, then you must lease a Rolls-Royce. Nobody will know it doesn't belong to you and besides the cost is tax deductible. Actor A will get a part in preference to actor B because he traditionally commands a higher salary and must therefore be a better actor. And so it goes up the scale: a man with two million dollars in the bank is only a winner when compared to a man with one million dollars in the bank. Compared to a man with three million dollars, he's a loser.

And so scores of enterprising shopkeepers and designers have established service industries to help the denizens of Hollywood flaunt their wealth even more openly. For example at Bejan on Rodeo Drive (possibly the most expensive men's outfitters in the world) you can buy an off-the-peg suit for 4,000 dollars, a mink-lined silk raincoat for 17,000 dollars, a chinchilla bedspread for 95,000 dollars or—and perhaps this could be the ultimate in status symbols —a twenty-four carat gold revolver, one of a numbered and limited edition of 200.

Who could possibly need such a thing is hard to say but presumably it might be used by one man in a Bejan suit while he mugs another man in a Bejan suit.

Ah, but wait . . . Perhaps a golden revolver is not quite the ultimate for the man who has more money than he knows what to do with. Consider the possibilities of a fully-equipped discotheque, constructed in the style of ancient Egypt (and never mind the fact that discotheques must have been comparatively rare in ancient Egypt) in *your own home* Alan Carr, the man behind *Grease* and other such films, has one of these, designed for him by Phyllis Morris.

Miss Morris is one of the best known designers in Hollywood and she has clients to match—Barbra Streisand, Hugh Hefner, Bernie Cornfeld and the like. And what she does, she says, is "try to give them the kind of fantasies they want and can afford and most of our people can afford to have just about anything they want."

Alan Carr, apparently, is hooked on the Cecil B. de Mille period of Hollywood—"all those great extravaganzas along the Nile, where everything was just very majestic and full of costumes and emperors and everything. And I think Alan visualises himself as living that kind of life, at least for a couple of hours a week when he's having a party down here in his basement." (The basement is where the discotheque is; before it was a discotheque it was a three-car garage.)

Other clients have other fantasies . . . "Harold Robbins, for instance, wanted to live the life of the kind of people he writes about. And so at his home in Beverly Hills we gave him this most majestic place with this fabulous master suite, with a fifty-foot mirrored ceiling and a satin bed, lit from underneath as though it's floating. And you look up into the mirror and you not only see yourself but you see the entire city of Beverly Hills reflected in it."

Well, no home should be without a bedroom like that. Not that any other home is ever likely to have one because Phyllis Morris deals only in one-offs. Harold Robbins' bedroom, she said, was his "statement" and she would never attempt to duplicate it for anybody else, just as she would never design another disco like Alan Carr's. "It's one of his little toys. He owns it. He paid for it. He wanted it. He got just what he wanted."

But not all her clients know precisely what they want. Sometimes they go to her, muttering vaguely, "Well, you know, I want it big and I want it soft and I want it gorgeous and I want the lights and I want . . ." and she takes it from there. In other words, I suggested, the clients provided the money and she provided the taste.

"No," she said, "they provide their dreams. The dreams of Hollywood are very important. This is a city that's built on dreams. I mean, this is not a *real* city; this is not Chicago or Cincinnati. This is very special. Once it was just another farm area with orange groves and horses where Hollywood Boulevard now is. But when the Hollywood people came here with their cameras and their films they brought a dream quality with them which they transmitted to the rest of the world and show business became part of people's lives. Even the doctors and the lawyers and the plumbers here, they're all living a dream. The plumber goes home and tells whose toilet he cleaned out that day and that's his big thrill. It's all part of the make-believe."

But if the plumbers and the lawyers and the doctors are led to believe by the works of Phyllis Morris and Bejan and their rivals and contemporaries that the stars lead glamorous lives, they are probably wrong.

"Most of the stars do *not* lead glamorous lives," said Miss Morris. "Most of the people on the edges, the producers, the writers, lead more glamorous lives than they do. The stars, for the most part, are wondering where their next picture is coming from . . ."

Annie Gaybis on movie stars . . .

"Last year I dated an actor—a big mistake, folks, if you're an actress. A *big* mistake. Dating an actor is about dating one of the most insecure people in the whole, entire world. I thought girls were insecure but dating an *actor* . . . I dated a very well known actor, known in London and known in America and—no names, please—an older, wiser, wealthier man that I'd been in love with from all the 2 a.m. movies I'd seen him in on TV. Well, when I started to date him I found out that he was very insecure about his looks (because he was ageing, though he looked fabulous); about his career, even though he had invested wisely and had a beautiful home and could buy any car he wanted at any time; and about the loyalty of his fans because they were getting older as he was getting older. And he was into things that were problems, things that I couldn't deal with—drugs and things and I wasn't into that sort of stuff . . . and dating an actor doesn't lead to any big roles, you know, because they don't want you to be more successful than them. They want the girl to be not successful and they want her to stay not successful and they want her to maybe ask for small favours from time to time, just so they can say, 'Well, darling, I can't do anything about it. This deal was closed by my agent and these people are all in Europe and such and such.' Now dating a producer, and I mean an established person, well he'd do anything to try to help you because that's a coup for him—to put you in a film in which you do wonderful and you get a terrific little notice, that's also wonderful for him because he's establishing a new name. But an *actor*—he's only worried about re-establishing his own . . ."

Hollywood has always been a self-admiring place, a society of Narcissi beating each other to death. On the surface it's a laidback town, a town where, so it has been sardonically said, they put valium in the drinking water. But beneath that surface . . . ah, beneath the surface neurosis rages. When David Niven said that he had lived in Hollywood for twenty years without once consulting a psychiatrist, he was speaking of a rare accomplishment. Nearly everyone in Hollywood consults a psychiatrist and the one they consult as often as any is Dr. Irene Kassorla, who is widely known as "the shrink to the stars" and as such has become something of a celebrity herself. Every day on a nationwide phone-in on KABC Radio in Hollywood she advises humbler people on their problems —emotional, psychological and sexual.

She enjoyed her fame, she said . . . "Fame is . . . is delicious. You know, it feels like you're the president of the class and the class is the world. It's fun."

Yes, no doubt. But what of her celebrated clients—do they, too, enjoy their fame? Well, she said, "they're very sweet and very fragile . . ."

Fragile? How?

"They're very needy. They need approval so desperately. I think everyone needs approval and I think needing approval is healthy. But perhaps the person who rises above the crowd has a little more intelligence and a little more need for approval."

That need for approval can be reflected in many ways and can lead people to somewhat excessive lengths. It has often occurred to me that in Hollywood the second greatest sin was to be old but the greatest sin of all was to look old. Dr. Kassorla didn't quite agree with that. She believed that the people there were more beautiful, better dressed, better groomed than in most other places anyway. But she conceded that "There is a tendency for people not to want to look old. Men and women colour their hair and probably more women wear make-up here than, say, in the mid-West. So there is an emphasis on appearance and it's very common to have something altered. Because I treat so many stars I'm very much involved with plastic surgery, both for men and women. The noses get done, this gets done, that gets done, and there is a great deal of alteration to make people look more attractive. It's very strange in other parts of the country, unheard of—but here it has become part of the culture."

Well, that, too, seemed to me to be part of the underlying neurosis, the fear of ageing, of losing out to someone who looks younger than you do. Dr. Kassorla, however, thought that the basic anxiety in Hollywood had another cause.

"I think there is a lot of fear because there are so many people and so few jobs and there's this phenomenon of, you know, heads rolling. At one time I was treating several people in the tower at Universal. (The tower is the executive block of Universal Studios.) And one year I had several executives as clients and the next year they were gone. They were fired. So there is that kind of fear. There's very little security for tomorrow in some jobs here."

At that time the death of the actor John Belushi from a massive overdose of drugs was still being discussed and analysed in the newspapers and on TV, not simply as an isolated incident but as an indication of the extent to which drugs were used in Hollywood. Dr. Kassorla pointed out that it would be a grave mistake to assume that every celebrity in the place was using the things but . . .

"Many of them suffer because they're not used to the kudos, they're not used to the fame, they're not used to the gorgeous feelings or to the marvellous things that happen to them."

In a large number of cases, she said, the stars had started off by having to struggle; for a long time they were accustomed to life being tough, both emotionally and financially. "And then, all of a sudden, they're thrust up here, where there's a great deal of money and everybody loves you. But they have the behaviour pattern to be down there and they can't quite adjust. So they create the pain—and drugs *are* pain, you know: they destroy your sexual performance, they destroy your mind. But they're also a way to get back to that place you're used to, where it's painful and where you feel you belong.

"The stars who suffer from drug addiction as adults suffered from something else as children. They may have been battered emotionally or physically; they may have been homely or had great difficulty at school. And then they get older and suddenly become stars and they have no skills to deal with this. They have the skills to be battered—so they batter themselves. And the drugs serve that purpose. Because when they're high, they feel good but the moment they come down they feel so inadequate and terrible and that's when the self-flagellation comes in. It's almost like them saying to themselves: how could you do that; why do you do the drugs, you darned fool?"

And so they use the drugs both to escape the fears and anxieties of being successful and to punish themselves for having had the effrontery to climb so high. As Dr. Kassorla said: "It's a very sad way to live." It's also a very sad way to die.

I would not wish however to give the impression that the entire population of Hollywood reels about, perpetually stoned out of its collective mind. Drugs are almost certainly more prevalent *there* than anywhere else in America but what most people are high on is optimism. As the British actress Juliet Mills put it: "There's a lot of unhappiness, there's a lot of envy, there's a lot of greed. But the people who do make it give others hope. It's like the football pools—you know, 'If he can do it there's still a chance that I can do it.'"

So to that extent I suppose that insofar as any such place can exist Hollywood is indeed the land of opportunity and those who have made it there, especially in show business, do appear to enjoy a kind of rich lifestyle and a degree of adulation that would be hard to find anywhere else. So it could be said that these fortunate people have indeed achieved the American Dream.

Ah, but what exactly *is* the American Dream? I find it hard to escape the conviction that it has hardly anything to do with accomplishment and almost everything to do with materialism. And a dream that aspires to nothing much more than fame and wealth is surely an empty sort of dream. All right, if the alternatives are obscurity and poverty then I daresay most of us would settle for fame and wealth but it's wise, I think, always to bear in mind the other side of the dream. Talking of his industry, the film industry, the director Peter Bogdanovich said: "I don't imagine we're any worse than any other big business except that we deal in people's lives and people's careers in a much more vulgar and exploitative way. The thing we're manufacturing really is people and the thing we're destroying is people, too." Success in Hollywood is much more visible than it is anywhere else; but then so, too, is failure—hence the constant fear of failure, the daily diet of terror that Jay Bernstein mentioned. To live with that, as so many people do, strikes me as an inordinately high price to pay for even the starriest success.

Index

ABC network, 246, 247
Actors' Studio, 63
Adams, Constance *see* De Mille, Constance
Adams, Neile *see* McQueen, Neile
Adams, Shirlee Mae *see* Fonda, Shirlee Mae
Alamo, The, 144, 145, 146
All the Winners, 28
Allen, Gracie, 208
Ambler, Eric, 36
American Federation of Radio Artists, 179
American Film Institute, 116
Annabella, 98
Apfel, Oscar, 164
Appointment with Venus, 40
Archard, Amy, 219–20
Armstrong, Louis, 218
Around the World in Eighty Days, 41, 44
Astaire, Fred, 219
Atkins, Christopher, 242

Bailey, Mildred, 197
Ball, Lucille, 98
Barbary Coast, 32
Barris, Harry, 198, 200, 203–4
Batjac Productions, 142, 145
Baur, Esperanza *see* Wayne, Esperanza
Bedtime Story, 46
Belasco, David, 162, 163, 165, 166
Belushi, John, 256
Bennett, Joan, 100
Bennett, Tony, 225
Benny, Jack, 224
Berlin, Irving, 216
Bernstein, Jay, 231–3, 242, 253
Better Late than Never, 48
Big Broadcast, The, 204
Big Jim McClain, 142
Big Trail, The, 132
Bing Crosby's Washington State, 222
Bishop's Wife, The, 38
Blanchard, Susan *see* Fonda, Susan
Blob, The, 65
Blow Ye Winds (play), 99
Blue Lagoon, The, 242
Bodeen, De Witt, 167, 179

Bogart, Humphrey, 86
Bogdanovich, Peter, 253
Boles, John, 199
Bond, Derek, 161
Bond, Ward, 112, 135
Bonjour Tristesse, 42
Bonny Prince Charlie, 38–9
Bounty, The, 251
Boyer, Charles, 41
Bradley, Tom, 241
Brando, Dorothy, 93
Brando, Marlon, 46, 68, 93, 218
Brannigan, 149
Bring on the Empty Horses (Niven), 24, 47
Brokaw, Frances Seymour *see* Fonda, Frances Seymour
Brokaw, George, 98
Brokaw, Tom, 22
Brunswick Records, 204
Brynner, Yul, 68
Buccaneer, The, 184
Bullitt, 66, 71, 74, 75
Burns, George, 208
Burton, Richard, 44

CBS network, 66, 202, 204, 246
Cabot, Bruce, 136
Cagney, James, 209
Cahill, 148
Caine Mutiny Court Martial, The (play), 106
Cancel My Reservation, 222
Capra, Frank, 187
Cardinale, Claudia, 126
Carey, Harry, Jr, 135, 136, 139, 140, 152
Carlisle, Mary, 204–5
Carmen, 165
Carr, Alan, 248, 249
Carrington VC, 41
Carroll, Carroll, 202, 211–12, 213, 214, 215, 217, 226
Cassie and Company (TV series), 246
Cast a Giant Shadow, 151
Cat on a Hot Tin Roof, 42
Central Casting, 31
Chaplin, Charles, 160
Charge of the Light Brigade, The, 32–3

Cheat, The, 165
Churchill, Sir Winston, 130
Cincinnati Kid, The, 58, 70, 73–4
Cinerama's Russian Adventure, 222
Circus World, 126
Cleopatra, 174, 175
Clooney, Rosemary, 221, 223, 224, 225, 226, 227
Clothier, Bill, 136
Coburn, James, 58, 66, 70, 75, 80–1
Coca, Imogene, 97
Cohn, Harry, 133
Colbert, Claudette, 174
College Humour, 204–5
Collins, Joan, 218
Colman, Ronald, 30, 33, 41
Columbia Pictures, 32, 133
Como, Perry, 225
Comyn-Platt, Lady Henrietta *see* Niven, Henrietta
Comyn-Platt, Sir Thomas, 24, 25
Connolly, Marc, 97
Cooper, Gary, 97, 132, 141, 205
Cornfeld, Bernie, 253
Corrigan, Ray, 134
Country Girl, The, 217–18, 225
Coward, Noel, 36, 151
Cowboys, 148, 152
Crawford, Julia, 59
Crawford, Victor, 59
Crosby, Bing, 7, 8
    character, 194, 200, 201, 206–8, 212–13, 214, 219, 220–21, 226–7
    early life, 194–6
    early films, 199, 200, 204
    box office success, 205
    begins the "*Road . . .*" series, 208
    records "White Christmas", 209
    makes *Going My Way*, 209–11
    peak years, 213–14
    acting ability, 217, 225, 227–8
    as a popular singer, 200, 225–6, 228
Crosby, Bob, 195, 205, 224
Crosby, Dennis, 205, 213
Crosby, Dixie (Wilma Winifred Wyatt), 200, 201, 202, 203, 205–6, 208, 214, 215, 216, 217, 221, 224
Crosby, Everett, 204
Crosby, Gary, 195, 202–3, 205–7, 208, 213, 214, 215, 220–1, 226–7
Crosby, Harry Lillis, Jr, 218, 220, 221, 223, 227
Crosby, Harry Lowe, 195, 196
Crosby, Kate, 195, 196, 207, 210

Crosby, Kathryn, 216, 217, 218–19, 220, 221, 223, 224, 226, 227
Crosby, Lindsay, 205, 215
Crosby, Mary Frances, 218, 220, 222, 224
Crosby, Mary Rose, 224
Crosby, Nathaniel, 218, 220
Crosby, Philip, 205, 213
Curtis, Tony, 42
Curtiz, Michael, 32

Dailey, Dan, 41
Damita, Lily, 34
Daniels, Bebe, 200
Davies, Marion, 197
Davis, Bette, 99, 100
Day, Chico, 172, 173, 176, 185
De Mille, Agnes, 162, 163, 167, 168, 174, 175, 178, 185, 186, 187
De Mille, Beatrice, 162
De Mille, Cecil Blount, 9, 249
    early years, 161–2
    success of *The Squaw Man*, 163–4
    character, 165, 169, 171, 172, 173, 175, 176, 177, 185, 186, 187, 188
    and *The Ten Commandments*, 169–70, 183–4
    and *King of Kings*, 170, 171
    political involvement, 179–81
    wins Oscar, 183–4
De Mille, Cecilia, 168, 176, 185
De Mille, Constance, 166, 167, 168
De Mille, Henry, 161
De Mille, John, 168
De Mille, Katherine, 168, 171, 172, 176, 184
De Mille, Richard, 168
De Mille, William, 162
De Sylva, Buddy, 210
Dean, James, 68, 86
Deer Hunter, The, 150
Defiant Ones, The, 42
Denham Studios, 36
Devine, Andy, 135
Dickinson, Angie, 246–7
Dietrich, Marlene, 139
Dixie Dynamite, 81–2
Don't Change Your Husband, 168
Double or Nothing, 205
Douglas, Kirk, 151
Douglas, Melvyn, 63
Drums Along the Mohawk, 101
Dunaway, Faye, 85
Dwan, Allan, 140
Dynamite, 174

Dynasty (TV series), 231

E.T., 230
Eisenstein, Sergei, 187
Ekins, Bud, 58, 66, 67, 81
Elusive Pimpernel, The, 39
Enemy of the People, An, 82
Evans, Joshua, 79
Evans, Linda, 231
Evans, Robert, 79

Fairbanks, Douglas, Jr, 28, 29, 38, 39, 43, 200
Farmer Takes a Wife, The, 97
Farmer Takes a Wife, The (play), 97
Farrar, Geraldine, 165
Fawcett, Farrah, 231, 232
Faye, Alice, 217, 219
Faye, Julia, 167, 173, 179
Feather in her Hat, A, 32
Feldman, Marty, 247
Field, Shirley Anne, 69
55 Days in Peking, 46
First Artists, 82
First Monday in October (play), 115
First of the Few, The, 35
Fisher, Alan, 218, 221, 223
Fleming, Victor, 97
Flynn, Errol, 33, 34
Fonda, Afdera, 96, 100, 109–12, 113, 114
Fonda, Amy, 106, 108
Fonda, Frances Seymour, 98, 99, 100, 102, 103–4, 105
Fonda, Harriet, 93
Fonda, Henry, 8
    character, 92–3, 94, 102, 103, 104–5, 108, 109, 110, 112, 113
    childhood, 93
    acting ability, 97, 114–16, 119
    first films, 97–8, 100
    war service, 101–2
    and *Mister Roberts* episode, 106–7
    illness, 115, 116, 118
    reconciliation with daughter, 117
    awards, 116, 118–19
Fonda, Herberta, 93
Fonda, Jane, 99, 100, 103, 105, 108, 111, 112, 116, 117, 118
Fonda, Jayne, 93
Fonda, Margaret, 95, 96, 99, 100
Fonda, Peter, 99, 100, 102, 103, 105, 108, 111, 112, 116, 117, 118
Fonda, Shirlee Mae, 113–14

Fonda, Susan, 92, 104, 105, 106, 108–9, 111, 113, 114
Fonda, William, 93, 94
Fonda: My Life (Teichmann), 96, 114
Forbes, Bryan, 43, 48
Ford, John, 100, 101, 102, 106–7, 130, 131, 132, 134, 135, 136, 137, 140, 142, 145, 181, 188
Foreman, Carl, 141
Fort Apache, 102, 140
Four Star Playhouse, 41
Fox Studios, 132, 133
Franchetti, Afdera *see* Fonda, Afdera
Frank, Melvin, 211
Fugitive, The, 102

Gable, Clark, 31, 144, 194, 199
Gabor, Zsa Zsa, 235–7
Gap, The (play), 63
Garbo, Greta, 98
Gardner, Ava, 41
Gaybis, Annie, 233–4, 245–6, 250
Gaynor, Janet, 97
Gazzara, Ben, 63
Getaway, The, 78, 243, 245
Girls Demand Excitement, 133
Go Slowly, Come Back Quickly (Niven), 48
Godless Girl, The, 173
Going My Own Way (Crosby), 206
Going My Way, 208, 209–11
Goldwater, Barry, 126
Goldwyn, Sam, 7, 31, 32, 33, 34–5, 36, 37, 39, 41, 163
Goodbye Columbus, 247
Gordon, Don, 66, 71, 74, 75, 80
Grandstaff, Olive *see* Crosby, Kathryn
Granger, Stewart, 41
Grant, Cary, 38, 41, 80
Grant, Kathryn *see* Crosby, Kathryn
Grapes of Wrath, The, 101, 102
Grease, 248
Great Escape, The, 58, 70, 71, 72, 73, 76
Great St Louis Bank Robbery, The, 65
Greatest Show on Earth, The, 183
Greatest Story Ever Told, The, 145
Green Berets, The, 146, 147
Greene, Graham, 187, 188, 205
Griffith, D. W., 161
Guns of Darkness, The, 43
Guns of Navarone, The, 45

Hamish Hamilton, 47
Hammerstein, Oscar, II, 104

Hangman's House, 132
Happy Days (TV show), 241
Happy Go Lovely, 40
Harper, Jody, 176
Harris, Jed, 96
Harris, Phil, 200, 212–13, 214, 217, 219, 224, 226, 227
Harris, Radie, 103
Hatful of Rain, A (play), 63
Hathaway, Henry, 146, 147, 172
Hawks, Howard, 140
Hay, Ian, 26
Hayakawa, Sessue, 165
Hayward, Leland, 97, 99, 100
Hayworth, Rita, 41, 42
Hearst, William Randolph, Jr, 197
Hefner, Hugh, 249
Heggen, Tom, 102
Hell is for Heroes, 68, 69
Hepburn, Katharine, 117, 118, 148
Heston, Charlton, 165, 183, 184, 241–2, 247
High and the Mighty, The, 142
High Noon, 141
High Society, 218, 226
Hitchcock, Alfred, 110, 183
Hoffman, Dustin, 85, 144
Holden, William, 217
Holiday Inn, 209
Hollywood Greats, The (Norman), 7, 8
Hondo, 142
Honeymoon Machine, The, 68–9
Hope, Bob, 195, 201–2, 208, 211, 212, 215, 218, 219, 222, 224
Horse Soldiers, The, 136
Houseman, John, 94, 113, 114, 115, 119
How the West was Won, 145
Hunter, The, 83
Hustler, The, 73
Hutchinson, Tom, 35
Hutton, Barbara, 28
Hyams, Joe, 220

Ibsen, Henrik, 82
Island in the Sky, 142
It Pays to Advertise (play), 26

Jaffe, Sam, 63
Jazz Singer, The, 173
Jewison, Norman, 58, 70, 73–4, 85, 86
Jezebel, 100
Joan the Woman, 169
Johnson, Ben, 142, 150
Jolson, Al, 212

Junior Bonner, 78

KABC Radio, 251
Kael, Pauline, 187
Kassorla, Dr Irene, 251–2
Katzin, Lee H., 78
Kelley, Dr William, 84
Kelly, George, 94
Kelly, Grace, 217, 218
Kerr, Deborah, 42, 43, 45
King of Jazz, The, 199
King of Kings, 170, 171, 173
Kipling, Rudyard, 40, 178
Kiss for Corliss, A, 39
Korda, Sir Alexander, 34, 38, 39
Kosygin, Alexei Nikolayevich, 127
Kurosawa, Akira, 67

Lady Says No!, The, 40
Lamarr, Hedy, 182
Lamour, Dorothy, 208, 218, 224
Lancaster, Burt, 41, 42
Landi, Elissa, 32
Lang, Fritz, 99
Laski, Marghanita, 215
Lasky, Jesse, Jr, 166, 170, 177, 188
Lasky, Jesse L., 163
Lasky Company, 163, 164, 165
Laughton, Charles, 31
Laurentiis, Dino de, 108
Le Mans, 76, 78
Lee, Dixie *see* Crosby, Dixie
Leigh, Vivien, 42
Lemmon, Jack, 107, 113, 114, 116, 119
Leonard, Sugar Ray, 238
Leroy, Mervyn, 107
Lewis, Jerry, 215
Little, Rich, 49
Little Boy Lost, 215
Little Hut, The, 41
Logan, Joshua, 94–104 *passim*, 112, 114
Long Voyage Home, The, 136
Longest Day, The, 145
Losey, Joseph, 181
Love Lottery, The, 41
Love Story, 243, 245
Love With a Proper Stranger, 73
Lubitsch, Ernst, 30, 161
Lumet, Sidney, 110, 111, 114, 115, 119
Lust for Life, 151
Lux Theatre of the Air (radio programme), 179

MGM, 31, 64, 144, 174, 210

McCarey, Leo, 209, 210
McCarthy, Joseph, 126, 180
McCormick, Myron, 96, 97
McCrea, Joel, 97
MacGraw, Ali, 78, 79, 80, 81, 82, 85,
    86, 243–4, 245
McLaglen, Andrew, 130, 139, 152
MacMurray, Fred, 208
MacPherson, Jeannie, 167, 168, 173,
    178–9
McQ, 149
McQueen, Ali *see* MacGraw, Ali
McQueen, Barbara Jo, 82, 84, 85
McQueen, Chadwick, 61, 66, 79, 80,
    84
McQueen, Julian, 59–60, 61
McQueen, Neile, 63–5, 66, 68, 73, 75,
    76–8, 79, 80, 82, 83–4, 85, 86
McQueen, Steve, 232, 243
    character, 58–9, 63, 65, 66, 69–70,
        71, 72–3, 74–6, 79, 80, 81, 83, 85,
        86
    obsession with machines, 58, 61,
        66–7, 71–2, 79, 80
    childhood, 59–61
    in Marines, 61–2
    illness, 62, 83–4
    early films, 64, 65
    established as a star, 67–8
    acting ability, 68, 85, 86
McQueen, Terri, 66, 79, 80, 84
McQueen, William, 59
Madam Satan, 174
Magnificent Doll, 37
Magnificent Seven, The, 58, 67–8, 70
Male and Female, 160, 168
Mamoulian, Reuben, 181
Man Who Shot Liberty Valance, The,
    136, 145
Mankiewicz, Joseph L., 180, 181, 182
Mann, Delbert, 42, 43
Mann, Roderick, 23–4, 38, 46, 47, 48,
    49, 50
Marchetti, Roger, 204
Marsh, Mae, 135
Martin, Dean, 215, 225
Marx, Groucho, 182
Mascot Films, 133
Mason, Peter, 84
Mason, Sammy, 58, 59, 83, 84
Matter of Life and Death, A, 36
Mature, Victor, 182
Maxwell, Elsa, 30
Mayer, Louis B., 174
Men without Women, 132

Mengers, Sue, 242–3, 244–5
Merrill, Gary, 63
Merton of the Movies (play), 94
Michael Parkinson Show (TV show),
    22, 48
Mills, Juliet, 253
Minty, Barbara Jo *see* McQueen,
    Barbara Jo
Mister Roberts, 106–8
Mister Roberts (play), 102–3, 104, 105
Mitchell, Thomas, 222
Mix, Tom, 130
Monogram Pictures, 133
Monroe, Marilyn, 232
Moon is Blue, The, 40–1
Moon's a Balloon, The (Niven), 24, 29,
    46, 47
Moore, Roger, 50
Morris, Phyllis, 248–50
Morrison, Clyde L., 129
Morrison, Mary, 129
Mortimer, John, 23, 43, 45, 48, 49,
    50–1, 52
Moss, Stirling, 66
Mother Machree, 130
Motion Picture Academy, 148
Motion Picture Alliance, 140, 141, 142
Motion Picture Patents Company, 164
Movie Greats, The (Norman), 7
Muir, Florabelle, 214
Mutiny on the Bounty, 31

NBC network, 22, 246
"Nessie", 25
Never Love a Stranger, 65
Never So Few, 67, 68
Newman, Paul, 42, 64, 76, 85
Nina, 40
Niven, David, 8, 251
    illness, 22, 48–50
    character, 22–4, 26, 29, 30, 42–3,
        50–2
    childhood, 24–5
    army career, 25–9
    signs with Goldwyn, 31
    early films, 32–3
    war years, 34–6
    makes *Separate Tables*, 41–2
    acting ability, 43–4, 51
    memoirs published, 46–8
Niven, David, Jr, 23, 36, 37–8, 40, 43,
    45, 47–8, 50
Niven, Fiona, 46
Niven, Henrietta, 24, 25, 28
Niven, Hjordis, 39, 44, 45, 46, 50

Niven, Jamie, 22, 37, 38, 40, 44, 46, 48–50, 51
Niven, Kristina, 46
Niven, Max, 25
Niven, Primula, 36, 37–8, 39
Niven, William, 24
Niven's Hollywood (Hutchinson), 35
Nixon, Richard, 235, 236
Northwest Mounted Police, 179

Oakie, Jack, 208
Oberon, Merle, 33–4
O'Brien, Margaret, 63
O'Connell, William, 167, 173, 179
Oh Men! Oh Women!, 41
O'Hara, Maureen, 150
Old Man and the Sea, The, 42
Old Wives for New, 168
Olivier, Sir Laurence, 42, 44
On Golden Pond, 116, 117, 118
On Golden Pond (play), 117
On the Waterfront, 218
O'Neill, Eugene, 136
Other Love, The, 38
Ox-Bow Incident, The, 101

Padre, The see Going My Way
Palette, Pilar *see* Wayne, Pilar
Panama, Norman, 211
Panter, Lloyd, 61
Papillon, 81
Paramount, 32, 161, 165, 166, 168, 170, 174, 182, 184, 204, 210
Parker, Dorothy, 9
Parrish, Robert, 161, 172, 175, 176, 177, 178, 180, 181, 182, 185, 186
Peckinpah, Sam, 78
Peg O' My Heart (play), 63
Perfect Marriage, The, 37
Philadelphia Story, The, 101, 218
Pickford, Mary, 161
Pinero, Manuel, 223
Pink Panther, The, 46
Plainsman, The, 179
Point of No Return (play), 106
Poitier, Sidney, 42
Police Woman (TV series), 246
Powell, Dick, 41
Power, Tyrone, 37
Preminger, Otto, 40
Presley, Cecelia, 176, 177, 180
Pyjama Game, The (play), 63

Quiet Man, The, 134, 142
Quinn, Anthony, 184, 186

Raffles, 34
Rattigan, Terence, 41
Reagan, Ronald, 142, 235, 236
Red River, 140
Reivers, The, 85
Republic, 134
Reynolds, Burt, 239
Rhythm on the Range, 205
Richardson, Sir Ralph, 23, 44
Rinker, Al, 196, 197, 198, 199, 200, 203
Rio Grande, 140
Rio Lobo, 148
Rivera, Geraldo, 224
Road to Hong Kong, 218
Road to Mandalay see Going My Way
Road to Singapore, The, 208
Road to Utopia, 211
Robbins, Harold, 65, 249
Robinson, Edward G., 73–4, 85
Rockefeller, Winthrop, 235
Rogers, Ginger, 37, 41, 98
Rollo, Bill, 36
Rollo, Lady Kathleen, 36
Rollo, Primula *see* Niven, Primula
Rooster Cogburn, 148
Round the Ragged Rocks (Niven), 47
Russell, Rosalind, 34
Rydell, Mark, 62–3, 85, 116–18, 119, 152

Saenz, Dr Jose Sainte, 132
Saenz, Josephine *see* Wayne, Josephine
Samson and Delilah, 182
Sand Pebbles, The, 73
Sands of Iwo Jima, 140
Scared Stiff, 215
Screen Actors' Guild, 142
Screen Directors' Guild, 180, 181, 187
Sea Chase, The, 142
Searchers, The, 134
Selznick, David, 37
Separate Tables, 41–2, 43, 44
Seven Samurai, 67
Shaw, Artie, 200, 202, 225–6
She Wore a Yellow Ribbon, 134, 140
Sherman, George, 134, 140, 143
Shields, Brooke, 242
Shootist, The, 149
Sign of the Cross, 174, 175
Silken Affair, The, 41
Sinatra, Frank, 67, 194, 208, 218, 225, 226
Soldiers Three, 40
Somebody Up There Likes Me, 64

Sons of Katie Elder, The, 146
Sound City, 28
Spielberg, Steven, 230
Splendour, 32
Squaw Man, The, 163, 164, 165, 174
Stacy, Pat, 149
Stagecoach (1938), 134, 135, 136, 137
Stagecoach (1965), 222
Stanwyck, Barbara, 38, 100
Steinbeck, John, 101
Sternberg, Josef von, 161, 164
Stevens, George, 145
Stevens, Rise, 209–10, 225
Stewart, James, 80, 92, 95, 96, 97–8,
    101, 119, 235
Strasberg, Lee, 63
Streisand, Barbra, 249
Sturges, John, 58, 62, 66, 67, 68, 70,
    71, 72–3, 76, 78, 80, 81
Sullavan, Margaret *see* Fonda,
    Margaret
Summer, Donna, 237–8
Sunset Boulevard, 182
Swanson, Gloria, 40, 160, 165, 166,
    169, 172, 182

Tall Story, 112
Teichmann, Howard, 96, 114
Temple, Shirley, 40
Ten Commandments, The (1923), 169,
    170
Ten Commandments, The (1956), 183,
    184
Tersmeden, Hjordis *see* Niven,
    Hjordis
Thalberg, Irving, 31
Thank You, Jeeves, 32
That Certain Woman, 99
Thierry, Gabe, 238, 239, 240–1
This Could be the Night, 64
Thomas Crown Affair, The, 58, 70
Thomson, Claude, 60
Three Girls Lost, 133
Three Godfathers, The, 135
Tiller Girls, 197
Time Out for Ginger (play), 63
Tin Star, The, 110
Toast of New Orleans, The, 40
Today (TV show), 22
Todd, Ann, 25, 26, 30, 38
Todd, Mike, 41
Tom Horn, 82
Tootsie, 144
Torch Bearer, The (play), 94
Towering Inferno, The, 76, 81

Tracy, Spencer, 42, 110, 118
Trail of the Pink Panther, The, 49
Trevor, Claire, 134, 135, 139, 140,
    143, 153
Trubshawe, Michael, 27, 28, 35, 36,
    37, 39, 46
True Grit, 126, 147, 148
Turkish Delight, 167
Twelve Angry Men, 110
Twelve Angry Men (TV play), 110
20th Century-Fox, 32, 97, 101, 102,
    112, 222
Two for Tonight, 205

US Marshall, 148
Union Pacific, 179
Universal Studios, 199, 252
Ustinov, Peter, 23, 36, 37, 43–4, 48

Viertel, Peter, 45
Virginian, The (play), 99

Wagner, Robert, 73
Wallach, Eli, 68, 85
Walsh, Raoul, 132, 133
Wanger, Walter, 97, 134
Wanted – Dead or Alive (TV series),
    66, 67
War and Peace, 108, 109
War Lover, The, 69, 70
War Wagon, The, 151
Ward, Fanny, 165
Warner, H. B., 170, 171
Warner Brothers, 133
Way Ahead, The, 35, 36
Wayne, Aissa, 143
Wayne, Antonia Maria (Toni), 134,
    143
Wayne, Esperanza (Chata), 137, 138,
    143
Wayne, John, 119, 235
    adulation of, 128–9, 153, 225
    childhood, 129–30
    character, 130, 139–40, 141–2, 143,
        144, 148, 151–2
    early films, 132–3
    stars in *Stagecoach*, 134–6
    acting ability, 134, 151
    as voice of America, 140–2, 152–3
    failure of *The Alamo*, 144–5
    illness, 145, 149–50, 153
Wayne, John Ethan, 143, 148
Wayne, Josephine, 132, 133, 137, 138
Wayne, Marisa, 143
Wayne, Melinda, 134

Wayne, Michael, 129, 130, 131, 132, 134, 136, 137, 139, 141, 142, 143, 146, 147, 148, 150, 152
Wayne, Patrick, 134
Wayne, Pilar, 139, 142, 143, 146, 148
Weigall, Priscilla, 28, 30
Weingand, Al, 30, 31, 33
Welles, Orson, 197
Whatever Happened to Hollywood? (Lasky), 170
White Christmas, 216
Whiteman, Paul, 198, 199
Widmark, Richard, 144
Whitney, Jock, 212
Wilcoxon, Henry, 175, 177, 185
Wilder, Billy, 181, 182
Williams, Bernard, 247–8
Wills, Chill, 145
Wilson, Karen, 83, 84
Winds of War, The (TV series), 245

Wings of the Morning, 98
Winkler, Henry, 241
Wise, Robert, 64, 181
Without Regret, 32
Wood, Natalie, 73
Woods, Robert, 230
Words and Music, 132
Wouk, Herman, 106
Wrong Man, The, 110
Wuthering Heights, 34
Wyler, William, 181, 187

Yates, Peter, 74
Yorkin, Bud, 247
You Only Live Once, 99
Young, Loretta, 37, 38, 133
Young Mr Lincoln, The, 100, 101

Zanuck, Darryl, 101, 102, 112
Zukor, Adolf, 170